Mathematics Bible

Edition 3

Table of Contents

(All items are in the Public Domain. No rights are reserved.)

* * *

(blank page)

Algebraic Manipulation Exercise 10001

preliminaries:

In the development leading to the presentation of a specific result, it often happens that we wish to use certain theorems as axioms. That is, we do not wish to prove those theorems – their proof being readily available in the literature – nor do we wish to focus attention on them. To this end, we will use the term 'synapse' for such theorems.

Synapse 1. $PQ = 0$ if, and only if, $P = 0$ or $Q = 0$

Theorem 1. $P^2 - Q^2 = (P - Q)(P + Q)$
Proof:
$(P - Q)(P + Q) = (P - Q)P + (P - Q)Q = (P^2 - PQ) + (PQ - Q^2) = P^2 - Q^2$ ∎

Theorem 2. $P^2 = Q^2$ if, and only if, $P = \pm Q$.
Proof: $P^2 = Q^2$
if, and only if,
$P^2 - Q^2 = 0$
if, and only if,
$(P - Q)(P + Q) = 0$
if, and only if,
$P - Q = 0$ or $P + Q = 0$
if, and only if,
$P = Q$ or $P = -Q$
if, and only if,
$P = \pm Q$
∎

Theorem 3. If each of a, b, and c is a constant and $a \neq 0$, then $ax^2 + bx + c = 0$ if, and only if, $x = (-b \pm \sqrt{(b^2 - 4ac)})/(2a)$.
Proof:
$ax^2 + bx + c = 0$
if, and only if,
$x^2 + (b/a)x + c/a = 0$
if, and only if,
$x^2 + (b/a)x = -c/a$
if, and only if,
$x^2 + (b/a)x + b^2/(4a^2) = b^2/(4a^2) - c/a$
if, and only if,
$(x + b/(2a))^2 = (b^2 - 4ac)/(4a^2)$
if, and only if,
$(x + b/(2a))^2 = (\sqrt{(b^2 - 4ac)}/(2a))^2$
if, and only if,
$x + b/(2a) = \pm\sqrt{(b^2 - 4ac)}/(2a)$
if, and only if,

x = -b/(2a) ± √(b² − 4ac)/(2a)
if, and only if,
x = (-b ± √(b² − 4ac))/(2a)
∎

Definition 1. A root is a number that makes the equation true.

Theorem 4. If each of a, b, and c is a constant, and a ≠ 0, then the sum of the two (possibly equal) roots of ax² + bx + c is -b/a.
Proof:
By Theorem 3, the two (possibly equal) roots are (-b ± √(b² − 4ac))/(2a). Their sum is -b/a. ∎

Theorem 5. If each of a, b, and c is a constant, and a ≠ 0, then the product of the two (possibly equal) roots of ax² + bx + c is c/a.
Proof:
By Theorem 3, the two (possibly equal) roots are (-b ± √(b² − 4ac))/(2a). Their product is c/a. ∎

Synapse 2. (Well-Ordering Principle) Every nonempty set of positive integers has a minimum element.

Definition 2. x divides y, written x | y, means that, for integers x and y, there exists an integer k such that kx = y.

Definition 3. x is said to be a square if, and only if, there exists an integer y such that x = y².

Definition 4. A quadratic equation is an equation of the form
ax² + bx + c = 0, where a, b, and c are constants, and a ≠ 0.

The Task:

This algebraic manipulation exercise consists of proving the following theorem:

Theorem 6. If each of a and b is a positive integer such that (1 + ab) | (a² + b²), then
(a² + b²)/(1 + ab) is a square.

We will use indirect proof, that is, we will assume that the result is false, then obtain a contradiction, and then conclude that the result must be true. Along the way we will use the Well-Ordering Principle, and the formulas for the sum and product of the roots of a quadratic equation. The contradiction obtained will be in regard to the minimality condition initially invoked via the Well-Ordering Principle.

Proof:
Suppose that there exist positive integers a and b such that (1 + ab) | (a² + b²) and

$(a^2 + b^2)/(1 + ab)$ is not a square. Let $a = A$ and $b = B$ be values of a and b such that $(a^2 + b^2)/(1 + ab)$ is not a square, and such that $A + B$ is minimum.

Without loss of generality, let $B \leq A$.

Let $k = (A^2 + B^2)/(1 + AB)$.

Then A is a root of the equation $k = (x^2 + B^2)/(1 + xB)$.

Then A is a root of the equation $k - (x^2 + B^2)/(1 + xB) = 0$.

Then A is a root of the quadratic equation $x^2 + (-Bk)x + (B^2 - k) = 0$.

Let the two roots of this quadratic equation be denoted by x_1 and x_2, with $x_1 = A$.

(We are going to show that x_2 also satisfies the hypothesis and is less than A, thereby contradicting the minimality of $A + B$.)

By Theorem 4, the sum of the roots of this quadratic equation is $(-(-Bk))/1 = Bk$.

Thus, $x_1 + x_2 = Bk$.

Thus, $A + x_2 = Bk$.

Thus, $x_2 = Bk - A$.

Thus, x_2 is an integer.

By Theorem 5, the product of the roots of this quadratic equation is $B^2 - k$.

Thus, $Ax_2 = B^2 - k$.

Thus, $x_2 = (B^2 - k)/A$.

Thus, since k is not a square, $x_2 \neq 0$.

Since $(x_2^2 + B^2)/(1 + x_2B) = k > 0$, and $x_2 \neq 0$, $x_2 > 0$.

Thus, x_2 is a positive integer satisfying the hypothesis.

Then:

$B \leq A$

implies

$B^2 \leq A^2$

implies

$B^2 - k < A^2$

implies

$(B^2 - k)/A < A$

implies

$x_2 < A$

implies

$x_2 + B < A + B$

which contradicts the supposed minimality of $A + B$.

Thus, the result holds.

∎

Note: This algebraic manipulation exercise is based on the Wikipedia article (February 2018) on problem #6 of the International Mathematical Olympiad of the year 1988.

Algebraic Manipulation Exercise 10001

Examination Version

Synapse 1. PQ = 0 if, and only if, P = 0 or Q = 0

Theorem 1. $P^2 - Q^2 = (P - Q)(P + Q)$

Theorem 2. $P^2 = Q^2$ if, and only if, $P = \pm Q$.

Theorem 3. If each of a, b, and c is a constant and $a \neq 0$, then $ax^2 + bx + c = 0$ if, and only if, $x = (-b \pm \sqrt{(b^2 - 4ac)})/(2a)$.

Definition 1. A root is a number that makes the equation true.

Theorem 4. If each of a, b, and c is a constant, and $a \neq 0$, then the sum of the two (possibly equal) roots of $ax^2 + bx + c$ is -b/a.

Theorem 5. If each of a, b, and c is a constant, and $a \neq 0$, then the product of the two (possibly equal) roots of $ax^2 + bx + c$ is c/a.

Synapse 2. (Well-Ordering Principle) Every nonempty set of positive integers has a minimum element.

Definition 2. x divides y, written x | y, means that, for integers x and y, there exists an integer k such that kx = y.

Definition 3. x is said to be a square if, and only if, there exists an integer y such that $x = y^2$.

Definition 4. A quadratic equation is an equation of the form $ax^2 + bx + c = 0$, where a, b, and c are constants, and $a \neq 0$.

Theorem 6. If each of a and b is a positive integer such that $(1 + ab) \mid (a^2 + b^2)$, then $(a^2 + b^2)/(1 + ab)$ is a square.

(end of document

Sum of the First 100 Numbers

The sum of the first 100 numbers (that is, $1 + 2 + 3 + ... + 98 + 99 + 100$), is 5050.
There is a way of obtaining this answer that is much easier than a brute-force approach.

Let S be the sum. That is, $S = 1 + 2 + 3 + ... + 98 + 99 + 100$.
Then it is also true that $S = 100 + 99 + 98 + ... + 3 + 2 + 1$.
Then, adding these two equations, we get:
$2S = 101 + 101 + 101 + ... + 101 + 101 + 101$.
Then:
$2S = 101 \times 100$.
Then:
$S = (101 \times 100)/2$.
Then:
$S = 101 \times (100/2)$.
Then:
$S = 101 \times 50$.
Then $S = 5050$.

■

(end of document)

(blank page)

How many customers?

Name: _____   Date: _____

1. On a day on which the temperature exceeded 100 degrees Fahrenheit, a certain store sold 36 bottles of liquid-form dihydrogen monoxide. Each customer bought one bottle, and was a member of the local debating club. As the last bottle was being bought, the wind was out of the SE at 3 mph, and the relative humidity was 57%, and a dog was barking in the distance. How many customers were there? _____

2. On a certain day a certain store sold 36 bottles of water. Each customer bought one bottle. How many customers were there? _____

3. On a certain day a certain store sold 12 bottles of water in the morning and 24 bottles of water in the afternoon. Each customer bought one bottle. How many customers were there?
_____

4. On a certain day a certain store sold 36 bottles of water. Each customer bought 2 bottles. How many customers were there? _____

5. On a certain day a certain store sold 12 bottles of water in the morning, and 24 bottles in the afternoon. Each customer bought 2 bottles. How many customers were there? _____

6. On a certain day a certain tire store sold 36 tires. Each customer bought 4. How many customers were there? _____

7. On a certain day a certain tire store sold 12 tires in the morning and 24 in the afternoon. Each customer bought 4. How many customers were there? _____

8. On a certain day a certain fast-food vendor sold 36 tacos. Half the customers bought 2 tacos each, and half the customers bought 4 tacos each. How many customers were there? _____

9. On a certain day a certain fast-food vendor sold 36 tacos. One fifth of the customers bought one taco each, and four fifths of the customers bought 2 tacos each. How many customers were there? _____

10. On a certain day a certain fast-food vendor sold 12 tacos at lunchtime and 24 tacos at dinnertime. One fourth of the customer bought one taco each. One fourth of the customers bought 2 tacos each. One fourth of the customers bought 3 tacos each. And one fourth of the customers bought 12 tacos each. How many customers were there? _____

Primes as Customers

Definition 1. $\pi(x)$ is the number of primes less than or equal to x. For example, $\pi(11)$ is 5, since the primes less than or equal to 11 are the five primes 2, 3, 5, 7, and 11.

Theorem 1. For large x, $\pi(x)$ is approximately $x/\log(x)$.

11. A large number, x, of identical hand-held calculators were bought by a store. The total cost of the collection of calculators was $\log(x)$. All the calculators were sold by the store to individual customers, many of whom purchased multiple calculators for re-sale or gifting. Give a guess as to the number of customers that bought the calculators. _____

(end of document)

(blank page)

Infinitude of the Primes

Definition 1. A divisor of a given integer n is any integer d such that there exists an integer k such that kd = n. (For example, 3 is a divisor of 12, because 4 × 3 = 12.)

Definition 2. A prime is an integer p > 1 such that p has no divisor d such that 1 < d < p.

In the development leading to the presentation of a specific result, it often happens that we wish to use certain theorems as axioms. That is, we do not wish to prove those theorems – their proof being readily available in the literature – nor do we wish to focus attention on them. To this end, we will use the term 'synapse' for such theorems.

Synapse. For each integer n > 1, there exists a prime p such that p is a divisor of n.

Theorem. The number of primes is infinite.
Proof:
Suppose that the number of primes is finite.
Let t be their product.
Let u = t + 1.
Then no prime can divide u.
But by the synapse, there exists a prime that divides u,
a contradiction.
Thus, the number of primes is infinite. ■

(end of document)

(blank page)

Irrationality of √2

Definition 1. A real number x is said to be rational if, and only if, there exists an integer a and there exists an integer b, with b ≠ 0, such that x = a/b.

Definition 2. A real number x is said to be irrational if, and only if, x is not rational.

In the development leading to the presentation of a specific result, it often happens that we wish to use certain theorems as axioms. That is, we do not wish to prove those theorems – their proof being readily available in the literature – nor do we wish to focus attention on them. To this end, we will use the term 'synapse' for such theorems.

Synapse. If x is a nonzero integer, then the prime factorization of x^2 has an even (possibly 0) exponent for 2.

Theorem. √2 is irrational.
Proof:
Suppose that each of a and b is an integer, with b ≠ 0, such that √2 = a/b.
Then a is also nonzero, and $2 = a^2/b^2$. Then $2b^2 = a^2$. Then, since the prime factorization of b^2 has an even exponent for 2, the prime factorization of a^2 has an odd exponent for 2, which contradicts the synapse. Thus, √2 is irrational. ∎

(end of document)

(blank page)

Geometric-Mean – Arithmetic-Mean Inequality

Definition 1. If each of x and y is a real number, then the arithmetic mean of x and y is the number A(x,y) defined by the equation x + y = A(x,y) + A(x,y). (In other words, it is the number which leaves the sum unchanged when each of the given numbers is replaced by that number.)

Theorem 1. If each of x and y is a real number, then A(x,y) = (x + y)/2.
Proof: x + y = A(x,y) + A(x,y). Thus, x + y = 2A(x,y). Thus, 2A(x,y) = x + y.
Thus, A(x,y) = (x + y)/2. ■

We normally want to use the result of Theorem 1 as the definition of the arithmetic mean. Let us call the use of a theorem result in place of the 'raw' definition the 'kick start' definition of the term.

Definition 2. If each of x and y is a positive real number, then the geometric mean of x and y is the number G(x,y) defined by the equation xy = G(x,y)G(x,y). (In other words, it is the number which leaves the product unchanged when each of the given numbers is replaced by that number.)

Theorem 2. If each of x and y is a positive real number, then G(x,y) = √(xy).
Proof: xy = G(x,y)G(x,y). Thus, xy = (G(x,y))². Thus, (G(x,y))² = xy.
Thus, G(x,y) = √(xy). ■

The result of Theorem 2 is the 'kick start' definition of the geometric mean.

In the development leading to the presentation of a specific result, it often happens that we wish to use certain theorems as axioms. That is, we do not wish to prove those theorems – their proof being readily available in the literature – nor do we wish to focus attention on them. To this end, we will use the term 'synapse' for such theorems.

Synapse 1. For each real number x, $0 \leq x^2$.

Theorem 3. (Geometric-Mean – Arithmetic-Mean Inequality) If each of x and y is a positive real number, then G(x,y) ≤ A(x,y).
Proof: Let each of x and y be a positive real number. Then each of √x and √y is a positive real number. Then (√x – √y) is a real number. Then $0 \leq (\sqrt{x} - \sqrt{y})^2$.
Then $0 \leq (\sqrt{x})^2 - 2\sqrt{x}\sqrt{y} + (\sqrt{y})^2$. Then $0 \leq x - 2\sqrt{xy} + y$.
Then 2√(xy) ≤ x + y. Then √(xy) ≤ (x + y)/2. Then G(x,y) ≤ A(x,y). ■

(end of document)

(blank page)

Kaprekar's Constant

Consider any 4-digit number such that more than one digit appears in it. Rearrange the digits to form the largest possible number and the smallest possible number. Then subtract the smaller number from the larger number. Apply the same process to the resulting number. After at most 7 iterations, you will get the number 6174, which is known as Kaprekar's Constant.

(end of document)

(blank page)

Metric Paper Size

Definition. The aspect ratio of a rectangle is L/W, where L is the length of the rectangle, and W is the width of the rectangle.

Theorem. If a rectangle is such that each of its two halves when it is cut in half width-wise has the same aspect ratio as the original rectangle, then the original rectangle has an aspect ratio of $\sqrt{2}$, as do both halves.

Proof:

Let the length of the rectangle be L, and the width of the rectangle be W.

Let the rectangle be cut in half width-wise.

Case 1. $W < L/2$. Then the aspect ratio of each half is $(L/2)/W = L/(2W) \neq L/W$.

Case 2. $L/2 \leq W$. Then the aspect ratio of each half is $W/(L/2)$.

Then if $W/(L/2) = L/W$, we have:

$W^2 = L(L/2)$.

Then $W^2 = L^2/2$.

Then $L^2/W^2 = 2$. Then $L/W = \sqrt{2}$.

Also, $W/(L/2) = 2(W/L) = 2(1/\sqrt{2}) = 2/\sqrt{2} = \sqrt{2}$. ∎

For example, A4 paper has this aspect ratio.

(end of document)

(blank page)

Chinese Magic Square

Consider the following 3 × 3 matrix:
The 3 entries of the first row are: 8, 1, 6.
The 3 entries of the second row are: 3, 5, 7.
The 3 entries of the third row are: 4, 9, 2.

Then:
The sum of each row is 15.
The sum of each column is 15.
The sum of each major diagonal is 15.

(end of document)

(blank page)

Casting Out Nines

The remainder when 31415962 is divided by 9 is 4.
There is a way of obtaining this answer that is much easier than a brute-force approach.

It is a theorem that the number obtained from adding up the digits of a number has the same remainder when divided by 9 as does the original number. This can therefore be carried to the next step, that is, the number obtained from adding up the digits of this second number has the same reminder when divided by 9 as does the second number. So, all of the numbers in this sequence have the same remainder when divided by 9. We can continue this process until we have a number consisting of only one digit. This digit will be in the range $1 - 9$. If the number is 9, then the remainder when divided by 9 is 0. Otherwise, the remainder is simply the digit obtained.

Applying this to the number 31415962, we have as the second number 31. That is, $3 + 1 + 4 + 1 + 5 + 9 + 6 + 2 = 31$. The next step is to sum the digits of 31: $3 + 1 = 4$. We have arrived at a one-digit number: 4. So, the remainder when 31415962 is divided by 9 is 4.

This phenomenon is helpful in catching one common type of accounting error, namely, transposition of digits, because a transposition of digits does not change the sum of the digits. If two numbers are supposed to be the same, but are not, but they have the same remainder when divided by 9, that suggests that it might be worthwhile looking for an error consisting of transposition of digits. (While transposition of digits is sufficient to cause such an error, it is not necessary, and so this is only a partial check.)

(end of document)

(blank page)

Coin-Flipping

Definition. The probability of an event is the number of favorable outcomes divided by the number of possible outcomes.

Theorem. If two coins are tossed and at least one of them comes up heads, then the probability that they both came up heads is 1/3.
Proof:
The possible outcomes, given that at least one of them came up heads, are (H,H), (H,T), and (T,H). Thus, there are exactly 3 possible outcomes, and there is exactly one favorable outcome (namely, (H,H)). Thus, the probability that they both came up heads is 1/3. ■

(end of document

(blank page)

Summing a String of Odd Numbers

The odd numbers start out 1, 3, 5, 7, ...

Consider a unit square. It has an area of 1.

Consider 3 more unit squares. We can wrap them around the first unit square so as to form a 2×2 square. This square has an area of 4.

Those two results concerned the first 2 odd numbers.

Now consider the third odd number, namely 5.
We can wrap 5 unit squares around the 2×2 square so as to form a 3×3 square. This square has an area of 9.

The pattern that is emerging is that the sum of the first n odd number is n^2.

We now formally prove this, and also give some extra information.

Definition 1. If n is a positive integer, then the nth odd number is $(2n - 1)$.

Definition 2. If n is a positive integer, then the nth odd number is denoted by $\delta(n)$.

In the development leading to the presentation of a specific result, it often happens that we wish to use certain theorems as axioms. That is, we do not wish to prove those theorems – their proof being readily available in the literature – nor do we wish to focus attention on them. To this end, we will use the term 'synapse' for such theorems.

Synapse. (Well-Ordering Principle) Every nonempty set of positive integers has a minimum element.

Theorem 1. If n is a positive integer, then $\delta(1) + \delta(2) + \delta(3) + ... + \delta(n) = n^2$.
Proof:
Suppose that there exists a positive integer n such that $\delta(1) + \delta(2) + ... + \delta(n) \neq n^2$.
Let M be the set of all such n.
Then M is a nonempty set of positive integers.
Then, by the synapse, M has a minimum element.
Let us denote by h the minimum element of M.
Since $\delta(1) = 1 = 1^2$, $1 \notin M$.
Thus, $h > 1$.
Thus, $h - 1$ is a positive integer, and $h - 1 \notin M$.
Thus, $\delta(1) + \delta(2) + ... + \delta(h - 1) = (h - 1)^2$.
Then, adding $2h - 1$ to both sides, we have:
$\delta(1) + \delta(2) + ... + \delta(h - 1) + (2h - 1) = (h - 1)^2 + (2h - 1)$.
Then, since $2h - 1 = \delta(h)$, we have:
$\delta(1) + \delta(2) + ... + \delta(h) = (h - 1)^2 + (2h - 1)$.

Summing a String of Odd Numbers

Then, since $(h - 1)^2 + (2h - 1) = (h^2 - 2h + 1) + (2h - 1) = h^2$,
we have:
$\delta(1) + \delta(2) + ... + \delta(h) = h^2$.
Thus, $h \notin M$, a contradiction.
Thus, if n is a positive integer, then $\delta(1) + \delta(2) + \delta(3) + ... + \delta(n) = n^2$.
■

some extra information:

Theorem 2. The sum of 2 or more consecutive odd numbers is never a prime.
Proof:
Suppose that each of m and n is a positive integer, and $m < n - 1$.
Then $\delta(1) + \delta(2) + ... + \delta(m) = m^2$
and
$\delta(1) + \delta(2) + ... + \delta(n) = n^2$.
Subtracting the top equation from the bottom equation, we have:
$\delta(m + 1) + ... + \delta(n - 1) + \delta(n) = n^2 - m^2$.
Since $m < n - 1$, the left hand side contains at least 2 terms.
Since $n^2 - m^2 = (n - m)(n + m)$, we have:
$\delta(m + 1) + ... + \delta(n - 1) + \delta(n) = (n - m)(n + m)$.
Since $m < n - 1$, $n - m > 1$.
Thus, the right hand side is not a composite number, and therefore not a prime.
Thus we can conclude that the sum of two or more consecutive odd numbers is never a prime.
■

(end of document)

Remainder Theorem

Theorem. (Remainder Theorem) The remainder of the division of a polynomial f(x) by the linear polynomial x − a is f(a).

Proof:

The result follows from Euclidean division which, given two polynomials f(x) and g(x), asserts the existence and the uniqueness, when f(x) is divided by g(x), of a quotient q(x) and a remainder r(x) such that

f(x) = q(x)g(x) + r(x), and r(x) = 0 or deg(r) < deg(g).

For g(x) = x − a, then r = 0 or deg(r) = 0; in either case r is a constant independent of x; that is:

f(x) = q(x)(x − a) + r.

Then f(a) = q(x)(a − a) + r = q(x)(0) + r = 0 + r = r.

∎

(end of document)

(blank page)

Rational Root Theorem

Theorem. (Rational Root Theorem) If $u \neq 0$ is the leading coefficient of a given polynomial and $v \neq 0$ is the constant term and if each of p and q is a nonzero integer, and $\gcd(p,q) = 1$, and $r = p/q$ and r is a root of the polynomial, then $q \mid u$ and $p \mid v$.

Proof:
Suppose that the given polynomial is:

$$f(x) \equiv a_n x^n + a_{n-1} x^{n-1} + \ldots + a_1 x^1 + a_0$$

Suppose that $f(p/q) = 0$.
Then $a_n(p/q)^n + a_{n-1}(p/q)^{n-1} + \ldots + a_1(p/q) + a_0 = 0$.
Then $q^n(a_n(p/q)^n + a_{n-1}(p/q)^{n-1} + \ldots + a_1(p/q) + a_0) = 0$.
Then $a_n p^n + a_{n-1} p^{n-1} q + \ldots + a_1 p q^{n-1} + a_0 q^n = 0$.
Then, taking the constant term to the right-hand side,
$a_n p^n + a_{n-1} p^{n-1} q + \ldots + a_1 p q^{n-1} = -a_0 q^n$
Then $p(a_n p^{n-1} + a_{n-1} p^{n-2} q \ldots + a_1 q^{n-1}) = -a_0 q^n$
Then $p \mid -a_0 q^n$.
Then $p \mid a_0 q^n$.
Then $p \mid a_0$, since $\gcd(p,q^n) = 1$, since $\gcd(p,q) = 1$.
Then $p \mid v$.
Also:
Taking the leading term to the right-hand side,
$a_{n-1} p^{n-1} q + \ldots + a_1 p q^{n-1} + a_0 q^n = -a_n p^n$
Then $q(a_{n-1} p^{n-1} + \ldots + a_1 p q^{n-2} + a_0 q^{n-1}) = -a_n p^n$
Then $q \mid -a_n p^n$
Then $q \mid a_0 p^n$
Then $q \mid a_0$, since $\gcd(q,p^n) = 1$, since $\gcd(q,p) = 1$.
Then $q \mid u$.
∎

(end of document)

(blank page)

Vieta's Formulas

Definition. A root is an input value that gives an output value of 0.

Vieta's Formulas give the value of various combinations of the roots of a polynomial. Among the various combinations, two of particular interest are the sum of the roots and the product of the roots. (The other combinations are 'intermediate' between these two.)

The various combinations and their values can be obtained as follows:
Let the polynomial in question be of degree n, with x_1, x_2, ..., x_n being its roots.
Let h be the coefficient of the leading term of the polynomial.
Then set the polynomial equal to $h(x - x_1)(x - x_2)\cdots(x - x_n)$, and equate the coefficients of each power of x.

∎

(end of document)

(blank page)

Divisibility Criterion for Even Perfect Numbers

The divisibility criterion for even perfect numbers is that every even perfect number is divisible by a Mersenne prime.

We develop this idea, and add some extra information afterwards.

Definition 1. If n is a positive integer, then $\sigma(n)$ is the sum of the positive divisors of n.

Definition 2. If f is a function whose domain is the set of positive integers, then f is said to be multiplicative if, and only if, for each positive integer x and for each positive integer y, if $\gcd(x,y) = 1$, then $f(xy) = f(x)f(y)$.

In the development leading to the presentation of a specific result, it often happens that we wish to use certain theorems as axioms. That is, we do not wish to prove those theorems – their proof being readily available in the literature – nor do we wish to focus attention on them. To this end, we will use the term 'synapse' for such theorems.

Synapse 1. σ is multiplicative.

Synapse 2. If p is a prime and m is a positive integer, then $\sigma(p^m) = (p^{m+1} - 1)/(p - 1)$.

Theorem 1. If m is a positive integer, then $\sigma(2^m) = 2^{m+1}$.
Proof:
The result follows immediately from Synapse 2.

Definition 3. A positive integer n is said to be perfect if, and only if, $\sigma(n) = 2n$.

Theorem 2. If n is an even perfect number, then there exists a positive integer m such that $2^m - 1$ is a prime and $n = (2^m - 1)2^{m-1}$.
Proof:
Suppose that n is an even perfect number. Let m be the positive integer such that there exists an odd number x such that $n = 2^m x$. Since n is perfect, $\sigma(n) = 2n = 2(2^m x) = 2^{m+1}x$. Then since $\gcd(2^m,x) = 1$, $\sigma(n) = \sigma(2^m x) = \sigma(2^m)\sigma(x) = (2^{m+1} - 1)\sigma(x)$.
Thus, $(2^{m+1} - 1)\sigma(x) = 2^{m+1}x$. Therefore $(2^{m+1} - 1)$ is odd and is a proper divisor of x.
Let $y \equiv x/(2^{m+1} - 1)$.
Then y is a proper divisor of x.
Then $\sigma(x) = x + y + z$, where z is the sum of the divisors of x other than x and y.
Then, since $\sigma(x) = 2^{m+1}y$, we have:
$2^{m+1}y = x + y + z$.
Since $x + y = x + x/(2^{m+1} - 1) = (x(2^{m+1} - 1))/(2^{m+1} - 1) + x/(2^{m+1} - 1)$
$= (x(2^{m+1} - 1) + x)/(2^{m+1} - 1) = (x((2^{m+1} - 1) + 1))/(2^{m+1} - 1)$
$= (x(2^{m+1}))/(2^{m+1} - 1) = (2^{m+1})(x/(2^{m+1} - 1) = 2^{m+1}y$,
we have:
$x + y + z = 2^{m+1}y + z$.
Therefore, combining the two results above, we have:

$2^{m+1}y = 2^{m+1}y + z$.
Therefore, $z = 0$.
Therefore, x has exactly two positive divisors, namely, x and y.
Therefore, x is a prime, $y = 1$, and $x = 2^{m+1} - 1$.
Therefore, $n = 2^m(2^{m+1} - 1)$.
Therefore, $n = (2^{m+1} - 1)2^m$.
Therefore, replacing m by $m - 1$, we have:
$n = (2^m - 1)2^m$.
∎

Definition 4. A Mersenne prime is a prime p such that there exists a positive integer m such that $p = 2^m - 1$.

Theorem 3. (Divisibility Criterion for Even Perfect Numbers) If n is an even perfect number, then n is divisible by a Mersenne prime.
Proof:
This follows immediately from Theorem 2.
∎

some extra information:

Synapse 3. If x is a number and m is a positive integer, then
$(x^{m+1} - 1) = (x - 1)(1 + x + x^2 + ... + x^m)$.

Synapse 4. If x is a number and each of a and b is a positive number, then $(x^a)^b = x^{ab}$.

Theorem 4. If m is a positive integer such that $2^m - 1$ is a prime, then m is a prime.
Proof:
Suppose that m is a positive integer such that $2^m - 1$ is a prime.
Then $m > 1$.
Suppose that m is not a prime.
Then there exists an integer a and there exists an integer b such that $a > 1$ and $b > 1$ and $m = ab$.
Then $2^m - 1 = 2^{ab} - 1 = (2^a)^b - 1$
$= (2^a - 1)(1 + (2^a) + (2^a)^2 + ... + (2^a)^{b-1})$.
Since $a > 1$, $(2^a - 1) > 1$,
and since $b > 1$, $(1 + (2^a) + (2^a)^2 + ... + (2^a)^{b-1}) > 1$.
Thus, $2^m - 1$ is not a prime, a contradiction.
Thus, m is a prime.
∎

(end of document)

Wilson's Theorem

In the development leading to the presentation of a specific result, it often happens that we wish to use certain theorems as axioms. That is, we do not wish to prove those theorems – their proof being readily available in the literature – nor do we wish to focus attention on them. To this end, we will use the term 'synapse' for such theorems.

Synapse 1. If p is a prime greater than 3, then the list of integers 2, ..., p – 2 is nonempty, has an even number of entries, and for each x in the list there exists exactly one y in the list such that $xy \equiv 1$ (mod p), and for each x in the list and for each y in the list, if $xy \equiv 1$ (mod p), then $x \neq y$.

Theorem 1. If n is a positive integer, then $n - 1 \equiv -1$ (mod n).
Proof:
Suppose that n is a positive integer.
Then:
$n - 1 \equiv -1$ (mod n)
if, and only if,
n is a divisor of $(n - 1) - (-1)$
if, and only if,
n is a divisor of $(n - 1) + 1$
if, and only if,
n is a divisor of n, which is a true statement.
Thus, the result holds. ∎

Theorem 2. (Wilson's Theorem) n is a prime if, and only if, n is an integer greater than 1 such that n is a divisor of $(n - 1)! + 1$.
Proof:
Part 1. We show that if n is an integer greater than 1 such that n is a divisor of $(n - 1)! + 1$, then n is a prime.
Suppose that n is an integer greater than 1 such that n is a divisor of $(n - 1)! + 1$.
Suppose that n is not a prime.
Then there exists a prime p such that p is a divisor of n and p is less than n. Therefore, p, too, is a divisor of $(n - 1)! + 1$, by transitivity of the divisor relationship. But since p is less than n, p occurs as a factor in the factorial $(n - 1)!$. Thus, p is a divisor of $(n - 1)!$. However, $(n - 1)!$ and $(n - 1)! + 1$ are consecutive positive integers, and the only positive integer that can be a divisor of two consecutive positive integers is 1. Thus, p = 1, which contradicts the supposition that p is a prime. Obtaining this contradiction shows that p must be a prime.
Part 2. We show that if n is a prime, then n is a divisor of $(n - 1)! + 1$.
Suppose that n is a prime.
Case 1. n = 2.
Then, since 2 is a divisor of $(2 - 1)! + 1$, because $(2 - 1)! + 1 = 1! + 1 = 1 + 1 = 2$, the result holds.
Case 2. n = 3.
Then, since 3 is a divisor of $(3 - 1)! + 1$, because $(3 - 1)! + 1 = 2! + 1 = 2 + 1 = 3$, the result holds.
Case 3. n is greater than 3.

Then, by Synapse 1, the list of integers 2, ..., n – 2 is nonempty, has an even number of entries, and for each x in the list there exists exactly one y in the list such that $xy \equiv 1$ (mod p), and for each x in the list and for each y in the list, if $xy \equiv 1$ (mod p), then $x \neq y$. Therefore, the entries in the list can be grouped into pairs of distinct entries such that the product of each such pair is congruent to 1 (mod n). Therefore, the product of the entries in the list is congruent to 1 (mod n). But the product of the entries in the list is equal to $(n – 2)!$. Therefore, $(n – 2)! \equiv 1$ (mod n). But by Theorem 2, $(n – 1) \equiv -1$ (mod n). Multiplying these last two congruences together, we have $(n – 1)! \equiv -1$ (mod n). Therefore, n is a divisor of $(n – 1)! – (-1)$. Therefore, n is a divisor of $(n – 1)! + 1$.

■

(end of document)

Heine-Borel Covering Theorem

Definition 1. An upper bound for a given set is any number h such that no member of the given set is greater than h.

Axiom. (Least Upper Bound Axiom) Every nonempty set of real numbers that has an upper bound has a least upper bound.

Definition 2. If M is a set of real numbers and G is a collection of sets of real numbers, then G is said to cover M if, and only if, every element of M is an element of some member of G.

Definition 3. An open interval is a set of real numbers such that there exists a real number a and there exists a real number b such that the open interval, denoted by (a,b) is equal to $\{x \mid x$ is a real number such that $a < x < b\}$.

Definition 4. A closed interval is a set of real numbers such that there exists a real number a and there exists a real number b such that the closed interval, denoted by [a,b] is equal to $\{x \mid x$ is a real number such that $a \leq x \leq b\}$.

Theorem. (Heine-Borel Covering Theorem) If each of a and b is a real number, and G is a collection of open intervals covering [a,b], then there exists a finite sub-collection G' of G such that G' covers [a,b].
Proof:
Suppose that each of a and b is a real number and G is a collection of open intervals covering [a,b].
Case 1. $b \leq a$.
Then [a,b] contains at most one element, and so the result follows.
Case 2. $a < b$.
Let M = $\{x \mid x \in [a,b]$ and there exists a finite sub-collection G' of G such that G' covers [a,x]$\}$. Since $a \in [a,b]$, there exists a member (t,u) of G such that $t < a < u$. Thus, there exists a member c of [a,b] such that $a < c$ and $c \in M$. Since M is nonempty and b is an upper bound of M, M has a least upper bound. Let us call this least upper bound h. Then $h \in [a,b]$. Therefore, there exists an open interval (v,w) in G such that $v < h < w$. However, there exists a member p of [a,b] such that $a < p < h$ and $v < p$. Let H be a finite sub-collection of G such that H covers [a,p]. Then there exists an open interval (e,f) in G such that $e < p < f$. Let G' $\equiv$ H $\cup$ $\{(e,f)\}$. Then G' is finite and covers [a,h], since $e < p < f$ and $v < p < w$. Thus, $h \in M$. However, if $h < b$, then there exists an element d of (e,f) such that $h < d < b$, and therefore G' is a cover for [a,d], and therefore h is not an upper bound of M, a contradiction. Thus, $h = b$. Thus, G' covers [a,b]. ∎

(end of document)

(blank page)

Bézout's Identity

Theorem. If each of a and b is an integer, and not both are 0, then there exists an integer x and there exists an integer y such that ax + by = gcd(a,b).

Proof:

Suppose that each of a and b is an integer, and not both are 0.

Let S = {ax + by | each of x and y is an integer, and ax + by > 0}.

Clearly, S is nonempty.

Let d be the smallest member of S, and let each of x and y be an integer such that d = ax + by.

If we can show that d is a common divisor of a and b, and that every common divisor of a and b divides d, then we have the result.

Suppose that d does not divide a. Then there exists integers q and r such that a = qd + r, with q ≥ 0 and 0 < r < d. Then qd = a − r. Then q(ax + by) = a − r.

Therefore, r = a − q(ax + by) = a − qax − qby = a(1 − qx) + (-qb)y. Thus, there exists an integer x' and there exists an integer y' such that r = ax' + by', and since r > 0, r ∈ S. But r < d. Thus, r is an element of S less than d, a contradiction. Thus d divides a. Similarly, d divides b. Thus, d is a common divisor of a and b.

Suppose that c is a common divisor of a and b. Then there exists an integer u and there exists an integer v such that uc = a and vc = b. Then d = ax + by = (uc)x + (vc)y = c(ux + vy). Thus, c divides d. ∎

(end of document)

(blank page)

Birthday Problem

Theorem. Ignoring leap years, if a group of 23 people is selected at random, then the probability that at least two of members of the group have the same birthday (month and day) is greater than 1/2.

Proof:

The probability that at least two of members of the group have the same birthday (month and day) is the complement of the probability that no two members of the group have the same birthday, which is $1 - P(A)$, where A is the event that at least two members of the group have the same birthday, and P denotes the probability function.

The probability that two members of the group do NOT have the same birthday is 364/365. The probability that NO two members of the group have the same birthday is 364/365 raised to the power equal to the number of combinations of 23 things taken 2 at a time. The number of combinations of 23 things taken 2 at a time is the binomial coefficient $C(23,2)$, which equals $23!/(2! \times (23 - 2)!)$, which equals $23!/(2 \times 21!)$, which equals $(22 \times 23)/2$, which equals 11×23, which equals 253. Then 364/365 raised to this power (253) is the probability that NO two members of the group have the same birthday. Subtracting this from 1 gives the probability that at least two members of the group have the same birthday, and this value is greater than 1/2.

(end of document)

(blank page)

Liouville's Theorem

Theorem. (Liouville's Theorem) Every non-constant entire function is unbounded.
(For a proof, see the treatise by A. I. Markushevich.)

With Liouville's Theorem in hand, we can easily prove the Fundamental Theorem of Algebra, namely, that every non-constant polynomial has a root, because if a non-constant polynomial had no root, then the reciprocal of the polynomial would be a non-constant bounded entire function, which would contradict Liouville's Theorem.

Note: Picard's Little Theorem is a considerable strengthening of Liouville's Theorem. Picard's Little Theorem states that any entire function that omits two or more points from its range is constant.

(end of document)

(blank page)

Remainder Theorem

Theorem. (Remainder Theorem) The remainder of the division of a polynomial f(x) by the linear polynomial x − a is f(a).

Proof:

The result follows from Euclidean division which, given two polynomials f(x) and g(x), asserts the existence and the uniqueness, when f(x) is divided by g(x), of a quotient q(x) and a remainder r(x) such that

$$f(x) = q(x)g(x) + r(x), \text{ and } r(x) = 0 \text{ or } \deg(r) < \deg(g).$$

For g(x) = x − a, then r = 0 or deg(r) = 0; in either case r is a constant independent of x; that is:

$$f(x) = q(x)(x − a) + r.$$

Then f(a) = q(x)(a − a) + r = q(x)(0) + r = 0 + r = r.

∎

(end of document)

(blank page)

Schröder-Bernstein Theorem

Definition. An injective function is a function that maps distinct points to distinct points.

Theorem. (Schröder-Bernstein Theorem) If each of A and B is a nonempty set and there exists an injective function from A into B, and there exists an injective function from B into A, then there exists a bijective function between A and B.
Proof:
Assume without loss of generality that A and B are disjoint.
Suppose that f is an injective function from A into B, and that g is an injective function from B into A.
For any a in A or b in B we can form a unique two-sided sequence of elements that are alternately in A and B, by repeatedly applying f and g (to go to the right) and g^{-1} and f^{-1} (where defined, to go to the left).

$$\cdots \rightarrow f^{-1}(g^{-1}(a)) \rightarrow g^{-1}(a) \rightarrow a \rightarrow f(a) \rightarrow g(f(a)) \rightarrow \cdots$$

For any particular a, this sequence may terminate on the left at a point where f^{-1} or g^{-1} is undefined.

Because f and g are injective functions, each a in A and b in B is in exactly one such sequence. Therefore the sequences form a partition of the (disjoint) union of A and B. Hence it suffices to show the existence of a bijection between the elements of A and B in each of the sequences separately, which we do as follows:

Call a sequence an A-stopper if it stops at an element of a, or a B-stopper if it stops at an element of b. Otherwise call it doubly infinite if all the elements are distinct, or cyclic if it repeats.

For an A-stopper, f is a bijection between its elements in A and its elements in B.

For a B-stopper, g is a bijection between its elements in B and its elements in A.

For a doubly infinite sequence or a cyclic sequence, either f or g will do.
∎

(end of document)

(blank page)

Well-Ordering Theorem

Definition 1. If each of A and B is a set, then the Cartesian product of A and B, denoted by A × B, is the set {(a,b) | a ∈ A and b ∈ B}.

Definition 2. A binary relation on a given set is any subset of the Cartesian product of the set with itself.

Definition 3. If R is a binary relation on a given set, then aRb means (a,b) ∈ R.

Definition 4. If R is a binary relation on a given set, then R is said to be reflexive if, and only if, for each x in the given set, xRx.

Definition 5. If R is a binary relation on a given set, then R is said to be symmetric if, and only if, for each x in the given set and for each y in the given set, if xRy, then yRx.

Definition 6. If R is a binary relation on a given set, then R is said to be anti-symmetric if, and only if, for each x in the given set and for each y in the given set, if xRy and yRx, then x = y.

Definition 7. If R is a binary relation on a given set, then R is said to be transitive if, and only if, for each x in the given set and for each y in the given set and for each z in the given set, if xRy and yRz, then xRz.

Definition 8. A partial order on a given set is a binary relation on the set such that the binary relation is reflexive, anti-symmetric, and transitive. The set, with regard to a given partial order on it, is called a partially ordered set.

Definition 9. If R is a binary relation on a given set, then for each x in the set and for each y in the set, x and y are said to be related (with respect to R) if, and only if, xRy or yRx.

Definition 10. A totally ordered subset of a given partially ordered set is a subset of the given partially ordered set such that every two members of the subset are related.

Definition 11. If H is a subset of a given partially ordered set, then an upper bound for H is any member p of the given partially ordered set such that for each x in H, xRp, where R is the given partial order.

In the development leading to the presentation of a specific result, it often happens that we wish to use certain theorems as axioms. That is, we do not wish to prove those theorems – their proof being readily available in the literature – nor do we wish to focus attention on them. To this end, we will use the term 'synapse' for such theorems.

Synapse. (Zorn's Lemma) If every totally ordered subset of a given partially ordered set has an upper bound, then the partially ordered set has a maximal element.

Theorem. (Well-Ordering Theorem) Every set can be well-ordered.

Well-Ordering Theorem

Proof:

Suppose X is a set.

Let A be the set of well-orderings on subsets of X. (That is, an element of A is an ordered pair (a,b), where a is a subset of X and b is a well-ordering of a.)

A can be partially ordered by continuation. That is, $E \leq F$ if, and only if, E is an initial segment of F and the ordering of the members of E is the same as their ordering in F. If T is a totally ordered subset of A, then the union of the sets in T can be ordered in a way that makes it a continuation of any set in T; this ordering is a well-ordering, and therefore an upper bound of T in A. Therefore, by Zorn's Lemma, A has a maximal element, say (M,R).

Suppose that M does not equal X.

Then there exists an element x of X such that $x \notin M$.

Then $M \cup \{x\}$ has a well-ordering that restricts to R on M, and for which x is larger than each element of M. This well-ordered set is a continuation of (M,R), contradicting maximality.

Therefore, M = X. Therefore, R is a well-ordering for X. Therefore, X can be well-ordered. ∎

(end of document)

Inferential Equivalence

Definition 1. Two statements are said to be inferentially equivalent if, and only if, each implies the other.

Many theorems are of the form of an inferential equivalence. Let us consider Wilson's Theorem as an example.

Wilson's Theorem. n is a prime if, and only if, n is an integer > 1 such that $n \mid (n-1)! + 1$.

Let A be the statement 'n is a prime', and let B be the statement 'n is an integer > 1 such that $n \mid (n-1)! + 1$'.

Then Wilson's Theorem can be stated as 'A if, and only if, B'.

So, an inferential equivalence is a theorem of the form 'A if, and only if, B'.

Definition 2. The right-pointing arrow $\rightarrow$ means 'only if', and the left-pointing arrow $\leftarrow$ means 'if', and the double-pointing arrow $\leftrightarrow$ means their logical conjunction.

So, an inferential equivalence is a theorem of the form 'A $\leftrightarrow$ B'. In other words, 'A $\leftrightarrow$ B' is an abbreviation for '(A $\rightarrow$ B) and (A $\leftarrow$ B)', which can be also written as '(A $\rightarrow$ B) and (B $\rightarrow$ A)'.

It sometimes happens that more than two statements of interest are all inferentially equivalent to each other. For example, suppose that three statements A, B, and C are all inferentially equivalent to each other. In such a case, a common proof technique is to prove them in a circle. For example, we prove A $\rightarrow$ C and then we prove C $\rightarrow$ B and then we prove B $\rightarrow$ A. This establishes that they are all inferentially equivalent to each other. In making this circle, we can choose any order we wish. Going from one inferentially equivalent statement to another can vary greatly in difficulty. That is why we wrote C after A in this example – to emphasize our option to choose the order.

To appreciate the difference in difficulty, let us consider the 'A' and 'B' components of Wilson's Theorem again. Going from A to be is very difficult, but going from B to A is very easy.

The following statements are all inferentially equivalent to each other:

The Axiom of Choice
Zorn's Lemma
The Well-Ordering Theorem
Tukey's Lemma

Going from the Axiom of Choice to the Well-Ordering Theorem is difficult, but going from Zorn's Lemma to the Well-Ordering Theorem is relatively easy, and going from the Well-Ordering Theorem to the Axiom of Choice is extremely easy.

(end of document)

(blank page)

! → factorial

⊂ → (is) a subset of

⊆ → (is) a subset of

⊃ → (is) a superset of

⊇ → (is) a superset of

∈ → (is) an element of

= → (is) equal to

≠ → (is) not equal to

< → (is) less than

≤ → (is) less than or equal to

<< → (is) much less than

> → (is) greater than

≥ → (is) greater than or equal to

>> → (is) much greater than

≈ → (is) approximately equal to

≅ → (is) congruent to (in Geometry)

≡ → (is) congruent to (in modular arithmetic)

≡ → (is) defined to be

⊄ → (is) not a subset of

⊥ → (is) perpendicular to

∝ → (is) proportional to

| → (is) a divisor of

∧ → and

× → cross product

× → multiplication

× → times

÷ → divided by

∃ → existential quantifier

∃! → uniqueness existential quantifier

∀ → universal quantifier

∞ → infinity

∫ → integral sign

∩ → intersected with

∞ → lazy 8

∅ → null set

∨ → or

∂ → boundary

∂ → partial derivative

% → percent

± → plus-or-minus

∋ → such that

Σ → summation symbol

∪ → unioned with

$\sqrt{(x^2 + y^2)} \to$ usual norm for the plane

(0,1)

$(0,1) \cup (1,2) \cup \{3\} \cup ([4,5] \cap Q) \to$ 14-set

(0,1]

$\sqrt{2} \to$ aspect ratio $\to$ A4 paper size

$\sqrt{2} \to$ metric paper $\to$ A4 paper size

$\sqrt{2} \to$ square root of 2

$\sqrt{2} \to$ unit hyperbola

$\sqrt{5} \to$ square root of 5

$\sqrt{5} \to$ square root of 5 $\to$ Binet's formula

$\gamma \to$ Euler's constant gamma

$\delta \to$ Dirac Delta Function

ε-δ proof

ζ function $\to$ zeta function

$\zeta(2) \to$ Basel Problem

$\lambda W \to L = \lambda W \to$ Little's Law

$\mu \to$ population mean

$\mu(n) \to$ Möbius function

π

$\pi \to$ calculation of $\pi \to$ Buffon Needle Problem

$\pi \to$ Chinese approximation of π

$\pi \to$ Greek approximation of π

$\pi \to$ Machin's formula

$\pi \to$ simple proof that π is irrational

$\pi(x) \to$ number of primes not exceeding x

$\pi^2 \to$ Basel problem

$\pi^2 \to$ fraction of primitive Pythagorean triples with perimeter $< p$

$\sigma \to$ population standard deviation

$\sigma(n) \to$ sum of the divisors of a given positive integer

$\sigma^2 \to$ population variance

$\tau(n) \to$ number of divisors of a given positive integer

$\tau(n) \to$ Ramanujan tau function

$\varphi(n) \to$ Euler's totient function

$\chi^2 \to$ chi-squared distribution

$\sqrt{x} \to$ square root

$\forall x \, \exists y \, [P(x,y)]$

$(xx)y = x(xy) \to$ left-alternative magma

$(xy)^{-1} = y^{-1}x^{-1} \to$ socks-shoes property

$(y_2 - y_1)/(x_2 - x_1) \to$ slope

$/ \to$ divided by

$\{ \to$ left curly brace

$\{\,\} \to$ empty set

$\{...\} \to$ curly braces

$| \to$ (is) a divisor of

$\|x\| \rightarrow$ norm

$|x| \rightarrow$ absolute value

$\} \rightarrow$ right curly brace

$<...> \rightarrow$ angle-brackets

$<0,1>$

$<a,b>$

$(a - b)/(a + b) = ... \rightarrow$ Law of Tangents

(a,b)

$(a,b]$

$[0,1)$

$[0,1]$

$[a,b)$

$[a,b]$

$(a^2 + b^2)/(ab + 1) \rightarrow$ Vieta jumping

$(ab + 1) \mid (a^2 + b^2) \rightarrow$ Vieta jumping

$(\cos x - 1)/x$

$(f(y) - f(x))/(y - x) \rightarrow$ difference-quotient

$(n - 1)$ in denominator instead of $n \rightarrow$ sample standard deviation

$(n - 1)! + 1 \rightarrow$ Wilson's Theorem

$(\text{observed} - \text{expected})^2 \rightarrow$ chi-squared test

$(\sin x)/x$

$(x - y)(x + y) \rightarrow$ factorization of the difference of two squares

$(x - y)(x^2 + xy + y^2) \rightarrow$ factorization of the difference of two cubes

0

$0 \le (\sqrt{x} - \sqrt{y})^2 \rightarrow$ Geometric-Mean – Arithmetic-Mean Inequality

$0 \rightarrow$ identity element for addition

$0 \rightarrow$ impossibility of dividing by 0

$0 \rightarrow$ setting the derivative to zero

$0.999... = 1$

1

$1 \rightarrow$ determinant of $1 \rightarrow$ indefinite special orthogonal group

$1 \rightarrow$ identity element for multiplication

$1 \rightarrow$ indicator function

$1 + 2 + 3 + ... + 98 + 99 + 100$

1/3-2/3 conjecture

$1/x \rightarrow$ multiplicative inverse

$10^1 \rightarrow$ order of magnitude

$10^{100} \rightarrow$ googol

$10^{\text{googol}} \rightarrow$ googolplex

$11 \rightarrow$ Casting Out Elevens

1-1 function $\rightarrow$ injective function

$12 \rightarrow$ dozen

$12 \rightarrow$ superior highly composite number

$14 \rightarrow$ Kuratowski's 14-Set Theorem

144 → gross

14-set

1729 → Hardy's taxicab number

18 countably infinite families → finite simple group

1988 → problem #6-IMO-1988

1-space → one-dimensional space

20 → score

22/7 → Greek approximation of π

23 problems → Hilbert's problems

24 → Cannonball Problem

24 → Ramanujan tau function

26 exceptions → sporadic group

2^A → power set

2-form

2mn → primitive Pythagorean triple

2nd moment of area

2p + 1 is also a prime → Sophie Germain prime

2-space → two-dimensional space

3 gloves implies either 2 left gloves or 2 right gloves → Pigeonhole Principle

3 mutual acquaintances → Ramsey Theory

3 mutual strangers → Ramsey Theory

3.14 → π

355/113 → Chinese approximation of π

3n + 1 → Collatz conjecture

3-space

3-term arithmetic progression

4 → Lagrange's 4-square theorem

5 → five number summary

5040 → 7!

5050 → sum from 1 to 100

6174 → Kaprekar's Constant

68-95-99.7 Rule → Empirical Rule

7 → genus seven → curve of genus seven → butterfly curve

7 → seven number summary

7! (already > 5000)

70 → Cannonball Problem

70 → Rule of 70

8/5 → Koch Snowflake

80/20 rule → Pareto Principle

9 → Casting Out Nines

3 primes problem → Goldbach's Weak Conjecture

100 → fake projective plane

25/78 → orchard-planting problem

2-dimensional surface in 3-space → two dimensional surface in 3-space

3/2 model

4-momentum operator

5/12 fraction of something → quincunx

50 → fake projective plane

6 → double six → Schläfli double six

7th degree equation → Hilbert's 13th problem

a (beginning of entries for A)

$A - B$

$a \times ab \times abc$, where a, b, and c are positive integers → harmonic brick

A → Axiom A

$A \cap B$

$A \cup B$

A → upside-down A → $\forall$ → universal quantifier

$a + (b + c) = (a + b) + c$ → Associative Property for Addition

$a + (n - 1)d$ → arithmetic progression

$a + b = b + a$ → Commutative Property for Addition

$a \cosh(x/a)$ → catenary

a feasible region in the parameter space

a more refined notion of limit

a number raised to a power

a number raised to a power → exponentiation

a random surface that exhibits fractal behavior

a set is called flat

a set is called flat → Cayley-Menger determinants

a set is called plane

a set is called plane → Cayley-Menger determinants

a set is called straight

a set is called straight → Cayley-Menger determinants

a simpler object that retains enough information about the object of interest

a simpler object that retains enough information about the object of interest → homotopy group

a situation in which for each $\varepsilon > 0$, there exists a $\delta > 0$ such that if $|x - a| < \delta$, then $|f(x) - f(a)| < \varepsilon$

$a(b + c) = ab + ac$ → Distributive Property

$a(bc) = (ab)c$ → Associative Property for Multiplication

$a(n)$ → number (up to isomorphism) of abelian groups of order n

$a, a + d, a + 2d, ..., a + (n - 1)d, ...$ → arithmetic progression

$a, ar, ar^2, ..., ar^{(n - 1)}, ...$ → geometric progression

a.e. → almost everywhere

$a/(1 - r)$ → geometric series

$a/(s^2 + a^2)$ → Cesàro equation

a/b → fraction

A4 paper size

a^b → a number raised to a power

$ab = ba$ → Commutative Property for Multiplication

abacus

abacus → slide rule
abc conjecture
Abel Ruffini Theorem
Abel Ruffini Theorem → topological proof of the Abel Ruffini Theorem
abelian extension
abelian group
abelian group → number (up to isomorphism) of abelian groups of order n
abelian variety
abelian variety → elliptic curve
about a given number
about a given number → sth moment about a given number
above or below the axis of symmetry → Lorenz asymmetry coefficient
absolute continuity
absolute convergence
absolute dispersion
absolute error
absolute pseudoprime
absolute pseudoprime → pseudoprime
absolute value
absolute value → Markov brothers' inequality
absolutely continuous function
absorption
absorption and closure properties → ideal
Abstract Algebra
Abstract Algebra → magma
abstract elliptic operators on arbitrary metric spaces
abstract resource semantics → Cirquent Calculus
abstract rewriting system
abstract simplicial complex
abstract structure versus concrete representations
abstract Volterra equation
abstraction
abstraction → concrete object
abstraction → intrinsic point of view
abundant number
acceptable level of false negatives
acceptable level of false positives
acceptance criterion
acceptance level
accessible pointed graph → rooted graph
accumulation point
accumulation point → adherent point
accumulation point → limit point
accumulator
accuracy

accuracy → going to higher degrees does not always improve accuracy → Runge's phenomenon

accuracy → precision

action of the Galois group on the roots of a polynomial

acute triangle

acyclic orientation

Aczel's anti-foundation axiom

adapted process

adapted process → stochastic process

adaptive path integral

added constraint

added constraint → circulation problem

added to

addend

adding equals to equals

adding inconvenience → just adding inconvenience, with no real benefit

addition

addition → Associative Property for Addition

addition → carry

addition → Commutative Property for Addition

addition chart

addition chart → addition table

addition of like terms

addition rule for derivatives

addition table

addition table → addition chart

additive inverse

additive inverse → identity element for addition

additive property

additive property → additivity

additivity

additivity → additive property

additivity of χ^2

adherent point

adherent point → closure of a set

adjacency

adjacency matrix

adjoint

adjoint → commutes with its adjoint

adjoint → commutes with its adjoint → normal matrix

adjoint → equal to its adjoint

adjoint → equal to its adjoint → Hermitian matrix

adjoint → If a matrix has only real elements, then its adjoint is equal to its transpose.

adjoint → self-adjoint linear transformation

adjoint matrix

adjoint matrix → conjugate transpose matrix

adjoint operator

adjugate matrix

adjugate matrix → conjugate transpose matrix

adjunction space

adjustments → seasonal index adjustments

Adleman-Pomerance-Rumley Primality Test

Advanced Calculus

AF-algebra → approximately finite-dimensional algebra

affine connection

affine function

Affine Geometry

affine plane

affine space

affine space → center of an affine space

aggregate index

aggregate index → simple aggregate index

aggregate index → weighted aggregate index

aggregation

aggregation → diffusion-limited aggregation

Agnesi → witch of Agnesi

agreement → final allocations of two goods between two people → contract curve

Ahlfors Finiteness Theorem

Airy function

aleph-null

Alexander duality

Alexander duality → Jordan Curve Theorem

Alexander duality → Spanier-Whitehead duality

Alexander invariants

Alexandroff one-point compactification

Algebra

algebra → Algebra

algebra → algebraic expression

algebra → approximately finite-dimensional algebra

Algebra → Artin-Wedderburn Theorem

algebra → associative algebra

algebra → Banach algebra

algebra → Boolean Algebra

algebra → Bose-Mesner algebra

algebra → C* algebra

algebra → Clifford algebra

algebra → Commutative Algebra

algebra → computer algebra

algebra → Computer Algebra

algebra → differential algebra

algebra → finite-dimensional algebra

algebra → finitely generated free modal algebra
algebra → free modal algebra
algebra → Kac-Moody algebra
algebra → K-algebra
algebra → L-algebra
algebra → Lie Algebra
algebra → Linear Algebra
algebra → Linear Algebra → Controlled Linear Algebra
algebra → non-associative algebra
algebra → Stone space of the free modal algebra
algebra → Tarski's high-school algebra problem
algebra → term algebra
algebra → tilted algebra
algebra → unital algebra
algebra → Universal Algebra
algebra → vertex operator algebra
algebra over a field
algebraic basis for the real numbers as a vector space over the rationals → Hamel basis
Algebraic Combinatorics
Algebraic Combinatorics → Combinatorics
algebraic curve
algebraic curve → analytic structure of an algebraic curve in the neighborhood of a singular point
algebraic curve → gonality
algebraic differential equation
algebraic differential equation → differential algebra
algebraic differential equation → polynomial vector field
algebraic equation → homotopy continuation method
algebraic expression
algebraic function of two parameters → Hilbert's 13th problem
Algebraic Geometry
Algebraic Geometry → Intersection Theory
Algebraic Geometry → motive
algebraic geometry of complex projective varieties
algebraic geometry of complex projective varieties → Hodge Theory
algebraic group
algebraic group → Jordan-Chevalley decomposition
algebraic group → linear algebraic group
algebraic invariant of a topological space
algebraic invariant of a topological space → mapping class group
algebraic manipulation
algebraic manipulation → problem #6-IMO-1988
algebraic number
algebraic number → transcendent number
algebraic number field

algebraic number field → Hilbert's 9th problem
Algebraic Number Theory
Algebraic Number Theory → Kronecker-Weber Theorem
algebraic properties → based on some useful algebraic properties
algebraic sign
algebraic space
algebraic stability
algebraic structure
algebraic structure of group rings
algebraic surface
algebraic surface → singular point on an algebraic surface
Algebraic Topology
Algebraic Topology → K-Theory
algebraic variety
algebraic variety → scheme
algebraically closed
algebras → classification theorem for semisimple algebras → Artin-Wedderburn Theorem
algorithm
algorithm → algorithm terminates within how many iterations
algorithm → Algorithm Theory
algorithm → backtracking
algorithm → computational algorithm
algorithm → computational algorithm → Monte Carlo method
algorithm → deterministic algorithm
algorithm → diamond-square algorithm
algorithm → division algorithm
algorithm → eigenvalue algorithm
algorithm → Euclidean algorithm
algorithm → exact algorithm
algorithm → forward-backward algorithm
algorithm → Hilbert's 10th problem
algorithm → inference algorithm
algorithm → Karatsuba algorithm
algorithm → Machine Learning
algorithm → Nearest-Neighbor Algorithm
algorithm → out-of-kilter algorithm
algorithm → polynomial algorithm
algorithm → stable algorithm
algorithm → strongly polynomial algorithm
algorithm terminates within how many iterations
Algorithm Theory
algorithmic and geometrical characteristics of origami
algorithmic and geometrical characteristics of origami → Recreational Mathematics
alien → urelement

aliquot parts

all → for all → universal quantification

All models are wrong, but some are useful.

all points on a line between two given points

all points on a line between two given points → convexity

all points on a line between two given points → interval

All's well that ends well. → independence of path

Allan Krill's technique for memorizing large numbers

allocation → final allocations of two goods between two people → contract curve

allowed poles → prescribed zeroes and allowed poles

allowed poles → prescribed zeroes and allowed poles → Riemann-Roch Theorem

allowed to run for a long time → Ergodic Theory

almost a manifold → Singularity Theory

almost all → Empirical Rule

almost everywhere

alternate interior angles

alternate interior angles → parallel lines cut by a transversal

alternating series

Alternating Series Test

alternative → statistical convention that the alternative hypothesis is assumed to be wrong

alternative hypothesis

alternative hypothesis → hypothesis

alternative hypothesis → Inferential Statistics

alternative hypothesis → null hypothesis

alternative interpretation of 'closeness' → p-adic number system

alternative magma

alternative route to analytical results

alternative specification

alternative specification of a probability distribution

alternative specification of a probability distribution → moment-generating function

altitude

altitude of a triangle

alysoid → catenary

amalgam of groups

ambient isotopy

ambient space

ambiguity → free from vagueness and ambiguity

amenable group

amenable group → Følner sequence

amicable pair

amortization

ampersand curve

amplitude

an emergent property

an emergent property → Ramsey Theory

an emergent property $\rightarrow$ synchronization

$a_n(x - x_1)(x - x_2)\cdots(x - x_n) \rightarrow$ Vieta's formulas

anallagmatic curves

analog

analogous to the relationship between the rationals and the integers

analogous to the relationship between the rationals and the integers $\rightarrow$ meromorphic function

analogy $\rightarrow$ shoes and socks

Analysis

analysis $\rightarrow$ Analysis

analysis $\rightarrow$ Analysis of Variance

analysis $\rightarrow$ Combinatorial Analysis

analysis $\rightarrow$ Consistency Analysis

analysis $\rightarrow$ Data Analysis

analysis $\rightarrow$ Dimensional Analysis

analysis $\rightarrow$ Factor Analysis

analysis $\rightarrow$ Fourier Analysis

analysis $\rightarrow$ Fracture Analysis

analysis $\rightarrow$ Functional Analysis

analysis $\rightarrow$ Harmonic Analysis

analysis $\rightarrow$ Nonstandard Analysis

analysis $\rightarrow$ Numerical Analysis

analysis $\rightarrow$ Ordinal Analysis

analysis $\rightarrow$ Pattern Analysis and Recognition

analysis $\rightarrow$ Time Series Analysis

analysis $\rightarrow$ Topological Data Analysis

analysis and processing

analysis and processing of geometrical structures $\rightarrow$ Mathematical Morphology

Analysis of Variance

Analysis of Variance $\rightarrow$ Theory of Association Schemes

analytic continuation

analytic function

Analytic Geometry

analytic manifold

Analytic Number Theory

Analytic Number Theory $\rightarrow$ Hardy-Littlewood circle method

analytic set

analytic solution $\rightarrow$ Hilbert's 19th problem

analytic structure

analytic structure of an algebraic curve in the neighborhood of a singular point

analytic torsion

analytical index

analytical index $\rightarrow$ Atiyah-Singer Index Theorem

analytical result

analytical result $\rightarrow$ alternative route to analytical results

analytical result $\rightarrow$ quantitative result

analytics

and

angle

angle $\rightarrow$ construction of an angle

angle between two intersecting lines

angle measure $\rightarrow$ degree angle measure

angle measure $\rightarrow$ radian angle measure

angle of inclination

angle trisection

angle trisection $\rightarrow$ cubic parabola

angle trisection $\rightarrow$ limaçon trisectrix

angle trisection $\rightarrow$ Maclaurin trisectrix

angle trisection $\rightarrow$ Morley's Miracle

angle-brackets

angle-measure

angular frequency

angular momentum operator

angular momentum operator $\rightarrow$ Casimir operator

anharmonic

anisohedral tiling

anisohedral tiling $\rightarrow$ isohedral tiling

anisotropy

anisotropy $\rightarrow$ isotropy

anisotropy $\rightarrow$ wood being easier to split along its grain than across it

annihilator

annual percentage rate

annuity

annuity $\rightarrow$ annuity due

annuity $\rightarrow$ annuity immediate

annuity $\rightarrow$ ordinary annuity

annuity $\rightarrow$ present value of a deferred annuity

annuity $\rightarrow$ present value of an annuity

annuity due

annuity immediate

annulus

annulus $\rightarrow$ Mamikon's proof of the Pythagorean Theorem

Anosov diffeomorphism

ANOVA $\rightarrow$ Analysis of Variance

ansatz

antiderivative

antiderivative $\rightarrow$ indefinite integral

antilog

antipodal points

antipodes

anti-symmetric relation

anti-symmetry

anti-symmetry of cardinality → Schröder-Bernstein Theorem

any odd perfect number has at least seven distinct prime factors

any property of a topological space invariant under homeomorphisms → topological invariant

aphorism → All models are wrong, but some are useful.

Apollonius → Problem of Apollonius

Apollonius center

appearance of a star in a telescope → Airy functions

Applied Mathematics

Applied Statistics

Applied Statistics → Optimal Estimation

Applied Statistics → Statistics

Applied Topology

applying the equations for continuous distributions to sets of discrete data

approximate solution

approximate solution → Perturbation Theory

approximate test

approximate test → Wilks' Theorem

approximately finite-dimensional algebra

approximately, is known, approximately

approximating the roots of an equation

approximating the roots of an equation → Newton-Raphson method

approximation

approximation → Bernstein polynomial

approximation → polynomial approximation → Mergelyan's Theorem

approximation → polynomial approximation → Runge's Approximation Theorem

approximation → polynomial approximation → Weierstrass Approximation Theorem

approximation → Simpson's Rule

approximation → Trapezoidal Rule

approximation by linear equations

approximation by linear equations → linearization

approximation by polygons

Approximation by Polynomials

Approximation by Polynomials → Stone-Weierstrass Theorem

approximation of π → Machin's formula

Approximation Theory

Approximation Theory → unisolvent point set

APR → annual percentage rate

$ar^{(n-1)}$ → geometric progression

Arabic numerals

Arabic numerals → Roman numerals

arbitrary holding times → Renewal Theory

arc

arc → inverse trigonometric function

arc → node

arc length
arc length
arc length of an ellipse
arc length of an ellipse
arccos → arccosine
arccot → arccotangent
arccsc → arccosecant
ARCH → autoregressive conditional heteroscedasticity
arch → inverted catenary arch
ARCH model
Archimedean local field
Archimedean spiral
Archimedes' screw
arcsec → arcsecant
arcsin → arcsine
arctan → arctangent
arctangent → witch of Agnesi
arcwise-connected set
area
area → enclosing an area → Dido's problem
area → equal areas → Equal areas are swept out in equal time.
area → equal areas → trifolium
area → invariance of area → Horseshoe Map
area → square
area → surface area → situation in which the derivative of volume equals the surface area → sphere
area element
area enclosed by a curve
area of a triangle
area of a triangle → Heron's formula
area under the curve
area under the curve → integral
Arens regularity
Arf invariant
Argand diagram
argument → diagonalization argument
argument → plausibility argument
argument of a complex number
Arithmetic → primitive recursive arithmetic
arithmetic function
arithmetic function → number-theoretic function
arithmetic mean
arithmetic mean → weighted arithmetic mean
arithmetic operation
arithmetic progression
arithmetic progression → Roth's theorem on 3-term arithmetic progressions

arithmetic progression of primes → Green-Tao theorem
arithmetical truth
arithmetical truth → Tarski's Undefinability Theorem
arithmetic-geometric mean
arity
arity → binary operation
arity → n-ary operation
arity → nullary operation
arity → ternary operation
arity → unary operation
arm
arm → vector
array → matrix
arrow
arrow → dart
arrow → hooked arrow
Arrow's Impossibility Theorem
artifacts of sampling, noise, and particular choice of parameters
artifacts of sampling, noise, and particular choice of parameters → Persistent Homology
Artin root numbers
Artin-Wedderburn Theorem
as soon as significant results are observed
as soon as significant results are observed → sequential analysis
as the scale of production increases
ascending chain condition on ideals → Noetherian ring
Ascoli's Theorem
Askey tableau
aspect ratio
aspect ratio → A4 paper size
association scheme
association scheme → Bose-Mesner algebra
association scheme → combinatorial structure
association scheme → Theory of Association Schemes
associative algebra
associative property
associative property → Associative Property for Addition
associative property → Associative Property for Multiplication
associative property → associativity
associative property → semigroup
Associative Property for Addition
associativity
associativity → associative property
associativity → Associative Property for Addition
associativity → Associative Property for Multiplication
associativity → concatenation

associativity → power-associativity
assortment
assumed wrong → statistical convention that the alternative hypothesis is assumed to be wrong
A-stability
astroid
Astronomy → light curve
Asymmetric Cantor set
asymmetric cryptographic key
asymmetric cryptographic key → Cryptography
asymmetric cryptographic key → Public-Key Cryptography
asymmetry
asymmetry → asymmetric cryptographic key
asymmetry → Lorenz asymmetry coefficient
asymptote
asymptotic behavior → Ergodic Theory
asymptotic behavior of the gamma function → Stirling's formula
asymptotic density
asymptotic density → sphere packing
asymptotic representation of the gamma function
asymptotic solutions of ordinary differential equations
Atiyah-Singer Index Theorem
Atiyah-Singer Index Theorem → Differential Geometry
atlas (in Topology)
atlas (in Topology) → chart
atom → urelement
atomistic view to the laws of motion of continua, from the → Hilbert's 6th problem
atriphtaloid
atriphtothalassic curve → atriphtaloid
attractor
attractor → Feigenbaum attractor
attractor → Lorenz attractor
attractor → repelling set
augend
augmented matrix
autocorrelation
autocorrelation → correlation
automated proof checking
Automath
automorphic form
automorphic function
automorphic function → Hilbert's 22nd problem
automorphism
automorphism → derived automorphism (in Ergodic Theory)
automorphism → endomorphism
automorphism group

automorphisms of the plane

autoregressive conditional heteroscedasticity

autoregressive moving average model

average

average → averaging

average → mean

average → median

average → mode

average → moving average

average → moving average → autoregressive moving average model

average → Pythagorean means

average → semi-averages → method of semi-averages

average → time-average

average → time-average → Little's Law

average deviation

average of a truncated running sum

average of a truncated running sum → moving average

average rate of change → difference-quotient

average speed

average speed → weighted harmonic mean

averaging

averaging → average

averaging → Cesàro summation

averaging → fungibility

averaging → homogenization

averaging → smoothing

averaging → time series

averaging → uniformity

averaging operation on bounded functions → amenable group

avoiding Runge's phenomenon → spline function

ax + by = c → standard form of a linear equation

ax + by = gcd(a,b) → Bézout's Identity

$ax^2 + bx + c = 0$ → standard form of a quadratic equation

axes (plural of axis)

axiom

axiom → Aczel's anti-foundation axiom

axiom → definitional axiom

axiom → eleven axioms → Tarski's high-school algebra problem

axiom → first axiom of countability

axiom → postulate

axiom → second axiom of countability

axiom → separation axiom

axiom → the various exogenous variables one is faced with

Axiom A

Axiom of Choice

Axiom of Choice → Hausdorff Maximal Principle

Axiom of Choice → socks-and-shoes illustration of the Axiom of Choice

Axiom of Choice → Tukey's Lemma

Axiom of Choice → Tychonoff's Theorem

Axiom of Choice → Well-Ordering Theorem

Axiom of Choice → Zorn's Lemma

axiom of pairing

axiom of regularity

axioms of Arithmetic

axioms of Arithmetic → Hilbert's 2nd problem

axioms of Physics, mathematical treatment of → Hilbert's 6th problem

axis

axis → axes → rotation of axes

axis → axes → translation of axes

axis → major axis

axis → minor axis

axis → principal axis theorem

axis of symmetry

axis of symmetry → Lorenz asymmetry coefficient

azimuth

b (beginning of entries for B)

B2B-DC → Bound-to-Bound Data Collaboration

Babbage's criterion for primality

backtracking

backwards E → ∃ → existential quantifier

badly → point where the solution of the equation behaves badly → movable singularity

Baillie-PSW primality test

Baire → property of Baire

Baire Category Theorem

Baker's Theorem

Baker-Beynon duality

balance of trade model → J curve

balanced design → pairwise balanced design

balanced incomplete block design

balanced incomplete block design → Combinatorial Design Theory

ball → bouncing ball → length of path of a bouncing ball

ball → duplication of a solid ball → Banach-Tarski Paradox

Banach algebra

Banach space

Banach-Tarski Paradox

banana function → Rosenbrock's banana function

band → Möbius strip

bar chart

bar chart → horizontal bar chart

bar chart → vertical bar chart
bar graph
barrier
barrier → obstacle
barycenter
barycentric refinement
base → change of base
base → radix
base → shifting base
base 10 digits → Real numbers whose base 10 digits are even
base 3 → Cantor set
base field
base of a logarithm
base of a topological space
base of a topological space → sub base of a topological space
base of a triangle
base of an exponential function
base period
based on some useful algebraic properties
based on some useful algebraic properties → exponential family
Basel problem
basic shape of a topological space → homotopy group
basis
basis → basis for a module
basis → basis for a vector space
basis → basis for an abelian group
basis → change of basis
basis → Gröbner basis
basis → Hamel basis
basis → ordered basis
basis → orthogonal basis
basis → orthonormal basis
basis → spherical basis
basis → usual basis of R^n
basis for a module
basis for an abelian group
basis of a vector space
bathtub curve
bathtub curve → hazard function
Bayes' Theorem
Bayesian Probability
bean curve
bean machine
bean machine → Central Limit Theorem
bean machine → Galton board

bean machine → quincunx

bearing

Becker-Gottlieb transfer

behavior

behavior → fractal behavior

behavior → how an object behaves as it 'runs around' a singularity → monodromy

behavior of the characteristic function in a neighborhood of the origin

bell curve

bell curve → Gaussian function

bell curve → normal distribution

Bell's theorem

below or above the axis of symmetry → Lorenz asymmetry coefficient

benchmark series → test of convergence

benefit → just adding inconvenience, with no real benefit

benefits, comparing long-term → Renewal Theory

Benford's Law

Benjamin-Feir instability

Bernoulli → lemniscate of Bernoulli → hippopede

Bernoulli differential equation

Bernoulli numbers

Bernoulli process

Bernoulli scheme

Bernoulli scheme → Bernoulli shift

Bernoulli shift

Bernoulli shift → Bernoulli scheme

Bernoulli trial

Bernstein polynomial

Bernstein polynomial

Bernstein polynomial → approximation

Bernstein polynomial → De Casteljau's Algorithm

Bernstein Problem (in Differential Geometry)

Bernstein-Sato polynomial

Bernstein-Sato polynomial → differential operator

Bertrand Paradox (in Probability Theory)

Bertrand's box paradox

Bertrand's Postulate

Bertrand's Theorem

Berwald connection

Bessel functions

best strategy for replacing a worn-out widget → Renewal Theory

Betti number

Betti number → fake projective plane

betting → gambler's ruin

between → relationship between

between → relationship between

between factors → no substitutability between factors
between factors → no substitutability between factors → Leontief production function
between one or two parallel planes → frustum
Bézout coefficients
Bézout coefficients → Bézout's Identity
Bézout's Identity
Bézout's Lemma → Bézout's Identity
Bianchi group
bias
bias → difference between expected value and true value
bias → zero bias
biased
biased → nonzero bias
biased coin
biased estimate
biased estimate → unbiased estimate
biased estimator
biased estimator → unbiased estimator
BIBD → balanced incomplete block design
Biblical unit of measure → cubit
bicircular quartic
bicircular quartic → Cassini ovals
bicompact space
bicomplex numbers
bicorn (curve)
bicuspid curve
bifurcation
big number → billion
big number → googol
big number → googolplex
big number → Graham's number
big number → million
big number → thousand
big O notation
biholomorphism
bijective function
bijective function → Schröder-Bernstein Theorem
bilinear mapping
bilinear product
billion
bimodal distribution
bin
bin → data binning
binary
binary operation

binary quadratic form
binary quadratic form → positive definite binary quadratic form
binary relation
Binet's formula
binomial
binomial coefficient
binomial distribution
Binomial Theorem
Binomial Theorem → Generalized Binomial Theorem
bipartite graph
bipolar coordinates
biquadratic form
biquadratic form → theory of biquadratic forms
bi-quinary coded decimal
Birthday Problem
bisection of angles
bit
Black-Scholes equation
Black-Scholes equation → heat equation
Blissard's Symbolic Method → Umbral Calculus
block → Jordan block over a ring
block design → balanced incomplete block design
block diagonal matrix
blocking data in an experiment involving multiple measures
board → Galton board
BODMAS
Bohr-Mollerup theorem
Bolza surface
Bolzano's theorem
bone → dogbone space
book → Dutch book
Boolean Algebra
Boolean Algebra → Mathematical Logic
Boolean Algebra → Stone's representation theorem for Boolean Algebras
Booth → lemniscate of Booth → hippopede
Booth → oval of Booth → hippopede
bordering of a space
Borel set
Borel-Cantelli Lemma
Bose-Mesner algebra
Bose-Mesner algebra → association scheme
Bose-Mesner algebra → matrix
bottle → Klein bottle
bouncing ball → length of path of a bouncing ball
bound → Hamming bound

bound orbits versus closed orbits

bound orbits versus closed orbits → Bertrand's Theorem

bound variable

boundary

boundary → Caccioppoli set

boundary → distance around, measured along the boundary → perimeter

boundary → empty boundary

boundary → frontier

boundary → partitioned boundary

boundary → without boundary → two-dimensional compact manifold without boundary

boundary condition

boundary condition → Hilbert's 20th problem

boundary conditions

boundary-value problems

bounded → totally-bounded metric space

bounded → totally-bounded uniform space

bounded function

Bounded Inverse Theorem

bounded lattice

bounded mean oscillation

bounded sequence

bounded sequence → Kaprekar process

bounded set

bounded variation

bounded variation → difference of two functions of bounded variation

boundedness of compound interest

Bound-to-Bound Data Collaboration

bow curve

Bowditch curve → Lissajous figures

box

box → box and whiskers diagram

box → box plot

box → Is it bigger than a bread box?

box → non similarity of brick and box → de Bruijn's Theorem

box → parallelepiped

box → thinking outside the box → nine-point problem

box and whiskers diagram

box paradox → Bertrand's box paradox

box plot

Boy's surface

brachistochrone

brachistochrone → constrained motion under gravity

bracket → commutator bracket → commutator

branch cut

branch of the complex logarithm

branching

branching out → Ramification Theory

breakdown voltage → Paschen's curve

Breit-Wigner distribution → Cauchy distribution

brick → domino

brick → harmonic brick

brick → non similarity of brick and box → de Bruijn's Theorem

brick → packing congruent rectangular bricks into larger rectangular boxes → de Bruijn's Theorem

brick → Turán's brick factory problem

bridge → structural support → inverted catenary arch

bridge (in Graph Theory)

bridge of fools (in Geometry)

Briggs logarithms

broadcast → no-broadcast theorem

Brouwer's fixed-point theorem

Brownian motion → fractional Brownian motion

Brownian motion → Wiener process

Brun sieve

Brun's Constant

Brun's Theorem

B-stability

B-theorem

Buffon's Needle Problem

bullet-nose curve

bump function

bundle → canonical bundle

bundle → fiber bundle → induced fiber bundle

butterfly curve

Butterfly Effect

Butterfly Effect → Chaos Theory

Butz Algorithm

Butz Algorithm → space-filling curve

c (beginning of entries for C)

C (set of complex numbers)

C^∞ function

C^∞ function → infinitely-differentiable function

C(X) → space of continuous functions on a compact Hausdorff space

C* algebra

C[0,1]

C[0,1] → set of all continuous functions on [0,1]

$c^2 = a^2 + b^2 - 2ab \cos \theta$ → Law of Cosines

$c^2 = a^2 + b^2$ → Pythagorean Theorem

Caccioppoli set

càdlàg function

càglàd function

calculating the determinant of a matrix

calculating the determinant of a matrix → Gaussian elimination

calculation

calculation → computation

calculation → rapid calculation → Trachtenberg system of rapid calculation

calculation device → abacus

calculation device → slide rule

calculation method → algorithm

calculation of the inverse of an invertible square matrix

calculation of the inverse of an invertible square matrix → Gaussian elimination

calculation of π → Buffon Needle Problem

Calculus

Calculus → Advanced Calculus

Calculus → Calculus of Probability

Calculus → Calculus of Several Variables

Calculus → Calculus of Variations

Calculus → Calculus of Variations in the Large

Calculus → Calculus on Manifolds

Calculus → Cirquent Calculus

Calculus → derivative → Newton's notation for the derivative → fluxion

Calculus → Differential Calculus

Calculus → Integral Calculus

Calculus → Itô Calculus

Calculus → Multivariate Calculus

Calculus → Sequent Calculus

Calculus → Stochastic Calculus

Calculus → Tensor Calculus

Calculus → Umbral Calculus

Calculus → Vector Calculus

Calculus → Visual Calculus

Calculus → Visual Calculus → Mamikon's Theorem

Calculus of Probability

Calculus of Several Variables

Calculus of Variations

Calculus of Variations → Hilbert's 19th problem

Calculus of Variations → Hilbert's 23rd problem

Calculus of Variations in the Large

Calculus of Variations in the Large → Morse Theory

Calculus on Manifolds

Caley-Hamilton theorem

calibration curve

càllàl function (continuous on one side, limit on the other side)

can be expressed as the ratio of two holomorphic functions

can be expressed as the ratio of two holomorphic functions → meromorphic function

Can you hear the shape of a drum?

Can you hear the shape of a drum? → Helmholtz's equation

Can you hear the shape of a drum? → vibrating membrane

cancellation

cancellation → catastrophic cancellation

candlestick

cannon ball → Cannonball Problem

cannon ball → cannonball trajectory

cannon ball → Coriolis force

Cannonball Problem

cannonball trajectory

cannot be represented as

cannot be represented as → connected topological space

canonical bundle

canonical form

canonical representation of a positive integer

Cantor → Smith-Volterra-Cantor set

Cantor set

Cantor set → Asymmetric Cantor set

Cantor set → Generalized Cantor set

Cantor set → nowhere-dense set

cap → cross-cap

capacity

capacity constraint

capacity constraint → flow network

cardiac function curve

cardinal

cardinal → inaccessible cardinal

cardinal → no cardinal between that of Z and R → Continuum Hypothesis

cardinal → smallest infinite cardinal → aleph-null

cardinal number

cardinal number → uncountable cardinal number

cardinality

cardinality → Schröder-Bernstein Theorem

cardinality of the continuum

cardinality of the continuum → Continuum Hypothesis

cardioid

Carmichael number

carrier set

carry

carry and borrow operation

Cartan connection

Cartesian coordinates → rectangular coordinates

Cartesian plane

Cartesian product

case

case → necessarily the case

case → not necessarily the case

case → special case

Casimir operator

Casimir operator → angular momentum operator

Casimir operator → universal enveloping algebra

Cassini ovals

Cassinoide → Cassini ovals

Casting Out Elevens

Casting Out Nines

Casting Out Nines → sum of digits

casualness → heuristic argument

casualness → Naive Set Theory

casualness → plausibility argument

casualness → rigor

catalyst → Lagrange multiplier

Catastrophe Theory

catastrophic cancellation

Category Theory

catenary

catenary → inverted catenary arch

catenoid

Cauchy distribution

Cauchy principal value

Cauchy sequence

Cauchy sequence → completeness

Cauchy's integral formula

Cauchy-Lorentz distribution → Cauchy distribution

Cauchy-Riemann equations

Cauchy-Schwarz inequality

Cavalieri's Principle

Cayley's theorem

Cayley-Hamilton Theorem

Cayley-Klein metric

Cayley-Menger determinants

Cayley-Menger determinants → determinant

CDF → cumulative distribution function

ceiling function

ceiling function → floor function

Celestial Mechanics → Perturbation Theory

cellular automata

center

center → triangle center

center of a group

center of an affine space

center of curvature

center of curvature → evolute

centers of similitude of two circles

central chi-squared distribution → chi-squared distribution

central chi-squared distribution → noncentral chi-squared distribution

Central Limit Theorem

Central Limit Theorem → bean machine

Central Limit Theorem → Galton board

Central Limit Theorem → quincunx

central origin → issuing from a central origin → eutactic star

central tendency

centroid

centroid → ill defined centroid → witch of Agnesi

certain event

certain occurrence of an event → zero-one law

certain quadrilateral is a square → Finsler-Hadwiger Theorem

Cesàro equation

Cesàro summation

Cesàro summation → averaging

Cesàro summation → Hadamard regularization

CEV → constant elasticity of variance

CEV model

Ceva's Theorem

Ceva's Theorem → Menelaus's Theorem

chain

chain → continuous-time Markov chain

chain → countable-chain condition

chain → Markov chain

Chain Rule

Chain Rule → related rates

chain slipping over the edge of a table (classical problem)

chainette → catenary

chance

chance → occurs simply by chance, or not

chance → occurs simply by chance, or not → Inferential Statistics

chance → probability

change → how much an endogenous variable changes in response to an exogenous variable

change a denominate number to units of lower or higher denomination

change of base

change of basis

change of dependent variable

Change of Variables Formula

Change of Variables Formula → Substitution Theorem for Integrals

change sign infinitely often → J. E. Littlewood's Theorem of 1914

changes → reflect changes over a period of time
changing divergence into convergence
changing divergence into convergence → Cesàro summation
changing divergence into convergence → Hadamard regularization
chaos
chaos → Butterfly Effect
Chaos Theory
chaotic → Julia set
chaotic → nonlinear system
character → of finite character
character of a group representation
Character Theory
characteristic
characteristic → nonzero characteristic
characteristic 0
characteristic a prime
characteristic equation
characteristic equation → Cayley-Hamilton Theorem
characteristic function
characteristic function → behavior of the characteristic function in a neighborhood of the origin
characteristic of a field
characteristic of a field → characteristic 0
characteristic of a field → characteristic a prime
characteristic polynomial
characterization of the gamma function → Bohr-Mollerup theorem
Charlier's Check
chart
chart → addition chart
chart → atlas (in Topology)
chart → bar chart
chart → bar chart → horizontal bar chart
chart → bar chart → vertical bar chart
chart → circle chart
chart → control chart
chart → curved-line chart
chart → multiplication chart
chart → pie chart
chart → rectangle chart
Chebyshev polynomial
check → Charlier's Check
check digit
check sum
checking → proof checking → automated proof checking
Chen's theorem
Chen's theorem → Goldbach's Conjecture

cherry-picking → Hadamard regularization
chess → Eight-Queens Problem
Chevalley group
Chevalley group → Lie group over a finite field
Chinese approximation to π
Chinese Magic Square
Chinese Remainder Theorem
chirality
Chisanbop
Chisanbop → finger math
chi-squared distributed
chi-squared distribution
chi-squared distribution → gamma distribution
chi-squared distribution → Inferential Statistics
chi-squared distribution → k independent standard normal random variables
chi-squared distribution → noncentral chi-squared distribution
chi-squared test
choice → Axiom of Choice
choice function
Cholesky decomposition
Cholesky decomposition → matrix decomposition
chord parallel to the directrix → latus rectum
chord through a focus → latus rectum
chosen for mathematical convenience → special form chosen for mathematical convenience
Christoffel symbols
chromatic index
cipher
cipher → Cryptography
circle
circle → circle method → Hardy-Littlewood circle method
circle → disk
circle → great circle
circle → great circle → intersecting great circles
circle → great circle → intersecting great circles → Spherical Trigonometry
circle → great circle → Spherical Trigonometry
circle → osculating circle
circle → two circles → generated by two circles → Watt's curve
circle → unit circle
circle chart
circle method → Hardy-Littlewood circle method
circle rolling along a line → cycloid
circular → bicircular quartic
circular → tricircular plane algebraic curve of degree six → Watt's curve
circular algebraic curve
circular conic

circular conic → circle
circular cubic
circular cubic → conchoids of de Sluze
circular function
circular function → Trigonometry
circular symmetry
circular symmetry around an axis
circular symmetry around an axis → cylindrical symmetry
circularity
circulation
circulation problem
circulation problem → maximum flow problem
circumference
circumference → perimeter
circumference of a circle
circumscribed circle
Cirquent Calculus
cissoid of Diocles
city block → Taxicab Geometry
C^k function
clamped → first vibrational mode of a thin L-shaped membrane, clamped at the edges
class → residue class
class boundary
Class Field Theory
class frequency
class interval
class length
class limit
class mark
class midpoint
class number formula
class number of a cyclotomic field
class number problem
class size
class width
classical and quantum setting for all (nongravitational) physical phenomena → Lorentz group
classical group
Classical Mechanics
Classical Mechanics → Dynamics
Classical Mechanics → Mechanics
Classical Mechanics versus Quantum Mechanics → Bell's Theorem
classification of closed surfaces
classification of finite simple groups
classification of finite simple groups → Finite Group Theory
classification of singularities

classification theorem

classification theorem → classification of finite simple groups

classification theorem → finite-dimensional vector spaces

classification theorem → Jordan normal form

classification theorem → rank-nullity theorem

classification theorem → structure theorem for finitely generated modules over ...

classification theorem → Sylvester's Law of Inertia

classification theorem for closed surfaces

classification theorem for semisimple algebras → Artin-Wedderburn Theorem

classification theorem for semisimple rings → Artin-Wedderburn Theorem

Clifford algebra

Clifford Index

Clifford index → Clifford's theorem on special divisors

Clifford's theorem on special divisors

clique (in a graph)

clique (in a graph) → monochromatic clique (in a graph) → Ramsey's Theorem

clockwise versus counterclockwise

clockwise versus counterclockwise → Möbius strip

cloning → no-cloning theorem

clopen set

clopen set → closed set

clopen set → open set

close analogy with trigonometric series → Walsh series

closed and bounded set → Heine-Borel Covering Theorem

closed and open set → clopen set

closed disk

closed form

closed form → results not being obtainable in closed form

closed form, results not being obtainable in → unbiased estimation of standard deviation

Closed Graph Theorem

closed interval

closed interval → continuous image of a closed interval

closed operator

closed rectangle

closed set

closed set → clopen set

closed set → separating points from closed sets

closed subset of a compact space

closed subsets → family of all nonempty closed subsets → Wijsman convergence

closed surface

closed surface → classification theorem for closed surfaces

closed-form expression

closed-form expression

closed-form solution

closure

closure and absorption properties → ideal
closure of a set
closure of a set → adherent point
closure-complement problem → Kuratowski's 14-Set Theorem
cloud → point cloud
clover → four-leaved clover → quadrifolium
cluster
cluster → clustering
cluster → clustering → volatility clustering
cluster → growth of specific types of clusters
clustering → cluster
clustering → volatility clustering
coanalytic set
coarsest topology
coarsest topology on a set → indiscrete topology
coaxal systems of circles
Cobb-Douglas production function
cobordism
cobordism → h-cobordism
cocked hat curve → bicorn
cocountable subset
code → cipher
code-cracking → Cryptography
coded decimal → bi-quinary coded decimal
coefficient
coefficient → Bézout coefficients
coefficient → Bézout coefficients → Bézout's Identity
coefficient → binomial coefficient
coefficient → coefficient of contingency
coefficient → coefficient of correlation
coefficient → coefficient of variation
coefficient → confidence coefficient
coefficient → decaying Fourier coefficients
coefficient → Fourier coefficient
coefficient → Gini coefficient
coefficient → Hilbert's 11th problem
coefficient → incidence coefficient
coefficient → integer coefficients → polynomial with integer coefficients
coefficient → Lorenz asymmetry coefficient
coefficient → matrix of coefficients
coefficient → matrix of coefficients → Gaussian elimination
coefficient → method of undetermined coefficients
coefficient → Pearson's correlation coefficient
coefficient → square of half the coefficient of the middle term

coefficient of contingency
coefficient of correlation
coefficient of variation
coefficient of variation → relative standard deviation
cofactor
cofactor matrix
cofinite subset
coherent set of characters
coherent set of characters → Representation Theory
coherent topology
Cohomology
cohomology groups of a smooth manifold
cohomology groups of a smooth manifold → Hodge Theory
cohomology ring
coin-flipping
coin-flipping → Bernoulli process
collating the data
Collatz conjecture
collinear points
collinear points → Menelaus's Theorem
collision avoidance → convex hull
coloring → partition
column
column → matrix
column → row
comb space
comb space → deleted comb space
combination → convex linear combination
combination → linear combination
combination → linear combination → convex linear combination
combinations → number of combinations of n things taken k at a time
Combinatorial Analysis
Combinatorial Design Theory
Combinatorial Design Theory → Combinatorics
combinatorial structure
combinatorial structure → association scheme
Combinatorial Topology
Combinatorics
Combinatorics → Algebraic Combinatorics
Combinatorics → Combinatorial Design Theory
comfortable lighting → Kruithof curve
commodity
common denominator
common denominator → least common denominator
common difference

common difference → arithmetic progression
common divisor
common divisor → greatest common divisor of n and k
common fraction
common multiple
common multiple → least common multiple
common ratio
common ratio → geometric progression
common refinement of two partitions of an interval
common trochoid
commutant lifting theorem
Commutative Algebra
commutative group
Commutative Property for Addition
Commutative Property for Multiplication
commutative ring
commutativity
commutator
commutator → group
commutator → ring
commutes with its adjoint
commutes with its adjoint → normal matrix
compact
compact → countably compact
compact → equivalence of various notions of compactness under various conditions
compact → limit point compact
compact → sequentially compact
compact complex manifold
compact complex surface
compact complex surface → Enriques-Kodaira classification
compact Hausdorff space
compact Hausdorff space → continuous functions on a compact Hausdorff space
compact Hausdorff space → locally-compact Hausdorff space
compact Hausdorff space → Weierstrass Approximation Theorem
compact Lie group
compact manifold → two-dimensional compact manifold without boundary
compact manifolds, index of elliptic operators on → Atiyah-Singer Index Theorem
compact operator
compact orientable surface
compact orientable surface → Nielsen-Thurston classification
compact self-adjoint operator
compact self-adjoint operator → Spectral Theorem
compact subset of a Hausdorff space
compact support
compact support → homology with compact support

compact topological group → Tannaka-Krein duality
compact topological space
compactification → Alexandroff one-point compactification
compactification → Hausdorff compactification
compactification → Samuel compactification
compactification → Wallman compactification
compactness
compactness → force compactness
compactness of a closed and bounded set
compact-open topology
comparing long-term benefits
comparing long-term benefits → Renewal Theory
comparison of an angle and its sine → (sin x) / x
Comparison Test
compass geometry
complement
complement → complements → replacing them with their complements
complement of a set
complement of the error function
complementary angles
complement-closure problem → Kuratowski's 14-Set Theorem
complete bipartite graph
complete divisor
complete graph of n points
complete lattice
complete metric space
complete randomization
complete set of invariants
completely normal space
Completely Randomized Design
completeness
completeness → consistency
completeness → incompleteness → Gödel's Incompleteness Theorem
completeness → NP-completeness
completeness axiom
completion → smooth completion → hyperelliptic curve
complex → simplicial complex
complex analysis → Nevanlinna Theory
complex conjugate
complex conjugation → complex conjugate
Complex Dynamics
complex harmonic motion
complex harmonic motion → Lissajous figures
complex Lie group
complex logarithm

complex manifold

complex manifold → Picard-Lefschetz Theory

complex manifold → simply connected 1-dimensional complex manifold

complex number

complex number → cross ratio of four complex numbers

complex number → modulus of a complex number

complex numbers

complex numbers → bicomplex numbers

complex numbers → field of complex numbers → Frobenius Theorem

complex numbers → hypercomplex numbers

complex numbers → split-complex numbers

complex plane

complex projective plane

Complex Variables

Complex Variables → Theory of Functions of a Complex Variable

Complex Variables → Theory of Functions of Several Complex Variables

complexity

complexity → parameterized complexity

complexity → structural complexity

complexity measure

complex-valued function of frequency

complex-valued function of frequency → discrete Fourier transform

component

component → subcomponent → sharing of subcomponents → Cirquent Calculus

component function

component of a time series

component of a time series → cyclical movement

component of a time series → cyclical variation

component of a time series → random movement

component of a time series → random variation

component of a time series → seasonal movement

component of a time series → seasonal variation

component of a time series → trend

components of a vector

composite function

composite number

compound interest

compressive loading → stress → stress-strain curve

computability

computability → constructability

Computability Theory

Computable Analysis

computation

computation → calculation

computation → dominant computation

computation → secure two-party computation
computation → symbolic calculation
computation → symbolic computation
computational algorithm
computational algorithm → Monte Carlo method
Computational Complexity Theory
Computational Complexity Theory → Yao's Principle
computational formula
computational formula → moment-generating function
computational formula → simplified methods for computing
computational formula for the logarithm
Computational Geometry
Computational Geometry → convex hull
computationally unrealistic set
computer algebra
Computer Algebra
Computer Algebra → Gröbner basis
computer algebra → symbolic computation
computing → simplified methods for computing
computing f(a) → Remainder Theorem
concatenation
concatenation → associativity
concave figure
concave function
concavity
concavity → concave figure
concavity → convexity
concentric circles
concept → evolution of the volatility of an underlying asset
concept → the various exogenous variables one is faced with
conchoids of de Sluze
conclusion reached at a much earlier stage
conclusion reached at a much earlier stage → sequential sampling
concrete number
concrete number → denominate number
concrete object
concrete object → abstraction
concrete object → extrinsic point of view
concrete representations versus abstract structure
concrete representations versus abstract structure
concurrent lines
concurrent lines → Ceva's Theorem
condition → a set is called flat
condition → a set is called plane
condition → a set is called straight

condition → as soon as significant results are observed
condition → as the scale of production increases
condition → boundary condition
condition → conclusion reached at a much earlier stage
condition → conclusion reached at a much earlier stage → sequential sampling
condition → Constructing an embedding can be difficult.
condition → countable-chain condition
condition → exists under weaker hypotheses
condition → no substitutability between factors
condition → number of zeroes equals number of poles
condition → output not proportional to input
condition → output proportional to input
condition → pre-defined condition
condition → pre-defined stopping rule → pre-defined stopping time
condition → pre-defined stopping time
condition → reformulated as an optimization problem
condition → sample size not fixed in advance
condition → used in fixed proportions
condition → wood being easier to split along its grain than across it
conditional → autoregressive conditional heteroscedasticity
conditional convergence
conditional factor demand
conditional factor demand → level of input required to produce a given level of output
conditional factor demand function
conditional probability
conditional tautology
conditional tautology → Sequent Calculus
conductor of an elliptic curve
cone
cone → conic section
cone → ice cream cone proof
confidence coefficient
confidence interval
confidence intervals for differences and sums
confidence intervals for means
confidence intervals for proportions
confidence intervals for standard deviations
configuration of 30 points and 12 lines → Schläfli double six
confluent hypergeometric functions
confused with the normal curve → Hubbert curve
confusion of words → Devil's curve
confusion of words → witch of Agnesi
congruence
congruence → scissors congruence

congruence modulo m

congruent rectangular bricks → packing congruent rectangular bricks into larger rectangular boxes

conic → circular conic

conic section

conic section → Dandelin spheres

conic section → eccentricity

conic section → toric section

conjecture

conjecture → Hadwiger conjecture (in Graph Theory)

conjecture → Hodge conjecture

conjecture → Kummer-Vandiver conjecture

conjecture → Morita conjectures

conjecture → Szpiro's conjecture

conjugate

conjugate → complex conjugate

conjugate → harmonic conjugate

conjugate → harmonic conjugate → projective harmonic conjugate

conjugate → isogonal conjugate

conjugate matrix

conjugate transpose matrix

conjugation → complex conjugation → complex conjugate

conjunction converted to disjunction → DeMorgan's Laws

connected → simply-connected space

connected interior → i-connected set

connected interior → polyomino

connected set

connected space

connected subgraphs → disjoint connected subgraphs → Hadwiger conjecture

connected sum

connected sum of manifolds → adjunction space

connectedness

connectedness → arcwise-connected set

connectedness → i-connectedness

connection → Berwald connection

connection between the monster group and modular functions

conoid

consequences of certain string-manipulation rules → Formalism

conservation

conservation → flow conservation

conservation → flow conservation being required for the source and sink → circulation problem

consider → natural set of distributions to consider

consistency

consistency → completeness

Consistency Analysis

consistent estimator
constant
constant → Brun's Constant
constant → difference is a constant
constant → Kemeny's constant
constant elasticity of variance
constant function
constant of integration
constant of proportionality
constant-sum property
constrained motion under gravity
constrained motion under gravity → brachistochrone
constrained motion under gravity → lemniscate of Bernoulli
constrained motion under gravity → pendulum
constrained motion under gravity → spherical pendulum
constrained motion under gravity → tautochrone
constraint
constraint → added constraint
constraint → capacity constraint
constraint on rational solutions
constraint on rational solutions → Rational Root Theorem
constraint-satisfaction problem
constraint-satisfaction problem → Distance Geometry
constructability
constructability → computability
constructability → constructible angle
constructability → constructible figure
constructability → constructible number
constructability → constructible point
constructability → constructible polygon
constructability → construction of a line
constructability → construction of an angle
constructability → construction of the real numbers
constructability → constructive generating process
constructability → constructive mental activity → Intuitionism
constructible angle
constructible figure
constructible number
constructible point
constructible polygon
Constructing an embedding can be difficult.
Constructing an embedding can be difficult. → manifold
construction of a line
construction of an angle
construction of the real numbers

construction of the real numbers → Dedekind cut
construction of two mean proportionals to a given ratio
construction of two mean proportionals to a given ratio → cissoid of Diocles
constructive generating process
constructive generating process → Intuitionism
constructive generating process → result of performing some constructive generating process
constructive mental activity → Intuitionism
consumption → permanent income hypothesis
consumption function
consumption function → relationship between consumption and disposable income
consumption goods → trade away your preferred consumption goods → Siegel's paradox
contact number → kissing number
contact of order k
contained in
content
content → measure
contest → IMO
contingency → coefficient of contingency
contingency table
contingency table → paradox regarding contingency tables → Simpson's paradox
continuation
continuation → analytic continuation
continuation → homotopy continuation method
continuation → meromorphic continuation
continued fraction
continued fraction → periodic continued fraction
continued fractions → Pell's equation
continuity
continuity → absolute continuity
continuity → discontinuity
continuity → modulus of continuity
continuity → modulus of continuity → Lipschitz condition
continuity → uniform continuity
continuity point
continuous → discrete
continuous compounding
continuous deformation
continuous deformation of a circle → Jordan curve
continuous deformation of a donut into a coffee cup
continuous derivative
continuous distribution
continuous distribution → discrete distribution
continuous extension of the factorial function
continuous extension of the factorial function → gamma function
continuous flow stirred tank reactor (classical problem)

continuous flow stirred tank reactor (classical problem) → CSTR problem
continuous function
continuous function → continuous mapping
continuous function → set of all continuous functions on [0,1]
continuous function of two parameters → Hilbert's 13th problem
continuous functions on a compact Hausdorff space
continuous groups versus differential groups → Hilbert's 5th problem
continuous image of a closed interval
continuous image of a closed interval → high-point theorem
continuous image of a compact set
continuous mapping
continuous mapping → continuous function
continuous mapping → number of fixed points of a continuous mapping
continuous on one side, limit on the other side → càllàl function
continuous on the left, limit on the right → càglàd function
continuous on the right, limit on the left → càdlàg function
continuous random variable
continuous random variable → discrete random variable
continuous time Gaussian process
continuous time Gaussian process → continuous time stochastic provess
continuous time Gaussian process → fractional Brownian motion
continuous time stochastic process
continuous time stochastic process → continuous time Gaussian process
continuous transformation group → Lie group
continuous variable
continuous-time Markov chain
continuum
continuum → indecomposable continuum
continuum → Whitehead continuum → Whitehead manifold
Continuum Hypothesis
continuum hypothesis → Hilbert's 1st problem
contour → Jordan contour
contour integral
contract curve
contractibility
contractibility → manifold
contractibility → surprising result → Whitehead manifold
contractible 3-manifold not homeomorphic to R^3 → Whitehead manifold
contractible manifold
contraction
contraction → dilation
contraction mapping
contradiction
contradiction → indirect proof
contradiction → paradox

contradictory-sounding term → simple complex Lie group
contrapositive
contrast → phase-contrast microscopy → Zernike polynomials
control chart
control group
Controlled Linear Algebra
conundrum → problem
convection-diffusion-reaction equation
convenience → special form chosen for mathematical convenience
convention
convention → statistical convention
convergence
convergence → absolute convergence
convergence → changing divergence into convergence → Cesàro summation
convergence → changing divergence into convergence → Hadamard regularization
convergence → convergence in measure
convergence → Lebesgue's Dominated Convergence Theorem
convergence → Monotone Convergence Theorem
convergence → pointwise convergence
convergence → questionable convergence
convergence → questionable convergence → Benjamin-Feir instability
convergence → radius of convergence
convergence → test of convergence
convergence → topological convergence
convergence → uniform convergence
convergence → Wijsman convergence
convergence in measure
convergence in probability
convergence in the L^1 norm → Lebesgue's Dominated Convergence Theorem
convergence of expected values
convergence of expected values → Lebesgue's Dominated Convergence Theorem
convergence of random variables
convergence of random variables → Probability Theory
convergence theorem
convergence theorem → Lebesgue's Dominated Convergence Theorem
convergent integral
convergent of a continued fraction
convergent series
convergent series → monotone convergent series
convergent subsequence
convergent subsequence → uniformly convergent subsequence → Ascoli Theorem
converse
converse → implication
converse → partial converse
converse → partial converse → partial converse of the Second Borel-Cantelli Lemma

converse → partial converse of the Borel-Cantelli Lemma → Second Borel-Cantelli Lemma
converse → proof
converting a decimal to a fraction
converting a fraction to a decimal
converting between polar and rectangular coordinates
convex → logarithmically convex → Bohr-Mollerup theorem
convex → nonconvex → nonconvex regular polyhedron
convex bodies in R^n → valuations on convex bodies in R^n → Hadwiger's Theorem
convex figure
convex function
convex functions in R^n → Wijsman convergence
convex hull
convex hull → Computational Geometry
convex hull → Graham's Algorithm
convex linear combination
convex polyhedron
convex set
convex uniform tiling of the Euclidean plane
convexity
convexity → concavity
convexity → convex set
convolution
convolution → Hilbert transform
convolution of functions
Conway number
cooling → Newton's Law of Cooling
coordinate
coordinate → coordinate system
coordinate → coordinates
coordinate → coordinates → homogeneous coordinates
coordinate space
coordinate space → real coordinate space
coordinate system
coordinate system → coordinate space
coordinate-free → in a coordinate-free fashion
coordinate-free treatment
coordinates
coordinates → coordinate
coordinates → homogeneous coordinates
coordinates → hyperbolic coordinates
coprime
coprime → relatively prime
Coriolis force
corollary
corollary → result

corollary → theorem
corona
corona → tessellation
corona → tiling
correctness → oblivious polynomial evaluation
correlated data → non-normal correlated data
correlation → autocorrelation
correlation → Heston model
correlation → rank correlation
correlation → rank correlation → Spearman's Formula for Rank Correlation
correlation coefficient → Pearson's correlation coefficient
Correlation Theory
corresponding angles
corresponding angles → parallel lines cut by a transversal
cos → cosine
cosecant
cosecant → hyperbolic cosecant → Poinsot's spirals
coset
coset → group
coset → Vitali set
cosine
cosine → hyperbolic cosine
cost
cost → cost on the flow → circulation problem
cost → lower cost
cost curve
cost on the flow
cost on the flow → circulation problem
cost-minimization problem of producers
cost-minimization problem of producers → isoquant
cot → cotangent
cotangent
Cotes's spiral
count data
countability
countability → first axiom of countability
countability → second axiom of countability
countability → separable space
countability of the rational numbers
countable
countable → countable set
countable → large countable ordinal
countable chain condition
countable intersection of open sets → G_δ set
countable set

countably compact
countably infinite → 18 countably infinite families → finite simple group
countably infinite set
counted with multiplicity
counterexample
counterexample → disproof
counterexample → minimum counterexample
counterexample → spoiler
counterintuitive → nonlinear system
counting argument
counting argument → Pigeonhole Principle
counting methods
counting on your fingers efficiently → finger math
country status model → J curve
couple → Tusi couple
coupled oscillators
coupled oscillators → oscillator
cover
cover → graph cover
cover → open cover
cover → open cover → compactness
covering group
covering space
Cox's theorem
Cox's theorem → Probability Theory
Cramer's theorem on algebraic curves
creative set
creative toy → Spirograph
Cremona group
criterion → acceptance criterion
criterion → Eisenstein's Irreducibility Criterion
criterion → rejection criterion
criterion for compactness → Heine-Borel Covering Theorem
criterion for primality
criterion for primality → Babbage's criterion for primality
criterion for primality → primality test
criterion for primality → Wilson's Theorem
critical line → Riemann Hypothesis
critical point
critical point → stationary point
critical point (in Set Theory)
CR-manifold
Crofton formula
cross multiplication
cross product

cross ratio
cross ratio → Cayley-Klein metric
cross ratio of four complex numbers
cross section
cross section → Cavalieri's Principle
cross section → cross section of a single water wave
cross section → cross section of a single water wave → witch of Agnesi
cross section → prism
cross section of a single water wave
cross section of a single water wave → witch of Agnesi
cross section of a smooth hill → witch of Agnesi
cross-cap
cross-cap → Möbius strip
crossed module
crossing numbers (in Graph Theory)
cross-shaped curve → cruciform curve
cross-validation
cross-validation → partitioning a sample of data into complementary subsets
cruciform curve
crumpled paper will have a point above where it started → Brouwer's fixed-point theorem
cryptographically secure pseudorandom number generator
Cryptography
cryptography → asymmetric cryptographic key
cryptography → Cryptography
Cryptography → Cryptology
Cryptography → oblivious polynomial evaluation
Cryptography → Public-Key Cryptography
Cryptography → secure two-party computation
Cryptology
Cryptology → Cryptography
Cryptology → oblivious transfer
Cryptology → zero-knowledge proof
csc → cosecant
CSTR (continuous-flow, stirred tank reactor)
CSTR problem
cube
cube → difference of two cubes
cube → doubling a cube → cissoid of Diocles
cube → factorization of the difference of two cubes
cube → Tychonoff cube
cube root
cubic → circular cubic
cubic → Tschirnhausen cubic
cubic curve
cubic equation

cubic parabola
cubic plane curve
cubit
cumulative distribution function
cumulative distribution function → distribution function
cumulative distribution function → not working directly with cumulative distribution functions
cumulative frequency polygon
cumulative frequency polygon → ogive
cumulative proportion → Lorenz curve
cup product
curl
curl → gradient
curl → normal component of the curl → Stokes' Theorem
curly braces
Curry-Howard correspondence
curse of dimensionality
curtate trochoid
curvature
curvature → center of curvature
curvature → radius of cuvature
curvature → surface with constant curvature
curvature of an individual's utility function
curve
curve → algebraic curve
curve → algebraic curve → gonality
curve → ampersand curve
curve → astroid
curve → atriphtaloid
curve → bathtub curve
curve → bean curve
curve → bell curve
curve → bicorn
curve → bicuspid curve
curve → bow curve
curve → Bowditch curve → Lissajous figures
curve → bullet-nose curve
curve → butterfly curve
curve → calibration curve
curve → cardiac function curve
curve → cardiod
curve → Cassini ovals
curve → catenary
curve → circular algebraic curve
curve → cissoid of Diocles

curve → common trochoid
curve → contract curve
curve → cost curve
curve → Cramer's theorem on algebraic curves
curve → cruciform curve
curve → cubic curve
curve → cubic parabola
curve → cubic plane curve
curve → curtate trochoid
curve → curve fitting
curve → curve of constant width
curve → curve of pursuit
curve → curves generated by other curves
curve → cyclogon
curve → degree of peakedness of a curve
curve → deltoid curve
curve → demand curve
curve → Devil's curve
curve → dose-response curve
curve → elliptic curve
curve → epicycloid
curve → epispiral
curve → epitrochoid
curve → family of curves
curve → Fermat curve
curve → fish curve
curve → Fletcher-Munson curves
curve → folium of Descartes
curve → forgetting curve
curve → galaxy rotation curve
curve → generalized logistic function
curve → Gompertz curve
curve → grading on the curve
curve → growth curve
curve → hippopede
curve → Hubbert curve
curve → hyperelliptic curve
curve → hypocycloid
curve → hypotrochoid
curve → idealized symmetric curve → Hubbert curve
curve → income-consumption curve
curve → indifference curve
curve → isoquant

curve → J curve
curve → kampyle of Eudoxus
curve → kappa curve
curve → Kruithof curve
curve → Laffer curve
curve → learning curve
curve → lemniscate of Bernoulli
curve → lemniscate of Booth
curve → lemniscate of Gerono
curve → light curve
curve → limaçon
curve → limaçon trisectrix
curve → Lissajous figures
curve → logistic function
curve → Lorenz curve
curve → Maclaurin trisectrix
curve → nephroid
curve → oxygen-hemoglobin dissociation curve
curve → parallel curve
curve → Paschen's curve
curve → Phillips curve
curve → Poinsot's spirals
curve → prolate trochoid
curve → quadrifolium
curve → quartic plane curve
curve → rational curve
curve → rational normal curve
curve → rectifiable plane curve
curve → right strophoid
curve → rose
curve → roulette
curve → semicubical parabola
curve → serpentine curve
curve → sinusoidal curve
curve → space-filling curve
curve → species-area curve
curve → species-discovery curve
curve → Spirograph
curve → squircle
curve → stress-strain curve
curve → strophoid
curve → supply curve
curve → topologist's sine curve

curve → torsion of a curve in 3-space
curve → trend curve
curve → trident curve
curve → trifolium
curve → trochoid
curve → Tschirnhausen cubic
curve → unicursal curve → rational curve
curve → U-shaped curve
curve → Viviani's curve
curve → Viviani's curve → lemniscate of Gerono
curve → Watt's curve
curve → witch of Agnesi
curve fitting
curve fitting → smoothing
curve of constant diameter → curve of constant width
curve of constant width
curve of constant width → Reuleaux triangle
curve of fastest descent → brachistochrone
curve of genus seven → butterfly curve
curve of pursuit
curve of pursuit → logarithmic spiral
curve of pursuit → radiodrome
curve of pursuit → tractrix
curve with a loop in the first quadrant and a double-point at the origin → folium of Descartes
curved-line chart
curves generated by other curves
cusp
cuspidal point
cuspidal point → pinch point
cuspidal point → singular point on an algebraic surface
cut
cut → branch cut
cut → Dedekind cut
cut (in Graph Theory)
Cut-Elimination Theorem → Sequent Calculus
cut-point
CW complex
cycle → limit cycle
cycle graph → Perrin number
cyclic group
cyclical movement
cyclical movement → component of a time series
cyclical variation
cyclical variation → component of a time series

cyclogon

cycloid

cyclotomic extension

cyclotomic field

cyclotomic field → class number of a cyclotomic field

cyclotomic polynomial

cylinder

cylinder → intersection of a sphere and a cylinder → Viviani's curve

cylinder functions

cylindrical coordinates

cylindrical symmetry

cylindrical symmetry → circular symmetry around an axis

d (beginning of entries for D)

Damerau-Levenshtein distance

damped oscillation

Dandelin spheres

Dandelin spheres → ice-cream cone proof

Darboux's theorem

dart

dart → arrow

data

data → applying the equations for continuous distributions to sets of discrete data

data → Bound-to-Bound Data Collaboration

data → collating the data

data → count data

data → Data Analysis

data → data binning

data → Data Mining

data → framework for combining models and training data from multiple sources

data → framework for combining models and training data from multiple sources → B2B-DC

data → grouped data

data → network having the best performance on new data

data → non-normal correlated data

data → reduction in the amount of variation in a set of data

data → remove noise from data → smoothing operator

data → separation of the data into two parts

data → separation of the data into two parts → method of semi averages

data → shape of data

data → shape of data → Topological Data Analysis

data → sparse data

data → test data

data → topological data → topological index → Atiyah-Singer Index Theorem

data → training data

data → unknown data

data → validation data
Data Analysis
data analysis
data analysis → exploratory data analysis
data binning
Data Mining
Data Mining → Machine Learning
data mining model
data project
de Bruijn graph
de Bruijn sequence
de Bruijn torus
de Bruijn's Theorem
De Casteljau's Algorithm
de Longchamps point
de Mere's paradox
de Moivre's formula
de Rham cohomology
decaying Fourier coefficients
decaying Fourier coefficients → Gibbs phenomenon
decile
decimal
decimal → bi-quinary coded decimal
decimal → periodic infinite decimal
decimal fraction
decimal point
decision rules
decision tree
decomposition
decomposition → Cholesky decomposition
decomposition → LU decomposition
decomposition → matrix decomposition
decomposition → Peirce decomposition
decomposition → QR decomposition
decomposition → rank factorization
decrease
decrease → increase
decreasing function
decreasing sequence
Dedekind cut
Dedekind domain
deduction
deep-inference system
deep-inference system → Cirquent Calculus
defect → number of defectives in a lot

defective design → faulty design

defective matrix

deficient number

definability → undefinability → Tarski's Undefinability Theorem

defined piecewise

defined piecewise → spline function

definite integral

definite integrals related to the gamma function

definition → definability → undefinability → Tarski's Undefinability Theorem

definitional axiom

definitions → relationship between definitions → uniform integrability

deformation

deformation → continuous deformation of a circle → Jordan curve

deformation → isomonodromic deformation

deformation → strain → stress-strain curve

deformation of a function → homotopy

deformation of material → hodograph

degenerate interval

degenerate triangle

degenerate triangle → needle triangle

degree

degree → lowest degree → gonality

degree → Turing degree

degree angle-measure

degree of inequality → Gini coefficient

degree of inequality → Lorenz curve

degree of peakedness of a curve

degree of peakedness of a curve → kurtosis

degree of unsolvability

degree of unsolvability → Turing degree

degrees of freedom

degrees of freedom → k degrees of freedom

degrees of freedom, ten, → Minkowski space

del

del → nabla

deleted comb space

deleted interval

delta function → Dirac delta function

delta function → Kronecker delta function

delta invariant

deltoid curve

demand

demand → conditional factor demand

demand → supply

demand curve

DeMorgan's Laws
denominate number
denominate number → change a denominate number to units of lower or higher denomination
denominate number → concrete number
denominator
denominator → fraction
denominator → least common denominator
denominator → numerator
denominator → Pell number
dense graph
dense set
density
density → asymptotic density
density → probability density function
density function
density function → probability density function
density function → probability density function of the Cauchy distribution → witch of Agnesi
density function → probability density function of the Cauchy distribution
dependence → functional dependence
dependent events
dependent variable
dependent variable → response variable
depreciation
depreciation → double-declining balance method of depreciation
depreciation → straight-line depreciation
depreciation → sum-of-the-years-digits method of depreciation
depreciation → units-of-production method of depreciation
derivation
derivation → proof
derivation of elliptical orbits from Newton's laws of motion and gravitation
derivative
derivative → derivative with respect to arc length
derivative → derivative with respect to time → fluxion
derivative → Leibniz's notation for the derivative
derivative → logarithmic derivative of the gamma function → digamma function
derivative → Newton's notation for the derivative → fluxion
derivative → second-derivative test
derivative → situation in which the derivative of volume equals the surface area → sphere
derivative → The function itself need not be injective, only its derivative.
derivative → The function itself need not be injective, only its derivative. → immersion
derivative → zero derivative → Rolle's theorem
derivative → zero derivative → stationary point
derivative doesn't exist → critical point
derivative of the inverse of a function

derivative of the tangent

derivative similar to original function → Pfaffian function

derivative with respect to arc length

derivative with respect to time

derived automorphism (in Ergodic Theory)

derived set

derived set → limit point

Descartes → folium of Descartes

descending sequence → Euclidean Algorithm

describe relative positions of ovals → Hilbert's 16th problem

Descriptive Statistics

design

design → balanced incomplete block design

design → Combinatorial Design Theory

design → Completely Randomized Design

design → pairwise balanced design

Design of Experiments

Design of Experiments → Theory of Association Schemes

desired property of an estimator

destination state, transition from an initial state to a random → Kemeny's constant

detect and quantify (a phenomenon)

detect and quantify (a phenomenon) → Topological Data Analysis

determinant

determinant → Cayley-Menger determinants

determinant → Sard's Theorem

determinant → use of determinants → Eight-Queens Problem

determinant → Wronskian

determinant of 1 → indefinite special orthogonal group

determinant of a matrix

determining the curve → number of points ... → Cramer's theorem on algebraic curves

determining the length of a curve → rectification of a curve

deterministic algorithm

deterministic primality test

deterministic primality test → Adleman-Pomerance-Rumley Primality Test

deterministic versus randomized algorithm, expected costs of → Yao's Principle

deviation

deviation → average deviation

deviation → unbiased estimation of standard deviation

Devil's curve

DFT → discrete Fourier transform

diagonal

diagonal → block diagonal matrix

diagonal → incommensurability of the diagonal of a square with its side

diagonal → number of negative elements in the diagonal → Sylvester's Law of Inertia

diagonal → number of positive elements in the diagonal → Sylvester's Law of Inertia

diagonal matrix
diagonal uniformity
diagonalizable matrix
diagonalization
diagonalization → Spectral Theorem
diagonalization argument
diagonalization argument → countability of the rational numbers
diagonalization argument → uncountability of the real numbers
diagonalization of a linear operator
diagonalization of a linear operator → Spectral Theorem
diagonalization of a matrix
diagonalization of a matrix → Spectral Theorem
diagram → Argand diagram
diagram → box and whiskers diagram
diagram → Dynkin diagram
diagram → velocity diagram
diagram → Venn diagram
diagram → Voronoi diagram
diagram → Young diagram
diameter
diamond → rhombus
diamond-square algorithm
Dido's problem
die (plural: dice)
diffeomorphism
diffeomorphism → Anosov diffeomorphism
difference
difference → common difference
difference → common difference → arithmetic progression
difference → difference between two cubes
difference → difference between two sets
difference → difference between two squares
difference → difference between two strings
difference → difference between two strings → edit distance
difference → difference of two functions of bounded variation
difference → difference-quotient
difference → symmetric difference of two sets
difference between expected value and true value
difference between expected value and true value → bias
difference between two sets
difference between two strings
difference between two strings → edit distance
difference is a constant → Meyer's relation
difference of squares → product of difference of squares → Markov brothers' inequality
difference of two cubes

difference of two functions of bounded variation

difference of two squares

difference of two squares → factorization of the difference of two squares

difference-quotient

differences → sampling distribution of differences

differentiability

differentiability → differentiable function

differentiable function

differentiable manifold

differentiable system

differentiable system → overdetermined differentiable system

differential algebra

Differential Calculus

differential equation

differential equation → algebraic differential equation

differential equation → Bernoulli differential equation

differential equation → direction field

differential equation → exact differential equation

differential equation → first order differential equation

differential equation → general solution of a differential equation

differential equation → homogeneous equation

differential equation → integro-differential equation

differential equation → intervals of validity

differential equation → linear differential equation

differential equation → method of undetermined coefficients

differential equation → nonhomogeneous equation

differential equation → particular solution of a differential equation

differential equation → reduction of order

differential equation → retarded semilinear nonlocal differential equation

differential equation → second-order differential equation

differential equation → separable differential equation

differential equation → slope field

differential equation → transformation of nonlinear partial differential equations to linear

differential field

differential form

Differential Geometry

Differential Geometry → Atiyah-Singer Index Theorem

Differential Geometry → Bernstein Problem (in Differential Geometry)

Differential Geometry → Nash Theorems

differential geometry from a singularity theory viewpoint

differential groups versus continuous groups → Hilbert's 5th problem

differential manifold

differential manifold → shrinking space

differential operator

differential operator

differential operator → Bernstein-Sato polynomial
differential ring
Differential Topology
Differential Topology → Morse Theory
Differential Topology → sphere eversion
differentiation → implicit differentiation
differentiation behind the integral sign
diffusion
diffusion map
diffusion-limited aggregation
digamma function
digamma function → gamma function
digamma function → polygamma function
digit
digit → Benford's Law
digit → check digit
digit → Real numbers whose base 10 digits are even
digit → sum of digits
digit → transposition of digits
digit → transposition of digits → Casting Out Nines
digital
digital root
digital root → sum of digits
dihedral angle
dihedral group
dihedral group → tiling
dilation
dilation → contraction
dilation → group of dilations
dilation → homogeneous dilation
dilation → inhomogeneous dilation
dimension
dimension → dimension of a vector space
dimension → Hausdorff dimension
dimension → relevant low dimensional features → Topological Data Analysis
dimension → vanish above the dimension of a space → Betti number
dimension of a vector space
dimension of space of solutions
Dimension Theory
Dimensional Analysis
dimensionality
dimensionality → curse of dimensionality
dimensionality-reduction
dimensionality-reduction → Sammon mapping
dimensionless variable

dimensionless variable → independent of the dimensions used
Diocles → cissoid of Diocles
Diophantine equation
Diophantine equation → Cannonball Problem
Diophantine equation → Hilbert's 10th problem
Diophantine equation → Pell's equation
Dirac delta function
direct product group
directed graph
directed graph → Askey tableau
directed graph → flow network
directed graph → transition system
directed line segment
directed line segment → equipollence
direction field
direction field → slope field
direction of oscillation versus direction of propagation
direction of oscillation versus direction of propagation → wave
directional derivative
directionality
directly → not working directly with cumulative distribution functions
directly → not working directly with probability density functions
directrix
directrix → distance from the focus to the directrix
directrix → parallel to the directrix → latus rectum
Dirichlet series
Dirichlet's Principle
Dirichlet's Principle → Riemann Mapping Theorem
Dirichlet's Test
Dirichlet's theorem on primes in a proper arithmetic progression
disc → disk
discontinuity
discontinuity → continuity
discontinuity → punctuated equilibrium
discontinuous function
discounting
discounting → hyperbolic discounting
discrete → continuous
discrete data
discrete data → applying the equations for continuous distributions to sets of discrete data
discrete data → level of measurement
discrete distribution
discrete distribution → continuous distribution
discrete Fourier transform
Discrete Geometry

Discrete Geometry → orchard-planting problem
discrete probability distribution
discrete random variable
discrete random variable → continuous random variable
discrete topological space
discrete topology
discrete variable
discriminant
discriminant → quadratic function
disjoint
disjoint → axiom of regularity
disjoint → sum-free set
disjoint connected subgraphs
disjoint connected subgraphs → Hadwiger conjecture
disjoint sets
disjoint sets → mutually disjoint sets
disjunction converted to conjunction → DeMorgan's Laws
disk
disk → circle
dispersion
dispersion → measures of dispersion
dispersion → relative dispersion
dispersion model
disproof
disproof → counterexample
disproof → spoiler
dissection puzzle
dissection puzzle → optical illusion
dissections of polygons
dissections of polygons → Wallace-Bolyai-Gerwien Theorem
distance
distance → Distance Geometry
distance → edit distance
distance → Hamming distance
distance → length
distance → Levenshtein distance
distance → metric
distance → shortest distance between two points
distance around, measured along the boundary → perimeter
distance between two points
distance between two points → hypotenuse
distance from a point to a line
distance from the focus to the directrix
Distance Geometry
Distance Geometry → Cayley-Menger determinants

Distance Geometry → constraint-satisfaction problem
distance of travel
distance to points in a specific subset of the plane
distance to points in a specific subset of the plane → Voronoi diagram
distance to the horizon
distinct points
distinction between points
distinction between points → separation axiom
distinctions among infinities → cardinality
distinguishability
distinguishability → indistinguishability
distinguishability → indistinguishability → topological indistinguishability
distinguished element
distracting fluctuations
distracting fluctuations → unwanted fluctuations
distributed → chi-squared distributed
distribution
distribution → binomial distribution
distribution → Cauchy distribution
distribution → chi-squared distribution
distribution → continuous distribution
distribution → discrete distribution
distribution → distribution of digits
distribution → distribution of infinite order
distribution → distribution of the primes
distribution → distribution of zeros
distribution → distribution of zeros of the Riemann zeta function
distribution → energy distribution → spectral energy distribution → witch of Agnesi
distribution → Erlang distribution
distribution → exponential distribution
distribution → five number summary
distribution → gamma distribution
distribution → geometric distribution
distribution → hypergeometric distribution
distribution → identical distribution → independence and identical distribution property
distribution → leptokurtic distribution
distribution → mesokurtic distribution
distribution → multinomial distribution
distribution → natural set of distributions to consider
distribution → normal distribution
distribution → null distribution
distribution → outlier
distribution → platykurtic distribution
distribution → Poisson distribution

distribution → sampling distribution

distribution → sampling distribution → standard deviation of a sampling distribution

distribution → sampling distribution of differences

distribution → sampling distribution of proportions

distribution → sampling distribution of sums

distribution → set of distributions

distribution → seven number summary

distribution → skewed distribution

distribution → stable distribution

distribution → stationary distribution

distribution function

distribution function → cumulative distribution function

distribution function → cumulative distribution function

distribution function → probability distribution function

distribution of digits

distribution of digits → Benford's Law

distribution of infinite order

distribution of infinite order → hyperfunction

distribution of primes → Rosser's theorem

distribution of the primes

distribution of the primes → Oppermann's conjecture

distribution of zeros

distribution of zeros of the Riemann zeta function

Distributive Property

Distributive Property → factoring

divergence

divergence → changing divergence into convergence → Cesàro summation

divergence → changing divergence into convergence → Hadamard regularization

divergence → unexpected divergence → harmonic series

divergence of the harmonic series

Divergence Theorem

divergent integral

divergent integral → Hadamard regularization

divergent series

divergent series → Cesàro summation

divergent series → monotone divergent series

divergent series → Summability Theory

divided by

divided by sign

divided by sign → obelus

dividend

divides

divides → (is) a divisor of

dividing by 9 → Casting Out Nines

dividing fractions

dividing x – a into f(x) → Remainder Theorem
divisibility
divisible group
divisible group → Prüfer group
division
division → long division
division → synthetic division
division algorithm
division by a fraction
division ring
divisor
divisor → Clifford's theorem on special divisors
divisor → common divisor → greatest common divisor of n and k
divisor → complete divisor
divisor → composite number
divisor → divisor function
divisor → divisor of zero
divisor → factor
divisor → linear system of divisors
divisor → number of divisors of a given positive integer
divisor → practical number
divisor → trial divisor
divisor → unitary divisor
divisor → weak divisor
divisor → zero divisor
divisor function
divisor of the order of a group → theorem of Lagrange
divisor of zero
dodecahedron
dodecahedron → small stellated dodecahedron
dogbone space
domain
domain → Dedekind domain
domain → frequency domain → Hilbert transform
domain → integral domain
domain → structure theorem for finitely generated modules over a principal ideal domain
domain → wandering domain
domain of a function
Domain Theory
dominant computation
Dominated Convergence Theorem → Lebesgue's Dominated Convergence Theorem
domino
domino → brick
domino → dominoes stacked over the edge of a table
dominoes stacked over the edge of a table

door space
dose-response curve
dot plot
dot plot → stem and leaf plot
dot product
double helix
double periodicity
double periodicity → fundamental parallelogram
double periodicity → fundamental parallelogram → function of a complex variable
double points → number of double points concentrated at a point
double points → number of double points concentrated at a point → delta invariant
double root → n-fold root
double six → Schläfli double six
double-angle formula for the cosine
double-angle formula for the sine
double-angle formula for the tangent
double-declining balance method of depreciation
doubling a cube → cissoid of Diocles
doubling the cube
doubling the cube → kampyle of Eudoxus
doubly periodic function → elliptic function
doubly-infinite power series
doubly-periodic function
Dowker space
downsized version → homomorphism
dozen
drum → Can you hear the shape of a drum?
drum → vibrating membrane
dual
duality
duality → Baker-Beynon duality
duality → Pontryagin duality
duality → Serre duality
duality → Spanier-Whitehead duality
duality → Tannaka-Krein duality
duality theory
duality theory → Spanier-Whitehead duality
dummy variable
Dunford decomposition → Jordan-Chevalley decomposition
duodecimal number system
duplication formula
duplication of a solid ball → Banach-Tarski Paradox
dusts → Fatou set
Dutch book
DV → dependent variable

dy/dx → derivative

dyadic fraction

dyadic fraction → Urysohn's Lemma

dynamical system

dynamical system → Axiom A

dynamical system → Bernoulli scheme

dynamical system → Complex Dynamics

dynamical system → de Bruijn graph

dynamical system → Ergodic Theory

dynamical system → Horseshoe Map

dynamical system → Krylov-Bobolyubov Theorem

dynamical system → limit cycle

dynamical system → Poincaré Return Theorem

Dynamics

Dynamics → Classical Mechanics

Dynamics → Nonlinear Dynamics

Dynkin diagram

Dynkin diagram → Lie Theory

e (beginning of entries for E)

E → backwards E → ∃ → existential quantifier

e → base of the natural logarithms

e → eccentricity

e (multiple meanings)

each → for each → universal quantification

earlier stage → conclusion reached at a much earlier stage

Easter egg → hidden feature → true features of the underlying space

eccentricity

Econometrics → heteroscedasticity-consistent standard errors

economic growth

economic growth → long-run economic growth

economic growth → long-run economic growth → model of long-run economic growth

economic growth → Solow-Swan model

economics → final allocations of two goods between two people → contract curve

economics → Lorenz curve

economics → Phillips curve

economies of scale

Eden growth model

Eden growth model → growth of specific types of clusters

edge

edge → extreme edge

edge → first vibrational mode of a thin L-shaped membrane, clamped at the edges

edge → lower bound on edge flows

edge → lower bound on edge flows → circulation problem

edge → sum of the weights of the edges

edge → where two edges meet → vertex
edge-transitivity
edit distance
edit distance → Levenshtein distance
educated guess → ansatz
effect → substitution effect
effective medium approximation
effective medium approximation
effective results in Number Theory
effective yield
efficient estimate
eigendecomposition of a matrix
eigenvalue
eigenvalue → real eigenvalues
eigenvalue → Wigner's classification
eigenvalue algorithm
eigenvalue of unity → stationary distribution
eigenvector
Eight-Queens Problem
Eilenberg-Maclane space
Eilenberg-Mazur swindle
Eisenstein integer
Eisenstein series
Eisenstein's Irreducibility Criterion
element
element → area element
element → distinguished element
element → idempotent element
element → identity element
element → order of an element
element → volume element
Elementary Arithmetic
Elementary Arithmetic → aliquot parts
Elementary Arithmetic → change a denominate number to units of lower or higher denomination
Elementary Arithmetic → common fraction
Elementary Arithmetic → concrete number
Elementary Arithmetic → denominate number
Elementary Arithmetic → fraction
Elementary Arithmetic → improper fraction
Elementary Arithmetic → like fractions
Elementary Arithmetic → mixed number
Elementary Arithmetic → proper fraction
Elementary Arithmetic → raising a fraction to higher terms
Elementary Arithmetic → reducing a fraction to lowest terms
elementary method → Liouville's Theory of Elementary Methods

elementary row operation

eleven → Casting Out Elevens

eleven axioms → Tarski's high-school algebra problem

elimination → Cut-Elimination Theorem → Sequent Calculus

elimination → Gaussian elimination

elimination of extraneous roots

Elimination Theory

ellipse

ellipse → ice-cream cone proof

ellipsoid

elliptic curve

elliptic curve → abelian variety

elliptic curve → conductor of an elliptic curve

elliptic function

Elliptic Geometry

elliptic integral

elliptic modular function → modular function

elliptic operator

elliptic operator → abstract elliptic operators on arbitrary metric spaces

elliptic operators on compact manifolds, index of → Atiyah-Singer Index Theorem

elliptical orbit

elliptical orbit → derivation of elliptical orbits from Newton's laws of motion and gravitation

Elliptic-Curve Cryptography

Elliptic-Curve Cryptography → Public-Key Cryptography

embedding

embedding → normally-embedded subspace

embeddings of one manifold into another → Geometric Topology

emergence of order → Ramsey Theory

emergence of patterns as the scale of the objects grows → Ramsey Theory

emergence of structure → Ramsey Theory

emergent order → Ramsey Theory

emergent property → an emergent property

emergent property → an emergent property → synchronization

emergent structure → Ramsey Theory

empirical models unsupported by theory → volatility

Empirical Rule

Empirical Rule → normal distribution

empty boundary

empty set

empty set → null set

enclosing an area → Dido's problem

endogenous variable

endogenous variable → exogenous variable

endogeny

endogeny → exogeny

endomorphism

endomorphism → automorphism

endomorphism → Frobenius endomorphism

endpoint

energy → Willmore energy

energy distribution → spectral energy distribution → witch of Agnesi

enough information about the object of interest, a simpler object that retains → homotopy group

Enriques-Kodaira classification

entire function

entire function → Liouville's theorem

entropy → topological entropy

entropy pool → random-number generation

enumerable set

enumerable set → recursively enumerable set

Enumerative Geometry

envelope

envelope → two envelopes problem

envelope of normals to a curve

envelope of normals to a curve → evolute

environment → the various exogenous variables one is faced with

environment-harvesting → harvesting the environment

epicycloid

epispiral

epitrochoid

equal areas → Equal areas are swept out in equal time.

equal areas → trifolium

Equal areas are swept out in equal time.

equal to its adjoint

equal to its adjoint → Hermitian matrix

equal to its transpose → symmetric matrix

equality

equality of sets

equal-loudness contours → Fletcher-Munson curves

equally-spaced samples of a function

equally-spaced samples of a function → discrete Fourier transform

equation

equation → abstract Volterra equation

equation → algebraic equation → homotopy continuation method

equation → applying the equations for continuous distributions to sets of discrete data

equation → approximation by linear equations

equation → Cesàro equation

equation → convection-diffusion-reaction equation

equation → cubic equation

equation → differential equation

equation → differential equation → algebraic differential equation

equation → Diophantine equation

equation → equations → Navier-Stokes equations

equation → Euler's equation (V − E + F = 2)

equation → functional equation

equation → heat equation

equation → impossible Diophantine equation

equation → inequality

equation → integral equation

equation → integral equation → hypersingular integral equation

equation → integral equation → hypersingular integral equation → Hadamard regularization

equation → integro-differential equation

equation → Lane-Emden equation

equation → Laplace's equation

equation → linear equation

equation → linear equation → system of linear equations

equation → Meyer's relation

equation → partial differential equations → Leray-Schauder degree

equation → Pell's equation

equation → Poisson's equation

equation → polytropic process equation

equation → quadratic equation

equation → quadratic equation → standard form of a quadratic equation

equation → quartic equation

equation → quintic equation

equation → system of polynomial equations

equation → whether singularities of solutions occur only at singularities of the equation

equation→ Tsiolkovsky rocket equation

equator

equiangular triangle

equicontinuity

equicontinuity → Ascoli's Theorem

equilateral triangle

equilateral triangle → Morley's Miracle

equipollence

equispaced interpolation points

equispaced interpolation points → Runge's phenomenon

equivalence of various notions of compactness under various conditions

equivalence relation

equivalence relation → cobordism

equivalence relation → homeomorphism

equivalence relation → isomorphism

equivalence relation → Miller's rules

equivalence relation → partition

equivalence relation → quotient space

equivalent fractions
equivalent up to permutation and isomorphism → Jordan-Hölder Theorem
Eratosthenes → sieve of Eratosthenes
Erf
Erfc
Ergodic Theory
Erlang distribution
Erlangen program
error → catastrophic cancellation
error → grouping error
error → heteroscedasticity-consistent standard errors
error → standard error
error → type 1 error
error → type 2 error
error function
error-correction
error-correction → Casting Out Elevens
error-correction → Casting Out Nines
error-estimate
essential singularity
estimate
estimate → biased estimate
estimate → unbiased estimate
estimate for exponential sums
estimate for exponential sums → Hua's lemma
estimation
estimation → Interval Estimation
estimation → Optimal Estimation
estimation → Point Estimation
estimation → unbiased estimation of standard deviation
estimation of parameters
estimation of population parameters from the corresponding sample statistics
Estimation Theory
Estimation Theory → U-statistic
estimator
estimator → biased estimator
estimator → consistent estimator
estimator → desired property of an estimator
estimator → minimum-variance unbiased estimator
estimator → objective property of an estimator
estimator → unbiased estimator
Euclid's Algorithm → Euclidean Algorithm
Euclid's fifth postulate
Euclid's fifth postulate → Parallel Postulate
Euclid's Lemma

Euclid's Theorem
Euclid's Theorem → infinitude of the primes
Euclidean algorithm
Euclidean Geometry
Euclidean group
Euclidean tiling by convex regular polygons
Euler brick
Euler line
Euler spoiler
Euler spoiler → Graeco-Latin square
Euler spoiler → Graeco-Latin squares exist for all orders n ≥ 3 except n = 6.
Euler top
Euler's constant gamma
Euler's constant γ
Euler's equation (V – E + F = 2)
Euler's totient function
Eulerian path
Euler-Maclaurin summation formula
eutactic star
evaluation of a polynomial → polynomial evaluation
evaluation of an integral
evaluation of an integral → u substitution
even → If the number is even, divide it by 2. → Collatz conjecture
even → Real numbers whose base 10 digits are even
even function
even number
even perfect number
even permutation
event
event → favorable event
event → rejection of the null hypothesis
event → tail event
eversion → minimax eversion → half-way model
eversion → sphere eversion
Every finite group of odd order is solvable.
Every finite group of odd order is solvable. → Feit-Thompson Theorem
evolute
evolution of the volatility of an underlying asset
evolution of the volatility of an underlying asset → Heston model
exact algorithm
exact differential equation
exact form
exact significance test → exact test
exact solvability
exact test

exactly once → de Bruijn torus

exactly one member → singleton

exactly two possible outcomes

exactly two possible outcomes → Bernoulli trial

Exact-Sampling Theory

Exact-Sampling Theory → Small-Sampling Theory

example → butterfly curve

example → counter-example

example → minimum of two values → Leontief production function

example → one of the first examples of determining the tangent to a curve → kappa curve

example → wood being easier to split along its grain than across it → anisotropy

except for a set of isolated points

except for a set of isolated points → meromorphic function

exceptional isomorphism

exceptional object

exceptions → 26 exceptions → sporadic group

excluded middle

exclusive or

exhaustive collection of subsets

existence

existence of a prime in a certain place

existence of a prime in a certain place → Dirichlet's theorem on primes in a proper ...

existence of transcendental numbers

existential quantification

existential quantification → existential quantifier

existential quantifier

exists → there exists → existential quantification

exists under weaker hypotheses

exists under weaker hypotheses → Jordan-Chevalley decomposition

exogenous → externally determined

exogenous variable

exogenous variable → endogenous variable

exogenous variables → the various exogenous variables one is faced with

exogeny

exogeny → endogeny

exotic sphere

expansion path

expectation → mathematical expectation

expected costs → inequality regarding expected costs of various algorithms → Yao's Principle

expected costs of a deterministic versus randomized algorithm → Yao's Principle

expected income in future years → permanent income hypothesis

expected number of time-steps

expected number of time-steps → Kemeny's constant

expected value

expected value and variance are undefined → Cauchy distribution experiment

experiment → control group

experiment → Design of Experiments

experiment → Multiplication Principle

experiment → random experiment

experiment → same experiment a large number of times → Law of Large Numbers

experiment → treatment

experimental design

experimental design → Completely Randomized Design

experimental unit

explained and unexplained variation

explanation → intuitive explanation

explanation → shoes and socks

explanatory model versus predictive model

explanatory variable

explanatory variable → independent variable

explanatory variable → response variable

exploratory data analysis

exploratory data analysis → Sammon mapping

exponent

exponent → pretending indices are exponents → Umbral Calculus

exponent → singular exponents

exponent → volume raised to a power → polytropic process equation

exponent 2 → generalized mean with exponent 2 → root mean square

exponent to which an integer belongs

exponential

exponential curve → forgetting curve

exponential decay

exponential distribution

exponential family

exponential family → based on some useful algebraic properties

exponential family → special form chosen for mathematical convenience

exponential function → function having a constant subtangent

exponential growth

exponential growth → compound interest

exponential integral

exponential notation for the power set → function space

exponential polynomial

exponential sum

exponential sum → estimate for exponential sums → Hua's lemma

exponential sum → Kloosterman sum

exponentiation

exponentiation → a number raised to a power

exponentiation → modular exponentiation

expression

expression → algebraic expression
expression → closed-form expression
expression → term
extended plane
extension
extension → abelian extension
extension → field extension
extension → Galois extension
extension → substructure
extension → superstructure
extension field
extension of degree n over the field F
extension problem
exterior angle
exterior of a set
externally determined → exogenous
extraneous root
extrapolation
extrema
extrema → finding extrema of a function
extremally-disconnected space
extreme edge
extreme edge → convex hull
extremum (singular of extrema)
extrinsic point of view
extrinsic point of view → intrinsic point of view
f (beginning of entries for F)
F distribution
f is given and φ is sought → Poisson's equation
f(a) = remainder when f(x) is divided by x − a → Remainder Theorem
f(x) → function notation
f(x) → function of a real variable
f(x) → function of one variable
f(x) = x → fixed point
f(x,y) → function of two variables
f(x,y,z) → function of three variables
f(z) → function of a complex variable
f'(z) ≠ 0
face
face → true face → their true face → true features of the underlying space
face-transitivity
fact → Every finite group of odd order is solvable.
fact ≥ Graeco-Latin squares exist for all orders n ≥ 3 except n = 6.
fact → If a matrix has only real elements, then its adjoint is equal to its transpose.
fact → If each edge has integral capacity, then there exists an integral maximum flow.

factor

factor → conditional factor demand

factor → divisor

factor → factor of proportionality

factor → no substitutability between factors

Factor Analysis

factor demand function

factor group

factor of proportionality

factor of proportionality → multiplier

factorial

factorial → falling factorial

factorial → Stirling's formula

factorial function

factorial function → continuous extension of the factorial function

factoring

factoring → Distributive Property

factoring → factorization

factoring → term

factorization

factorization → integer factorization

factorization → Lenstra elliptic-curve factorization

factorization → matrix factorization → matrix decomposition

factorization → rank factorization

factorization → unique factorization

factorization of the difference of two cubes

factorization of the difference of two squares

failure → exactly two possible outcomes

failure → exactly two possible outcomes → Bernoulli trial

failure of the limit of a sequence of continuous functions to be a continuous function

failure to be simply-connected → fundamental group

fair

fair coin

faithful representation

faithful representation → Representation Theory

fake projective plane

falling factorial

false negative

false negative → acceptable level of false negatives

false positive

false positive → acceptable level of false positives

false prime → pseudoprime

families of topologies on a fixed set

family → exponential family

family of all nonempty closed subsets → Wijsman convergence

family of curves
fanciful name → dogbone space
Fano plane
Farey sequence
Fáry's Theorem
fast Fourier transform
fast multiplication → Karatsuba algorithm
fastest descent → curve of fastest descent → brachistochrone
Fatou set
Fatou set → Julia set
Faulhaber's formula
faulty design
favorable event
favorable event → frequentist definition of probability
feasible region
feature → true features of the underlying space
features → hidden features → true features of the underlying space
features → true features of the underlying space
Feigenbaum attractor
Feit-Thompson Theorem
Feit-Thompson Theorem → Every finite group of odd order is solvable.
Fejer's theorem
Fermat curve
Fermat number
Fermat primality test
Fermat prime
Fermat's Last Theorem
Fermat's little theorem
Feuerbach's theorem
FFT → fast Fourier transform
fiber bundle
fiber bundle → induced fiber bundle
fiber space
Fibonacci → Spectrum of the Fibonacci Hamiltonian
Fibonacci number → Binet's formula
Fibonacci sequence
Fibonacci sequence → missing square puzzle
field
field → algebra over a field
field → base field
field → characteristic of a field
field → class number of a cyclotomic field
field → cyclotomic field
field → differential field
field → extension field

field → field extension
field → field of quotients
field → finite field
field → finite field → Wedderburn's Theorem
field → global field
field → Hilbert class field
field → local field
field → local field → Archimedean local field
field → local field → non-Archimedean local field
field → perfect field
field → scalar field
field → splitting field
field → topological field
field → valued field
field → vector field
field → vector field on a manifold
field extension
field of complex numbers → Frobenius Theorem
field of quotients
field of real numbers → Frobenius Theorem
fifth postulate → Euclid's fifth postulate
figurate number
figure → isohedral figure
figure-eight knot
fill → filling → space-filling curve
filter
filter → ultrafilter
Filtering Theory
final allocations of two goods between two people → contract curve
final topology
finance → Mathematical Finance
financial time series → ARCH model
finding extrema of a function
finding the rank of a matrix
finding the rank of a matrix → Gaussian elimination
finding the slope of a line from two points
finding the trend line or trend curve of a time series
finding the trend line or trend curve of a time series → freehand method
finding the trend line or trend curve of a time series → method of least squares
finding the trend line or trend curve of a time series → moving-average method
finest topology on a set → discrete topology
finger math
finger math → Chisanbop
finite → of finite character

finite area with infinite perimeter → Koch Snowflake
finite area with infinite perimeter → Koch Snowflake
finite division ring → Wedderburn's Theorem
finite field → Wedderburn's Theorem
finite geometry
Finite Geometry
Finite Geometry → Fano plane
finite group
finite group → monomial representation of a finite group
Finite Group Theory
Finite Group Theory → classification of finite simple groups
Finite Group Theory → Feit-Thompson Theorem
Finite Group Theory → Group Theory
Finite Group Theory → rank 3 permutation group
Finite Group Theory → Schreier conjecture (theorem)
Finite Group Theory → Schur-Zassenhaus Theorem
Finite Group Theory → Sylow theorems
finite perimeter
finite perimeter → Caccioppoli set
finite ring
finite ring analogy of Bessel functions
finite ring analogy of Bessel functions → Kloosterman rum
finite set
finite set of points → given a finite set of points in the plane → Sylvester-Gallai Theorem
finite simple group
finite terms → integration in finite terms
finite volume with infinite surface area → Gabriel's horn
finite-dimensional algebra
finite-dimensional algebra → approximately finite-dimensional algebra
finite-dimensional vector space
finite-forking property
finite-intersection property
finitely generated free modal algebra
finitely generated group
finitely generated modules → structure theorem for finitely generated modules over a ...
finitely-presented group
finiteness
finiteness → Ahlfors Finiteness Theorem
Finsler Geometry
Finsler manifold
Finsler-Hadwiger Theorem
first
first → Which one was first? → Fisher's Exact Test
first algebraic curve (other than the line and circle) to be rectified → semicubical parabola
first axiom of countability

first countable space

first digit law → Benford's Law

first moment

first order differential equation

first seen data → unknown data

first uncountable ordinal

first vibrational mode of a thin L-shaped membrane, clamped at the edges

fiscal multiplier

fiscal multiplier: not to be confused with 'money multiplier'

fish curve

Fisher's Exact Test

fit → curve fitting

fit → goodness of fit

five number summary

five number summary → seven number summary

five points → patterns of five points → quincunx

fixed point

fixed point → Lefschetz Fixed-Point Theorem

fixed point → Schauder Fixed-Point Theorem

fixed point → trace of a fixed point of a small circle that rolls within a larger circle

fixed proportions

fixed proportions → Leontief production function

fixed proportions → used in fixed proportions

fixed-point iteration

flat → a set is called flat

flat → a set is called flat → Cayley-Menger determinants

flat module

flat topology

Fletcher-Munson curves

flexagon

flexagon → hexaflexagon

flexagon → Recreational Mathematics

flexagon → tetraflexagon

flip → coin-flipping → Bernoulli process

flip → flipping → root flipping → Vieta jumping

Floer homology

floor function

floor function → ceiling function

flow

flow → gradient flow structure

flow → lower bound on edge flows

flow → lower bound on edge flows → circulation problem

flow → vector flow

flow conservation

flow conservation being required for the source and sink

flow conservation being required for the source and sink → circulation problem
flow network
flow network → capacity constraint
flow network → directed graph
flow network → Operations Research
flow network → out-of-kilter algorithm
flow network → out-of-kilter algorithm
flow network → skew symmetry constraint
flow problem → maximum flow problem
fluctuations
fluctuations → distracting fluctuations
fluctuations → unwanted fluctuations
fluxion
focal property of the ellipse
focal property of the hyperbola
focal property of the parabola
focal tendencies in random data
focal tendencies in random data → Descriptive Statistics
foci (plural of focus)
focus
focus → distance from the focus to the directrix
focus → through a focus → latus rectum
folding
folding is done neatly → Horseshoe Map
folium of Descartes
folium of Descartes → right strophoid
Følner sequence
Følner sequence → amenable group
foot → perpendicular foot
for all → universal quantification
For all sufficiently large n, there are at most f(n) special objects. → orchard-planting problem
For all sufficiently large n, there are at most f(n) special objects.
for each → universal quantification
For each x, there exists a y such that P(x,y).
for each $\varepsilon > 0$
for some → existential quantification
forbidden graph
forbidden subgraph
forbidden subgraph → $K_{(3,3)}$
forbidden subgraph → K_5
forbidden subgraph → Kuratowski's Theorem
force compactness
forcing
Ford circle
foreign → urelement

forgetting curve
form
form → canonical form
form → closed form
form → differential form
form → exact form
form → integral quadratic form
form → modular form
form → presentational form
form → shape
form → special form chosen for mathematical convenience
form → waveform
Formal Logic
Formal Logic → Logic
Formal Logic → Mathematical Logic
formal power series
formal proof
Formalism
formula
formula → computational formula
formula → Laurent series
formula → midpoint formula
formula → polynomial
formula → power series
formula → reflection formula
formula → replacing subterms of a formula with other terms
formula → rewriting
formula → Weyl-Kac character formula
formula for compound interest
formula for simple interest
formula for the surface area of a sphere
formula for the volume of a sphere
forward problem
forward problem → inverse problem
forward problem → normal problem
forward-backward algorithm
founded → Non-Well-Founded Set Theory
founded → well-founded relation
four → Lagrange's 4-square theorem
four exponentials conjecture
four families → Padua points
four leaf clover → quadrifolium
Four-Color theorem
Fourier Analysis
Fourier coefficient

Fourier coefficients → decaying Fourier coefficients
Fourier expansion of modular forms
Fourier expansion of modular forms → Kloosterman sum
Fourier series
Fourier series approximation
Fourier series approximation → Gibbs phenomenon
Fourier transform
Fourier transform → discrete Fourier transform
Fourier transform → fast Fourier transform
Fourier transform → Pontryagin duality
four-sided figure → quadrilateral
fractal
fractal → Cantor set
fractal → Feigenbaum attractor
fractal → fractional Brownian motion
fractal → Generalized Cantor set
fractal → Koch Snowflake
fractal → Smith-Volterra-Cantor set
fractal → Spectrum of the Fibonacci Hamiltonian
fractal behavior
fractal landscape
fractal of Hausdorff dimension 1
fractal of Hausdorff dimension 1 → Smith-Volterra-Cantor set
fractal-generating software
fractal-generating software → Recreational Mathematics
fraction
fraction → common fraction
fraction → decimal fraction
fraction → denominator
fraction → division by a fraction
fraction → fixed proportions
fraction → fixed proportions → used in fixed proportions
fraction → fixed proportions → used in fixed proportions → Leontief production function
fraction → improper fraction
fraction → interesting fraction → Markov brothers' inequality
fraction → like fractions
fraction → mixed number
fraction → numerator
fraction → proper fraction
fraction → raising a fraction to higher terms
fraction → rational number
fraction → reducing a fraction to lowest terms
fraction → sequence of decreasing fractions
fraction of primitive Pythagorean triples with perimeter < p

fractional Brownian motion
fractional Brownian motion → Brownian motion
fractional Brownian motion → continuous time Gaussian process
fractional linear transformation → Möbius transformation
Fracture Analysis
frame → ordered basis
framework for combining models and training data from multiple sources
fraud-detection → Benford's Law
Fréchet space
Fredholm operator
Fredholm operator → Index Theory
free → coordinate-free treatment
free abelian group
free from vagueness and ambiguity
free from vagueness and ambiguity → null hypothesis
free modal algebra
free modal algebra → finitely generated free modal algebra
free modal algebra → Stone space of the free modal algebra
free module
free variable
freedom → degrees of freedom
freehand method
freehand method → finding the trend line or trend curve of a time series
frequency
frequency → frequencies → Hardy-Weinberg Principle
frequency distribution
frequency domain
frequency domain → Hilbert transform
frequency polygon
frequentist definition of probability
Fresnel integrals
Friedman test
Friedman-Savage utility function
frieze group
Frobenius endomorphism
Frobenius integrability
Frobenius integrability → overdetermined differentiable system
Frobenius Theorem
from (0,0) to (1,1) → Lorenz curve
from inside the model → endogenous variable
from outside the model → exogenous variable
from the atomistic view to the laws of motion of continua → Hilbert's 6th problem
frontier
frontier → boundary
frontier operator

frustum
Fubini's theorem
Fuchsian group
fully mechanized mathematics
function
function → absolutely continuous function
function → affine function
function → Airy function
function → analytic function
function → arithmetic function
function → automorphic function
function → automorphic function
function → bijective function
function → bounded function
function → bump function
function → C^∞ function
function → càdlàg function (continuous on the right, limit on the left)
function → càglàd function (continuous on the left, limit on the right)
function → càllàl function (continuous on one side, limit on the other side)
function → ceiling function
function → choice function
function → circular function
function → C^k function
function → component function
function → composite function
function → conditional factor demand function
function → confluent hypergeometric functions
function → constant function
function → consumption function
function → continuous function
function → continuous function → set of all continuous functions on [0,1]
function → continuous functions on a compact Hausdorff space
function → convex function
function → convolution of functions
function → convolution of functions
function → cylinder functions
function → diffeomorphism
function → differentiable function
function → digamma function
function → Dirac delta function
function → discontinuous function
function → distribution function
function → divisor function
function → doubly-periodic function

function → elliptic function
function → entire function
function → error function
function → exponential function
function → factor demand function
function → factorial function
function → finding extrema of a function
function → floor function
function → function composition
function → function convolution
function → function equal to its derivative → exponential function
function → function having a constant subtangent
function → function notation
function → function of a complex variable
function → function of a product
function → function of a real variable
function → function of bounded variation
function → function of one variable
function → function of several complex variables
function → function of several complex variables
function → function of three variables
function → function of two variables
function → functional dependence
function → gamma function
function → Gaussian function
function → generalized function
function → generating function
function → hazard function
function → holomorphic function
function → hyperfunction
function → identity function
function → indicator function
function → injective function
function → j function → j-invariant
function → Jacobi symbol
function → Kronecker delta function
function → Kronecker symbol
function → Legendre symbol
function → linear function
function → logarithm
function → logarithmically convex function
function → logistic function
function → measurable function

function → meromorphic function
function → Möbius function
function → modular function
function → moment-generating function
function → monotone function
function → multilinear function
function → nice function
function → non-decreasing function
function → non-increasing function
function → non-monotonic function
function → non-monotonic function → Uncanny Valley
function → nowhere differentiable continuous function
function → number-theoretic function
function → ogive
function → one-to-one function
function → operation
function → partial function
function → periodic function
function → periodic function → generalization of periodic functions → automorphic form
function → Pfaffian function
function → piecewise continuously differentiable function
function → polygamma function
function → primitive recursive function
function → probability density function
function → probability distribution function
function → production function
function → production function → Cobb-Douglas production function
function → production function → Leontief production function
function → quadratic function
function → Ramanujan tau function
function → random variable
function → rational function
function → recursive function
function → Riemann zeta function
function → ring of symmetric functions
function → Rosenbrock's banana function
function → salt-and-pepper function
function → sawtooth function
function → sequence of functions
function → sequence of functions → Lebesgue's Dominated Convergence Theorem
function → set function
function → set function → content
function → set function → measure

function → sigmoid
function → sign function
function → size function
function → smooth function
function → special functions
function → spline function
function → square wave function
function → square-integrable function
function → state function
function → step function
function → subadditive function
function → surjective function
function → symmetric function
function → symmetric function → ring of symmetric functions
function → total function
function → triangle wave function
function → uniformly continuous function
function → utility function
function → vector-valued function
function composition
function composition → Chain Rule
function convolution
function equal to its derivative → exponential function
function having a constant subtangent
function having a constant subtangent → exponential function
function notation
function of a complex variable
function of a product
function of a product → Paschen's curve
function of a real variable
function of bounded variation
function of several complex variables
function of several complex variables
function of three variables
function of two parameters → Hilbert's 13th problem
function of two variables
function resulting from the differentiation of another function
function space
function space → compact-open topology
function→ partial recursive function
functional
functional → Functional Analysis
functional → Willmore functional
Functional Analysis

Functional Analysis → C* algebra
functional dependence
functional equation
functional equation → reflection formula
functions regular in a disk → Landau theorems
functor
functor → morphism
fundamental group
fundamental group → homotopy group
Fundamental Lemma of Sieve Theory
fundamental parallelogram
fundamental parallelogram → function of a complex variable
fundamental queueing formula → Little's Law
fundamental theorem
fundamental theorem → fundamental theorem of symmetric polynomials
Fundamental Theorem of Algebra
Fundamental Theorem of Arithmetic
Fundamental Theorem of Calculus
Fundamental Theorem of Calculus → Fundamental Theorem of Calculus (first form)
Fundamental Theorem of Calculus → Fundamental Theorem of Calculus (second form)
Fundamental Theorem of Calculus (first form)
Fundamental Theorem of Calculus (second form)
fundamental theorem of group homomorphisms
fundamental theorem of ring homomorphisms
fundamental theorem of symmetric polynomials
fungibility
fungibility → averaging
fungibility → homogenization
fungibility → substitutability
funicular → catenary
Furstenberg's proof of the infinitude of the primes
future prices → Siegel's paradox
future years → expected income in future years → permanent income hypothesis
future-value formula
g (beginning of entries for G)
Gabriel's horn
gage of a uniform space
galaxy rotation curve
Galois → inverse Galois problem
Galois extension
Galois group
Galois group → action of the Galois group on the roots of a polynomial
Galois Theory
Galton board
Galton board → bean machine

Galton board → Central Limit Theorem
Galton board → quincunx
gambler's ruin
gambling → Dutch book
game
game → Game Theory
game → lotto game
game → zero-sum game
Game Theory
gamma distribution
gamma distribution → chi-squared distribution
gamma function
gamma function → Bohr-Mollerup theorem
gamma function → digamma function
gamma function → Raabe integral of the gamma function
gaps between
gaps between → gaps between the primes
gaps between primes
GARCH → generalized autoregressive conditional heteroscedasticity
GARCH model
Garfield's proof of the Pythagorean theorem
gauge integral
gauge integral → Henstock integral
Gauss's lemma on the factorization of polynomials
Gauss's summation formula
Gaussian elimination
Gaussian elimination → calculating the determinant of a matrix
Gaussian elimination → calculation of the inverse of an invertible square matrix
Gaussian elimination → finding the rank of a matrix
Gaussian elimination → matrix of coefficients
Gaussian elimination → sequence of elementary row operations
Gaussian elimination → upper-triangular matrix
Gaussian function
Gaussian function → bell curve
Gaussian integer
Gaussian process
Gaussian process → continuous time Gaussian process
Gauss-Markov Theorem
Gauss-Markov Theorem → linear regression
gcd → greatest common divisor
gcd(n,k) → greatest common divisor of n and k
Gegenbaur polynomials
Gelfond-Schneider Theorem → Hilbert's 7th problem
General Linear Models
general number field sieve

general solution

general solution of a differential equation

General Systems Theory → Ramsey Theory

General Topology

generality

generality → without loss of generality

generalization

generalization → non-linear generalization of Euclid's algorithm

generalization → sweeping generalization → Atiyah-Singer Index Theorem

generalization of Laplace's equation → Poisson's equation

generalization of periodic functions to topological groups → automorphic form

generalization of tangency

generalization of tangency → osculation

generalization of the Black-Scholes model

generalization of the Black-Scholes model → local volatility model

generalization of the concept of parallel lines → parallel curve

generalization of the Four Color Theorem

generalization of the Four Color Theorem → Hadwiger conjecture (in Graph Theory

generalization of the maximum flow problem → circulation problem

generalized autoregressive conditional heteroscedasticity

Generalized Binomial Theorem

Generalized Cantor set

generalized function

generalized homological manifold

generalized homological manifold → dogbone space

generalized intermediate-value theorem for integrals

generalized logistic function

generalized mean

generalized mean with exponent 2 → root mean square

Generalized Riemann Hypothesis

generated → finitely generated free modal algebra

generated by two circles → Watt's curve

generating function

generating function → moment-generating function

generating set of a group

generating set of an ideal

generating set of an ideal → Gröbner basis

generation → pseudo-random-number generation

generation → random-number generation

generator → cryptographically secure pseudorandom number generator

generator → reverse engineering the seed of a linear congruential random number generator

generator of a group

generic topographic obstacle in a flow in mathematical modeling

generic topographic obstacle in a flow in mathematical modeling → witch of Agnesi

genuine infinitesimals → Nonstandard Analysis

genus → geometric genus

genus (n − 1)(n − 2)/2 → Fermat curve

genus seven → curve of genus seven → butterfly curve

geodesic

geodesics → metrics where lines are geodesics → Hilbert's 4th problem

geometric distribution

geometric genus

Geometric Group Theory

Geometric Group Theory → Group Theory

geometric mean

geometric mean → weighted geometric mean

geometric object with flat sides → polytope

Geometric Probability

geometric progression

geometric progression → logarithmic spiral

geometric series

geometric series → length of path of a bouncing ball

Geometric Topology

Geometric Topology → mapping class group

geometric toy → Spirograph

geometrical properties of certain conformal mappings → Landau theorems

geometrical structure

geometrical structure → Mathematical Morphology

Geometric-Mean – Arithmetic-Mean Inequality

Geometry

geometry → Algebraic Geometry

geometry → Algebraic Geometry

geometry → Ceva's Theorem

geometry → Computational Geometry

geometry → Differential Geometry

geometry → Discrete Geometry

geometry → Distance Geometry

geometry → Elliptic Geometry

geometry → envelope

geometry → equipollence

geometry → Euclidean Geometry

geometry → finite geometry

geometry → Finite Geometry

geometry → Finsler Geometry

geometry → Geometry

geometry → geometry of motion

geometry → geometry of motion → Kinematics

geometry → Geometry of Triangles in the Euclidean Plane

geometry → Hyperbolic Geometry

geometry → Integral Geometry

geometry → Interior Geometry

geometry → isohedral figure

geometry → Lie Sphere Geometry

geometry → non-Euclidean Geometry

geometry → Parabolic Geometry

geometry → Partial Geometry

geometry → Plane Geometry

geometry → Projective Geometry

geometry → Riemannian Geometry

geometry → Solid Geometry

geometry → Synthetic Geometry

geometry → Taxicab Geometry

geometry → Thurston's geometrization conjecture

Geometry → unifying principle in Geometry → Group Theory

geometry of motion

geometry of motion → Kinematics

Geometry of Triangles in the Euclidean Plane

Gergonne triangle

gH → coset

ghosts of departing quantities → infinitesimal

Gibbs phenomenon

Gibbs phenomenon → Runge's phenomenon

gift problem for education majors

gift problem for education majors → How many pints are in a gallon?

Gini coefficient

Gini coefficient → Lorenz asymmetry coefficient

Gini coefficient → Lorenz curve

given a finite set of points in the plane → Sylvester Gallai Theorem

given and sought → Poisson's equation

given in a free-standing way

given in a free-standing way → intrinsic point of view

given number

given number → about a given number

given ratio → mean proportionals to a given ratio → cissoid of Diocles

global field

gloves → 3 gloves implies either 2 left gloves or two right gloves

Gödel number

Gödel's Incompleteness Theorem

going to higher degrees does not always improve accuracy → Runge's phenomenon

Goldbach's Conjecture

Goldbach's Conjecture → Chen's theorem

Goldbach's Conjecture → Goldbach's Weak Conjecture

Goldbach's Weak Conjecture

Goldbach's Weak Conjecture → Harald Helfgott's proof of Goldbach's Weak Conjecture

golden ratio

Gompertz curve

gonality (of an algebraic curve)

good → how good → information on how good the inference is

good integrator

good integrator → semimartingale

goodness of fit

goodness of fit → Kolmogorov-Smirnov Goodness-of-Fit Test

goods → final allocations of two goods between two people → contract curve

goods → trade away your preferred consumption goods → Siegel's paradox

googol

googolplex

Goryachev-Chaplygin top

Gothic arch → ogive

grade

gradient

gradient → curl

gradient → gradient flow structure

gradient flow structure

grading on the curve

grading on the curve → learning curve

Graeco-Latin square

Graeco-Latin squares exist for all orders $n \geq 3$ except $n = 6$.

Graeco-Latin squares exist for all orders $n \geq 3$ except $n = 6$. → Euler spoiler

Graham's Algorithm

Graham's Algorithm → convex hull

Graham's number

graph

graph → acyclic orientation

graph → bar graph

graph → clique

graph → cycle graph → Perrin number

graph → de Bruijn graph

graph → dense graph

graph → directed graph → Askey tableau

graph → forbidden subgraph

graph → graph cover

graph → Graph Minor Theory

graph → graph partition

graph → Graph Theory

graph → Graph Theory

graph → Graph Theory → Graph Minor Theory

graph → graphical representation

graph → graphical representation of a partition of a natural number

graph → graphical representation of a partition of a natural number → Young diagram

graph → graph-representation conjecture

graph → hypergraph

graph → magic graph

graph → planar graph

graph → planar graph → Fáry's Theorem

graph → plot → scatter plot

graph → rooted graph

graph → sparse graph

graph → subdivision of a graph

graph → subgraph

graph → subgraph → forbidden subgraph

graph cover

Graph Minor Theory

graph partition

Graph Theory

Graph Theory → cut (in Graph Theory)

Graph Theory → Hadwiger conjecture

Graph Theory → Kuratowski's Theorem

Graph Theory → shortest path problem

graphical representation

graphical representation of a partition of a natural number → Young diagram

graphical representation of income or wealth

graphical representation of income or wealth → Lorenz curve

graph-reconstruction conjecture

graph-representation conjecture

gravitation → Newton's laws of motion and gravitation

gravity → constrained motion under gravity

gravity → constrained motion under gravity → brachistochrone

gravity → constrained motion under gravity → pendulum

gravity → constrained motion under gravity → spherical pendulum

gravity → constrained motion under gravity → tautochrone

great circle

great circle → intersecting great circles → Spherical Trigonometry

great circle → Spherical Trigonometry

great icosahedron

great icosahedron → small stellated dodecahedron

greater cardinality of the power set (than of the original set)

greatest → maximum

greatest area → rectangle having greatest area for a given perimeter

greatest common divisor

greatest common divisor of n and k

greatest integer ≤ ... → floor function

greatest lower bound

greatest number that can be made from a given set of digits → Kaprekar's Constant

greatest possible effective yield

Greek → Graeco-Latin square

Greek approximation of π

Green's theorem

Green-Tao theorem

Gröbner basis

Gröbner basis → Computer Algebra

Gröbner basis computation

gross

group

group → abelian group

group → amalgam of groups

group → amenable group

group → automorphism group

group → Bianchi group

group → center of a group

group → classical group

group → cohomology groups of a smooth manifold

group → cohomology groups of a smooth manifold → Hodge Theory

group → commutative group

group → commutator

group → compact Lie group

group → complex Lie group

group → continuous groups versus differential groups → Hilbert's 5th problem

group → continuous transformation group → Lie group

group → control group

group → coset

group → covering group

group → Cremona group

group → cyclic group

group → dihedral group

group → direct product group

group → divisible group

group → Euclidean group

group → factor group

group → finite group

group → finite group → monomial representation of a finite group

group → finite simple group

group → finitely generated group

group → frieze group

group → Fuchsian group

group → fundamental group

group → Galois group
group → generating set of a group
group → generator of a group
group → group homomorphism
group → group of dilations
group → group of Lie type
group → group of orthogonal transformations
group → Group Theory
group → hyperbolic group
group → ideal class group
group → indefinite orthogonal group
group → isometry group
group → Kleinian group
group → Koebe group
group → Lie group
group → linear algebraic group
group → linear group
group → Lorentz group
group → Mathieu group
group → Möbius group
group → monster group
group → multiply transitive permutation group
group → nilpotent group
group → order of a group
group → orthogonal group
group → permutation group
group → Picard group
group → po-group
group → Poincaré group
group → Prüfer group
group → quantum group
group → rank 3 permutation group
group → renormalization group
group → scale-invariant group
group → semigroup
group → simple complex Lie group
group → simple group
group → simple Lie group
group → small group of Lie type
group → solvable group
group → space group
group → special linear group
group → split orthogonal group

group → sporadic group
group → Steinberg group
group → subgroup
group → Suzuki-Ree group
group → symmetry group
group → Tits group
group → transitive permutation group
group → unitary group
group → wallpaper group
group homomorphism
group of dilations
group of dilations → homothetic transformation
group of Lie type
group of Minkowski spacetime isometries
group of Minkowski spacetime isometries → Poincaré group
group of orthogonal transformations
group of symmetries of the square
Group Theory
Group Theory → Finite Group Theory
Group Theory → Geometric Group Theory
Group Theory → Hall-Higman Theorem
Group Theory → Schur multiplier
grouped data
grouping error
grouping error → Sheppard's Correction
grows exponentially → exponential growth
growth
growth → economic growth
growth → emergence of patterns as the scale of the objects grows → Ramsey Theory
growth → long-run economic growth
growth → long-run economic growth → model of long-run economic growth
growth curve
growth model
growth model → Eden growth model
growth of specific types of clusters
growth of specific types of clusters → Eden growth model
guaranteed loss → Dutch book
guaranteed win → Dutch book
guard against transmission error
guard against transmission error → check digit
guess → educated guess → ansatz
guess → estimate
Gutschoven's curve → kappa curve
gyroscope

gyroscope → top
G_δ set → countable intersection of open sets
h (beginning of entries for H)
H ≤ G ≤ A → relationships among the Pythagorean means
H test corrected for ties
Haar integral
Haar measure
Hadamard regularization
Hadamard regularization → Cesàro summation
Hadwiger conjecture (in Graph Theory)
Hadwiger's Theorem
Hadwiger-Finsler inequality
Hahn series
Hahn-Banach theorem
hairball → fixed point
Haken manifold
half-closed interval
half-life
half-line → ray
half-open interval
half-plane
half-space
half-way model
half-way model → Boy's surface
half-way model → sphere eversion
Hall-Higman Theorem
Hamel basis
Hamilton → Cayley-Hamilton Theorem
Hamiltonian → Spectrum of the Fibonacci Hamiltonian
Hamiltonian path
Hamiltonian vector flow
Hamming bound
Hamming code
Hamming distance
handedness → chirality
Handle Theory
Harald Helfgott's proof of Goldbach's Weak Conjecture
Hardy space
Hardy's taxicab number
Hardy-Littlewood circle method
Hardy-Weinberg Principle
harmonic
Harmonic Analysis
harmonic brick
harmonic conjugate
harmonic conjugate → projective harmonic conjugate

harmonic mean

harmonic mean → weighted harmonic mean

harmonic motion

harmonic motion → complex harmonic motion

harmonic oscillation

harmonic oscillator

harmonic series

harmonic series → surprising divergence

harmonics of a plucked string

harvesting the environment

harvesting the environment → random-number generation

hash total

Hausdorff compactification

Hausdorff dimension

Hausdorff Maximal Principle

Hausdorff Maximal Principle → Axiom of Choice

Hausdorff Maximal Principle → Tukey's Lemma

Hausdorff space

Hausdorff space → compact Hausdorff space

have at least 2 poles → elliptic function

hazard function

hazard function → bathtub curve

h-cobordism

heads

heart → cardiac function curve

heart-shaped curve → cardiod

heat equation

heat equation → Black-Scholes equation

heat equation → diffusion map

heat-conduction and -trapping in random media → Wiener sausage

Heaviside operator

height

Heine-Borel Covering Theorem

helicoid

Helicopter Paradox (rotor of infinite length and zero speed producing lift)

helix

helix → double helix

Helmholtz's equation

Helmholtz's equation → Can you hear the shape of a drum?

Helmholtz's equation → vibrating membrane

help → lemma

hemisphere

Henstock integral → gauge integral

Hermite polynomials

Hermitian matrix

Hermitian matrix → equal to its adjoint
Heron's formula
Heston model
heteroscedasticity → autoregressive conditional heteroscedasticity
heteroscedasticity-consistent standard errors
heuristic argument
Hewitt-Savage Zero-One Law
hexadecimal
hexaflexagon
hexagon
hidden features → true features of the underlying space
hidden Markov model
high degree of symmetry
high degree of symmetry → Roman surface
highly composite number
highly composite number → superior highly composite number
high-point theorem
Hilbert class field
Hilbert space
Hilbert space → Spectral Theorem
Hilbert space → Spectral Theory of Operators on a Hilbert Space
Hilbert space of states
Hilbert space of states → Wigner's Theorem
Hilbert transform
Hilbert's 1st problem
Hilbert's 2nd problem
Hilbert's 3rd problem
Hilbert's 4th problem
Hilbert's 5th problem
Hilbert's 6th problem
Hilbert's 7th problem
Hilbert's 8th problem
Hilbert's 9th problem
Hilbert's 10th problem
Hilbert's 11th problem
Hilbert's 12th problem
Hilbert's 13th problem
Hilbert's 14th problem
Hilbert's 15th problem
Hilbert's 16th problem
Hilbert's 17th problem
Hilbert's 18th problem
Hilbert's 19th problem
Hilbert's 20th problem
Hilbert's 21st problem
Hilbert's 22nd problem

Hilbert's 23rd problem
Hilbert's problems
hill → cross section of a smooth hill → witch of Agnesi
hippopede
hit or miss transform → Mathematical Morphology
Hodge conjecture
Hodge conjecture → Hodge Theory
Hodge Theory
Hodge Theory → Hodge conjecture
hodograph
hodograph → derivation of elliptical orbits from Newton's laws of motion and gravitation
hodograph → transformation of nonlinear partial differential equations to linear
hodograph → velocity diagram
hodograph → Visual Calculus
Holder inequality
holding small numbers with great precision
holding time
holding time → Renewal Theory
holes of a topological space → homotopy group
holomorphic function
homeomorphic image of a circle → Jordan curve
homeomorphic to R^3
homeomorphism
homeomorphism → topological invariant
homeomorphism-characterization → Nielsen-Thurston classification
homogeneity → effective medium approximation
homogeneity → indistinguishability
homogeneous → uniform
homogeneous coordinates
homogeneous dilation
homogeneous dilation → homothetic transformation
homogeneous equation
homogeneous equation → differential equation
homogeneous polynomial
homogenization
homogenization → averaging
homogenization → fungibility
homogenization → uniformity
homogenous (misspelling of homogeneous)
Homological Algebra
homological manifold → generalized homological manifold
homological manifold → generalized homological manifold → dogbone space
homology
homology → Floer homology
homology → Intersection Homology

homology → Persistent Homology
homology → Singular Homology
homology with compact support
homomorphism
homothecy
homothetic transformation
homothety → homothetic transformation
homotopy
homotopy → Rational Homotopy Theory
homotopy → stable homotopy theory
homotopy continuation method
homotopy group
homotopy group → fundamental group
homotopy manifold
homotopy theory → Spanier-Whitehead duality
hooked arrow
hooked arrow → embedding
hooked arrow → inclusion map
Hopf invariant
horizon → distance to the horizon
horizontal asymptote
horizontal bar chart
horizontal intercept
horizontal tangent → Rolle's theorem
Horner's Method
Horseshoe Map
how → not how, only what → flow network
how an object behaves as it 'runs around' a singularity → monodromy
how an object behaves as it runs around a singularity → monodromy
how good → information on how good the inference is
how many iterations → algorithm terminates within how many iterations
How many pints are in a gallon?
How many pints are in a gallon? → gift problem for education majors
how much a given surface deviates from a sphere → Willmore energy
how much an endogenous variable changes in response to an exogenous variable
how much axiomatic power you need to prove a particular theorem
how much axiomatic power you need to prove a particular theorem → reverse mathematics
how prime factors can be found by continued fractions
Hua's lemma
Hua's lemma → estimate for exponential sums
Hubbert curve
hundred
hyperbola
hyperbola → unit hyperbola
hyperbolic coordinates

hyperbolic coordinates → squeeze mapping
hyperbolic cosecant → Poinsot's spirals
hyperbolic cosine
hyperbolic discounting
Hyperbolic Geometry
hyperbolic group
hyperbolic secant → Poinsot's spirals
hyperbolic sine
hyperbolic spiral
hyperbolic tangent
hypercomplex numbers
hyperelliptic curve
hyperfunction
hyperfunction → distribution of infinite order
hypergeometric distribution
hypergeometric functions
hypergraph
hyperreal number
hyperreal number → Nonstandard Analysis
Hyperset Theory
hypersingular integral equation
hypersingular integral equation → Fracture Analysis
hyperspace over a given topological space
hypersurface
hypocycloid
hypotenuse
hypotenuse → right triangle
hypotenuse → square root
hypothesis
hypothesis → alternative hypothesis
hypothesis → exists under weaker hypotheses
hypothesis → exists under weaker hypotheses → Jordan-Chevalley decomposition
hypothesis → Inferential Statistics
hypothesis → null hypothesis
hypothesis → permanent income hypothesis
hypothesis → rejection of the null hypothesis
hypothesis testing → statistical hypothesis testing
hypotrochoid
i (beginning of entries for I)
(is) a divisor of
(is) a divisor of → divides
(is) a subset of
(is) a superset of
(is) an element of
(is) approximately equal to

(is) congruent to
(is) defined to be
(is) equal to
(is) greater than
(is) greater than or equal to
(is) less than
(is) less than or equal to
(is) maximized
(is) minimized
(is) much greater than
(is) much less than
(is) not a subset of
(is) not an element of
(is) not equal to
(is) perpendicular to
(is) proportional to
i → identity function
i → imaginary unit
ice-cream cone proof
ice-cream cone proof → Dandelin spheres
ice-cream cone proof → ellipse
i-connected set
i-connected set → i-connectedness
i-connectedness
i-connectedness → i-connected set
icosahedron
ideal
ideal → generating set of an ideal
ideal → maximal ideal
ideal → nil ideal
ideal → nilpotent ideal
ideal → prime ideal
ideal → structure theorem for finitely generated modules over a principal ideal domain
ideal class group
ideal number
ideal rocket equation → Tsiolkovsky rocket equation
idealized symmetric curve → Hubbert curve
idempotence
idempotent element
idempotent matrix
identical distribution → independence and identical distribution property
identification
identification space → quotient space
identification topology
identity

identity → Bézout's Identity

identity → Itô's lemma

identity → Tarski's high-school algebra problem

identity → trigonometry identity

identity element

identity element → identity element for addition

identity element → identity element for multiplication

identity element for addition

identity element for multiplication

identity function

identity function → inclusion map

If a matrix has only real elements, then its adjoint is equal to its transpose.

If each edge has integral capacity, then there exists an integral maximum flow.

If the number is even, divide it by 2. → Collatz conjecture

If the number is odd, multiply it by 3 and add 1. → Collatz conjecture

if x < y and y < z, then x < z → transitivity

i^i

IID property → independence and identical distribution property

ill defined

ill defined → Non-Well-Founded Set Theory

ill defined → undefined

ill defined centroid → witch of Agnesi

ill defined first moment → witch of Agnesi

ill-posed problem

ill-posed problem → introducing additional information in order to solve an ill-posed problem

ill-posed problem → well-posed problem

illusion → optical illusion → missing square puzzle

illustration → shoes and socks

image

image → homeomorphic image of a circle → Jordan curve

image → range of a function

imaginary number

imaginary taut string

imaginary taut string → involute

imaginary unit

imbedding → embedding

immersion

IMO → problem #6-IMO-1988

IMO (International Mathematical Olympiad)

IMO (International Mathematical Olympiad) → problem #6-IMO-1988

imperial units of measure

implication

implication → converse

implication → material implication

implication → proof

implicit differentiation

implicit differentiation → folium of Descartes

implied volatility

implied volatility as a function of strike price → volatility smile

important integral → integral of secant cubed

important integral → probability integral

impossibility of dividing by 0

impossibility of doubling the cube

impossibility of smoothly combing a hairy ball → fixed-point theorem

impossibility of squaring the circle

impossibility of trisecting an arbitrary angle

impossibility theorem

impossibility theorem → Arrow's Impossibility Theorem

impossibility theorem → doubling the cube

impossibility theorem → squaring the circle

impossibility theorem → trisection of angles

impossible Diophantine equation

improper fraction

improper integral

improper integral → Cauchy principal value

improper subset

impulse → Dirac delta function

in a coordinate-free fashion

in a coordinate-free fashion → universal enveloping algebra

inaccessible cardinal

incenter

incidence coefficient

incidence structure

incidence structure → Partial Geometry

incidence structure → points are on which lines

inclusion

inclusion → partially ordered by inclusion → Tukey's Lemma

inclusion → Tauberian theorems

inclusion map

inclusion map → identity function

income → graphical representation of income or wealth → Lorenz curve

income → permanent income hypothesis

income-consumption curve

incommensurability

incommensurability → irrationality

incommensurability of the diagonal of a square with its side

incomplete block design → balanced incomplete block design

incomplete gamma function

incompleteness → Gödels' Incompleteness Theorem

incompressible surface

inconvenience → just adding inconvenience, with no real benefit
increase
increase → as the scale of production increases
increase → decrease
increasing function
increasing sequence
increasing subsets → nested sequence of increasing subsets
indecomposable continuum
indefinite integral
indefinite integral → antiderivative
indefinite orthogonal group
indefinite special orthogonal group
independence and identical distribution property
independence of parameterization
independence of path
independence of starting state
independence of starting state → Kemeny's constant
independence of the Continuum Hypothesis
independent events
independent of the dimensions used
independent of the dimensions used → dimensionless variable
independent variable
independent variable
independent variable → explanatory variable
indeterminate form
index
index → aggregate index
index → aggregate index → simple aggregate index
index → aggregate index → weighted aggregate index
index → analytical index
index → Clifford Index
index → indices → pretending indices are exponents → Umbral Calculus
index → reflect changes over a period of time
index → seasonal index adjustments
index → single number
index → topological index
index of elliptic operators on compact manifolds → Atiyah-Singer Index Theorem
index theorem
index theorem → Atiyah-Singer Index Theorem
Index Theory
indicator function
indices → pretending indices are exponents → Umbral Calculus
indices (plural of 'index')
indifference curve
indifference curve → utility-maximizing problem of consumers

indirect proof
indiscernibles
indiscernibles → indistinguishability
indiscrete topology
indiscrete topology → trivial topology
indistinguishability
indistinguishability → distinguishability
indistinguishability → homogeneity
indistinguishability → indiscernibles
indistinguishability → topological indistinguishability
individual → urelement
induced fiber bundle
induced orientation
induced representation
induced subgraph
induced topology
induction → mathematical induction
inequality
inequality → Cauchy-Schwarz inequality
inequality → equality
inequality → equation
inequality → geometric mean – arithmetic mean inequality
inequality → Gini coefficient
inequality → Hadwiger-Finsler inequality
inequality → Holder inequality
inequality → inequality regarding expected costs of various algorithms → Yao's Principle
inequality → Jackson's Inequality
inequality → Jensen's inequality
inequality → Lorenz curve
inequality → Meyer's relation
inequality → triangle inequality
inequality → Young's inequality
inequality regarding expected costs of various algorithms → Yao's Principle
inertia → Sylvester's Law of Inertia
inevitable intersection
inevitable intersection → forbidden graph
inevitable order → Ramsey Theory
inevitable structure → Ramsey Theory
inference → deep-inference system
inference → statistical inference
inference algorithm
inferential equivalence
Inferential Statistics
Inferential Statistics → alternative hypothesis

Inferential Statistics → chi-squared distribution

Inferential Statistics → hypothesis

Inferential Statistics → Neyman-Pearson Lemma

Inferential Statistics → null hypothesis

Inferential Statistics → occurs simply by chance, or not

infimum

infimum → liminf

infinite

infinite → countably-infinite set

infinite continued fraction for π

infinite decimal

infinite decimal → periodic infinite decimal

infinite membership chain

infinite number of periodic orbits → Horseshoe Map

infinite order

infinite order → distribution of infinite order

infinite perimeter with finite area → Koch Snowflake

infinite regress

infinite sequence of random variables

infinite sequence of random variables → Kolmogorov's Zero-One Law

infinite sequences of abstract symbols → Symbolic Dynamics

infinite set

infinite sets which are of different sizes → cardinality

infinite surface area with finite volume → Gabriel's horn

infinitely-differentiable function

infinitely-differential function → C^∞ function

infinitesimal

infinitesimal → infinitesimals → Nonstandard Analysis

infinitesimal group → Lie algebra

infinitude of the primes

infinitude of the primes → Euclid's Theorem

infinity

infinity → distinctions among infinities → cardinality

inflection → point of inflection

inflection point

information → Information Theory

information about the object of interest, a simpler object that retains enough → homotopy group

information about the topology of singularities

information about the topology of singularities → algebraic curve

information on how good the inference is

Information Theory

inhomogeneous dilation

inhomogeneous linear ordinary differential equation

inhomogeneous linear ordinary differential equation

inhomogeneous system

initial conditions

initial conditions → ordinary differential equations → movable singularity

initial conditions → sensitivity to initial conditions → chaos

initial guess → ansatz

initial segment

initial state to a random destination state, transition from → Kemeny's constant

initial topology

initial value → seed of a random number generator

injection → natural injection

injective function

injective function → magic square (each cell contains a unique positive integer)

injective function → Schröder-Bernstein Theorem

injectivity → faithful representation

injectivity → natural injection

injectivity → The function itself need not be injective, only its derivative.

injectivity → The function itself need not be injective, only its derivative. → immersion

inner product

inner product → norm

inner product → usual inner product on R^n

inner-product space

input

input → level of input required to produce a given level of output

input → output

input-output model

input-output model → inter-industry relationships within an economy

inradius

inradius of a Pythagorean triple

inscribed circle

inscribed-square problem

inside out → turning a sphere inside out → sphere eversion

inside-out → eversion

instability

instability → Benjamin-Feir instability

instability → stability

instantaneous acceleration

instantaneous speed

instantaneous velocity

insurance policy → Renewal Theory

integer

integer → Eisenstein integer

integer → exponent to which an integer belongs

integer → Gaussian integer

integer → integer factorization

integer → positive integer → representation of a positive integer as the sum of four squares

integer → ring of integers

integer coefficients → polynomial with integer coefficients

integer coordinates → lattice point

integer factorization

integer factorization → modular root-extraction

integer solutions to $\alpha x + \beta y = \gamma$ with $\gcd(\alpha,\beta) = 1$

integrability

integrability → Frobenius integrability

integrability → Frobenius integrability → overdetermined differentiable system

integrability → uniform integrability

integrable function

integrable system

integral

integral → convergent integral

integral → divergent integral

integral → gauge integral

integral → improper integral

integral → improper integral → Cauchy principal value

integral → integral equation

integral → integral equation → hypersingular integral equation

integral → integral equation → hypersingular integral equation → Hadamard regularization

integral → integro-differential equation

integral → Itô integral

integral → Riemann integral

integral → Riemann-Stieltjes integral

integral → Stieltjes integral

Integral Calculus

integral domain

integral equation

integral equation → hypersingular integral equation

integral equation → hypersingular integral equation → Hadamard regularization

Integral Geometry

integral of a function

integral of a function → lower integral of a function

integral of a function → upper integral of a function

integral of secant cubed

integral of secant cubed → rectifying the Archimedean spiral

integral of secant cubed → rectifying the parabola

integral of secant cubed → surface area of the helicoid

integral quadratic form

integral representation of the logarithm

integral sign

Integral Test

integral transform

integrating factor

integration

integration → area element
integration → constant of integration
integration → integral
integration → numerical integration
integration → numerical integration → Simpson's Rule
integration → numerical integration → Trapezoidal Rule
integration → volume element
integration by partial fractions
integration by parts
integration by trigonometric substitution
integration in finite terms
integration in finite terms → Liouville's Theory of Elementary Methods
integration on chains
integrator
integrator → good integrator
integrator → good integrator → semimartingale
integrator → semimartingale
integro-differential equation
intercept
interchange of limits
interest
interest → nominal and effective interest rates
interest rates
interesting fraction → Markov brothers' inequality
inter-industry relationships within an economy
inter-industry relationships within an economy → input-output model
interior angle
Interior Geometry
interior of a set
interior operator
intermediate between a square and a circle → squircle
intermediate value property
intermediate-value theorem for integrals
International Mathematical Olympiad
International Mathematical Olympiad → IMO
interpolation
interpolation → Nevanlinna-Pick interpolation theorem
interpolation → polynomial interpolation of two variables → Padua points
interpolation → Sarason interpolation theorem
interpolation points
interpolation points → equispaced interpolation points
interpolation points → equispaced interpolation points → Runge's phenomenon
interquartile range
interrupt times from periodically interrupting devices
interrupt times from periodically interrupting devices → entropy pool

intersected with
intersecting great circles
intersecting great circles → Spherical Trigonometry
intersecting plane
intersection
intersection → Crofton formula
intersection → inevitable intersection → forbidden graph
intersection → self-intersecting mapping
intersection → self-intersection
intersection → union
intersection graph
Intersection Homology
intersection of a collection of sets
intersection of a sphere and a cylinder
intersection of a sphere and a cylinder → Viviani's curve
intersection of a sphere and a cylinder → Viviani's curve → lemniscate of Gerono
intersection of sets
intersection of two sets
intersection product
Intersection Theory
interval
interval → closed interval
interval → deleted interval
interval → half-open interval
interval → line segment
interval → open interval
interval → partition of an interval
interval data
interval data → level of measurement
interval estimate
Interval Estimation
intervals of validity
intrinsic point of view
intrinsic point of view → abstract manifold
intrinsic point of view → extrinsic point of view
introducing additional information in order to solve an ill-posed problem
Intuitionism
intuitive explanation
intuitive explanation → Kemeny's constant
invariance of area → Horseshoe Map
invariant
invariant → Alexander invariants
invariant → algebraic invariant of a topological space → mapping class group
invariant → complete set of invariants
invariant → Hopf invariant

invariant → j-invariant
invariant → topological invariant
invariant measure
invariant measure → Ergodic Theory
inverse
inverse → additive inverse
inverse → inverse image of an open set
inverse → inverse of a matrix
inverse → inverse problem
inverse → inverse proportionality
inverse → inversion → inversion of a point
inverse → multiplicative inverse
Inverse Function Theorem
inverse Galois problem
inverse image of an open set
inverse Laplace transform
Inverse Mapping Theorem
inverse of a matrix
inverse of the trigonometric cosecant → arccsc
inverse of the trigonometric cosine → arccos
inverse of the trigonometric cotangent → arccot
inverse of the trigonometric secant → arcsec
inverse of the trigonometric sine → arcsin
inverse of the trigonometric tangent → arctan
inverse problem
inverse problem → forward problem
inverse proportionality
inverse trigonometric function
inversion
inversion of a point
invert the fraction, then multiply → division by a fraction
inverted catenary arch
inverted catenary arch → structural support
invertible function
invertible square matrix
invertible square matrix → square matrix
involute
involution
IQR → interquartile range
irrational number
irrational number → most famous irrational number → square root of 2
irrationality
irrationality → incommensurability
irreducibility
irreducibility → Eisenstein's Irreducibility Criterion

irreducible fraction
irreducible over Q
irreducible over the integers
irreducible over the integers → Gauss's lemma on the factorization of polynomials
irreducible semiperfect number
Is it bigger than a bread box?
Is it bigger than a bread box? → estimate
is known, approximately
is known, precisely
isogonal conjugate
isohedral figure
isohedral tiling
isohedral tiling → anisohedral tiling
isolated point
isolated point → except for a set of isolated points → meromorphic function
isometric surfaces
isometry
isometry group
isomonodromic deformation
isomonodromic deformation → linear system of ordinary differential equations
isomorphism
isomorphism → equivalent up to permutation and isomorphism → Jordan-Hölder Theorem
isomorphism → exceptional isomorphism
isomorphisms of topology → homeomorphism
isoperimetric problem
isoquant
isoquant → cost-minimization problem of producers
isosceles triangle
isotopy
isotopy → ambient isotopy
isotropy
isotropy → anisotropy
isotropy → uniformity in all orientations
issuing from a central origin
issuing from a central origin → eutactic star
iterated extension
iterated integral
iterating the square → Horseshoe Map
iteration
iteration → algorithm terminates within how many iterations
iteration → fixed-point iteration
iteration → iterating the square → Horseshoe Map
iteration → Newton-Raphson method
iteration → rinse and repeat
Iteration Theory

Itô Calculus
Itô integral
Itô's lemma
IV → independent variable
j (beginning of entries for J)
j → imaginary unit
J curve → balance of trade model
J curve → country status model
J curve → medicine model
J curve → political science model
J curve → private equity model
J curve → Uncanny Valley
j function → j-invariant
J. E. Littlewood's Theorem of 1914
Jackson's Inequality
Jacobi polynomials
Jacobi symbol
Jacobian matrix
Jensen's inequality
j-invariant
j-invariant → modular function
join (of a lattice)
Jordan block over a ring
Jordan contour
Jordan curve
Jordan curve → polygon
Jordan curve → region bounded by a Jordan curve
Jordan Curve Theorem → Alexander duality
Jordan Curve Theorem → Lakes of Wada
Jordan matrix
Jordan normal form
Jordan-Chevalley decomposition
Jordan-curve theorem
Jordan-Hölder Theorem
J-shaped curve → J curve
juggling
juggling → patterns in juggling
Julia set
Julia set → Fatou set
jump → jumping → Vieta jumping
jump discontinuity
jump discontinuity → Gibbs phenomenon
just adding inconvenience, with no real benefit
just adding inconvenience, with no real benefit → unbiased estimation of standard deviation
juxtaposition

juxtaposition → adjacency
juxtaposition → magma operation
k (beginning of entries for K)
K (1024)
K (1024) → kilobyte
K (thousand)
k at a time → taken k at a time → binomial coefficient
k at a time → taken k at a time → permutation
k degrees of freedom
k degrees of freedom → degrees of freedom
k independent standard normal random variables
k independent standard normal random variables → chi-squared distribution
$K_{(3,3)}$
$K_{(3,3)}$ → forbidden graph
K_5
K_5 → forbidden graph
Kac-Moody algebra
Kähler manifold
Kähler manifold → Hodge Theory
K-algebra
kampyle of Eudoxus
Kaplansky density theorem
kappa curve
Kaprekar process
Kaprekar's Constant
Kaprekar's Constant → Recreational Mathematics
Karatsuba algorithm
Kemeny's constant
kernel of a homomorphism
kernel of an integral transform
kernelization
key → asymmetric cryptographic key
kidney-shaped curve → nephroid
Killing field → Killing vector field
Killing vector field
kiln → Turán's brick factory problem
kilo
kilobyte
kilobyte → denominate number
kilter → out-of-kilter algorithm
Kinematics
kissing → osculating
kissing number
kissing number problem
Klein bottle

Klein quartic

Klein's absolute invariant → j-invariant

Kleinian group

Kloosterman sum

Kloosterman sum → exponential sum

Kloosterman sum → finite ring analogy of Bessel function

Kloosterman sum → Fourier expansion of modular forms

knot

knot → figure-eight knot

knot → trefoil knot

knot → unraveling a knot

Knot Theory

knowledge management → mathematical knowledge management

Koch Snowflake

Koebe group

Kolmogorov quotient

Kolmogorov's axiomatics

Kolmogorov's axiomatics → Probability Theory

Kolmogorov's Zero-One Law

Kolmogorov-Smirnov Goodness-of-Fit Test

Koshlyakov's formula

Kovalevskaya top

Krill → Allan Krill's technique for memorizing large numbers

Kronecker delta function

Kronecker symbol

Kronecker-Weber Theorem

Kruithof curve

Kruskal-Wallis H test

Krylov-Bogolyubov Theorem

Krylov-Bogolyubov Theorem → dynamical system

k^{th} entry in the n-th row of Pascal's triangle

K-Theory

Kummer's Test

Kummer-Vandiver conjecture

Kuramoto model

Kuramoto model → synchronization

Kuratowski closure axioms

Kuratowski's 14-Set Theorem

Kuratowski's Theorem

Kurt Vonnegut → shape of stories

kurtosis

kurtosis → degree of peakedness of a curve

l (beginning of entries for L)

L → L = λW → Little's Law

L = λW → Little's Law

L'Hôpital's rule

L^1 norm

L^1 norm $\rightarrow$ convergence in the L^1 norm $\rightarrow$ Lebesgue's Dominated Convergence Theorem

labyrinth

labyrinth $\rightarrow$ maze

laces $\rightarrow$ Julia set

lack of a moment-generating function $\rightarrow$ Cauchy distribution

lacunary system

ladder $\rightarrow$ leaning ladder $\rightarrow$ related rates

ladder against a wall (classical problem)

ladder around a corner (classical problem)

lady tasting tea $\rightarrow$ Fisher's Exact Test

Laffer curve

Lagrange $\rightarrow$ method of Lagrange multipliers

Lagrange multiplier

Lagrange top

Lagrange's 4-square theorem

Lagrange's interpolation formula

Lagrange's method $\rightarrow$ method of Lagrange multipliers

Laguerre polynomials

lakes of Wada

Lakes of Wada $\rightarrow$ Jordan Curve Theorem

L-algebra

lamina

laminar flow

Landau theorems

landscape

landscape $\rightarrow$ fractal landscape

Lane-Emden equation

Lane-Emden equation $\rightarrow$ Poisson's equation

Langlands program

Laplace transform

Laplace's equation

Laplace's equation $\rightarrow$ Poisson's equation

Laplace-Runge-Lenz vector

Laplace-Runge-Lenz vector $\rightarrow$ shape and orientation of the orbit of one astronomical body ...

Laplacian operator

Laplacian operator

Laplacian operator $\rightarrow$ Hodge Theory

large $\rightarrow$ Calculus of Variations in the Large

large countable ordinal

large numbers $\rightarrow$ Allan Krill's technique for memorizing large numbers

large numbers $\rightarrow$ Law of Large Numbers

large oscillations near the jump $\rightarrow$ Gibbs phenomenon

large set

large-sampling methods
largest → greatest
largest number that can be made from a given set of digits → Kaprekar's Constant
largest sporadic simple group → monster group
largest topology on a set → discrete topology
latent Gaussian model
latent variable
lateral area of a cone
lateral surface
Latin rectangle
Latin rectangle → Combinatorial Design Theory
Latin rectangle → Latin square
Latin rectangle → Latin square → Combinatorial Design Theory
Latin square
Latin square → Combinatorial Design Theory
latitude
lattice
lattice → bounded lattice
lattice → complete lattice
lattice → elliptic function
lattice point
latus rectum
Laurent series
law → Benford's Law
law → DeMorgan's Laws
law → Hewitt-Savage Zero-One Law
law → Kolmogorov's Zero-One Law
law → Law of 70
law → law of averages
law → law of averages → Law of Large Numbers
law → Law of Cosines
law → Law of Large Numbers
law → Law of Quadratic Reciprocity
law → Law of Sines
law → Law of Tangents
law → Law of the Excluded Middle
law → Law of the Excluded Middle
law → law of the vital few
law → law of the vital few → Pareto Principle
law → Little's Law
law → Newton's Law of Cooling
law → Newton's laws of motion and gravitation
law → parallelogram law of vector addition
law → power law

law → rule
law → zero-one law
law → Zipf's Law
Law of 70
law of averages → Law of Large Numbers
Law of Cosines
Law of Large Numbers
Law of Quadratic Reciprocity
Law of Sines
Law of Sines → triangulation
Law of Tangents
Law of the Excluded Middle
law of the vital few → Pareto Principle
laws of motion of continua, from the atomistic view to the → Hilbert's 6th problem
lazy 8
LCG → linear congruential random-number generator
leading coefficient
leading coefficient → leading coefficient of 1
leading coefficient → leading coefficient of 1 → monic polynomial
leading coefficient of 1
leading coefficient of 1 → monic polynomial
leading digits
leading digits → first-digit law → Benford's Law
leading digits → trailing digits
leaning ladder → related rates
learning → Machine Learning
learning curve
learning curve → grading on the curve
least → minimum
least → smallest
least common denominator
least common multiple
least integer ≥ ... → ceiling function
least residue
least squares → method of least squares
least upper bound
least-squares parabola
Lebesgue constant → minimal growth of their Lebesgue constant → Padua points
Lebesgue integral
Lebesgue measure
Lebesgue's Dominated Convergence Theorem
Lebesgue-integrable
Lefschetz Fixed-Point Theorem
Lefschetz number
Lefschetz theorem on (1,1)-classes

Lefschetz theorem on (1,1)-classes → Hodge conjecture
left curly brace
left- or right-handed → chirality
left-hand side
left-sided limit
leg of a right triangle
Legendre polynomial
Legendre sieve
Legendre symbol
Legendre symbol → Law of Quadratic Reciprocity
Lehmer random number generator
Leibniz's notation for the derivative
Leigh Mercer's mathematical limerick
lemma
lemma → Bézout's Lemma → Bézout's Identity
lemma → Borel-Cantelli Lemma
lemma → Euclid's Lemma
lemma → Fundamental Lemma of Sieve Theory
lemma → Itô's lemma
lemma → Neyman-Pearson Lemma
lemma → Poincaré Lemma
lemma → Second Borel-Cantelli Lemma
lemma → theorem
lemma → Tukey's Lemma
lemma → Urysohn's Lemma
lemma → Zorn's Lemma
lemniscate
lemniscate → Devil's curve
lemniscate → lemniscate of Bernoulli
lemniscate → lemniscate of Booth
lemniscate → lemniscate of Gerono
lemniscate of Bernoulli
lemniscate of Bernoulli → hippopede
lemniscate of Booth
lemniscate of Booth → hippopede
lemniscate of Gerono
length
length → arc length
length → distance
length → interval
length → metric
length of a toilet roll (classical problem)
length of path of a bouncing ball → geometric series
length of path of a bouncing ball (classical problem)
length of run

length of run → algorithm terminates within how many iterations
Lenstra elliptic-curve factorization
Leontief production function
Leontief production function → no substitutability between factors
leptokurtic distribution
Leray-Schauder degree
level → acceptable level of false negatives
level → acceptable level of false positives
level → acceptance level
level → rate
level curve
level of input required to produce a given level of output
level of input required to produce a given level of output → conditional factor demand
level of measurement
level of measurement → discrete data
level of measurement → interval data
level of measurement → nominal data
level of measurement → ordinal data
level of measurement → ratio data
level of significance
level set
Levenshtein distance
Levenshtein distance → edit distance
lexicographical ordering
L-function
LHS → RHS
LHS (left-hand side)
Lie Algebra
Lie algebra
Lie algebra → Lie Algebra
Lie Algebra → Lie algebra
Lie algebra → universal enveloping algebra
Lie group
Lie group → compact Lie group
Lie group → continuous transformation group
Lie group → small group of Lie type
Lie group over a finite field
Lie group over a finite field → Chevalley group
Lie Sphere Geometry
Lie Theory
Lie Theory → Dynkin diagram
Lie type → group of Lie type
lies → Statistics
lifting theorem → commutant lifting theorem
light curve

lighting → comfortable lighting → Kruithof curve
like fractions
like terms
Likelihood Ratio Test
limaçon
limaçon trisectrix
limerick → Leigh Mercer's mathematical limerick
liminf → limit inferior
limit → a more refined notion of limit
limit → L'Hôpital's rule
Limit Comparison Test
limit cycle
limit inferior
limit inferior → limit superior
limit of a function at a point
limit of a sequence
limit ordinal
limit point
limit point → accumulation point
limit point → adherent point
limit point → derived set
limit point compact
limit superior
limit superior → limit inferior
limited → diffusion-limited aggregation
limsup → limit superior
Lindelöf space
Lindelof's theorem
line
line → concurrent lines
line → concurrent lines → Ceva's Theorem
line → configuration of 30 points and 12 lines → Schläfli double six
line → construction of a line
line → critical line
line → critical line → Riemann Hypothesis
line → Euler line
line → line segment
line → linear equation
line → Michael line
line → points are on which lines
line → points are on which lines → incidence structure
line → scattered line
line → sweeping line
line → trend line
line containing exactly 2 points of a given finite set of points → Sylvester-Gallai Theorem

line integral

line integral in the complex plane → contour integral

line segment

line segment → directed line segment

line segment → directed line segment → equipollence

line segment → interval

line→ skew lines

Linear Algebra

Linear Algebra → Controlled Linear Algebra

Linear Algebra → matrix

Linear Algebra → Matrix Theory

linear algebraic group

linear combination

linear combination → convex linear combination

linear congruences

linear congruential generator

linear congruential generator → Lehmer random number generator

linear congruential generator → linear congruential random-number generator

linear congruential random-number generator

linear congruential random-number generator → linear congruential generator

linear differential equation

linear differential equation → Hilbert's 21st problem

linear equation

linear equation → approximation by linear equations

linear equation → approximation by linear equations → linearization

linear equation → linear system

linear equation → point-slope form of a linear equation

linear equation → slope-intercept form of a linear equation

linear equation → standard form of a linear equation

linear equation → system of linear equations

linear equation → system of linear equations → Gaussian elimination

linear function

linear functional

linear group

linear model → General Linear Models

linear motion → Tusi couple

linear operator

linear operator decomposition → Jordan-Chevalley decomposition

linear order

Linear Point Set Theory

linear programming

linear regression

linear regression → Gauss-Markov Theorem

linear regression → heteroscedasticity-consistent standard errors

linear representations → Tannaka-Krein duality

linear separability
linear system
linear system → linear equation
linear system → output proportional to input
linear system of divisors
linear system of ordinary differential equations
linear system of ordinary differential equations → isomonodromic deformation
linear system of ordinary differential equations → singular exponents
linear transformation
linear transformation → order-preserving linear transformation → L-algebra
linear transformation → self-adjoint linear transformation
linearization
linearization → approximation by linear equations
linearly dependent
linearly independent
linearly-ordered set
linked relatives
Liouville's theorem
Liouville's Theory of Elementary Methods
Lipschitz condition
Lissajous figures
literacy → numeracy
little now versus more later
little now versus more later → discounting
little now versus more later → discounting → hyperbolic discounting
Little's Law
Little's Law → Queueing Theory
little-o notation
local extremum
local extremum → critical point
local extremum → relative extremum
local field
local field → Archimedean local field
local field → non-Archimedean local field
local volatility
local volatility model
local volatility model → generalization of the Black-Scholes model
locally-compact Hausdorff space
locally-compact topological group
locally-convex space
locally-convex topological vector space
locally-Euclidean → manifold
loci (plural of locus)
locked steering wheel → osculating circle
locus

log → logarithm

log(2) → fraction of primitive Pythagorean triples with perimeter < p

logarithm

logarithm → Cayley-Klein metric

logarithm → integral representation of the logarithm

logarithm → Napierian logarithm

logarithmic derivative of the gamma function

logarithmic derivative of the gamma function → digamma function

logarithmic differentiation

logarithmic integral

logarithmic spiral

logarithmically convex → Bohr-Mollerup theorem

logarithmically convex function

$\log_b(a)$

Logic

Logic → Formal Logic

Logic → Mathematical Logic

Logic → Mathematical Logic → Boolean Algebra

logistic function

logistic function → generalized logistic function

Logistics

long division

long division of polynomials

long division of polynomials → synthetic division

longitude

longitudinal wave

longitudinal wave → transverse wave

long-run economic growth

long-run economic growth → model of long-run economic growth

long-term benefits, comparing → Renewal Theory

long-term mean value

long-term movement

long-term movement → trend

loop

loop → phase-locked loop

Lorentz distribution → Cauchy distribution

Lorentz function → Cauchy distribution

Lorentz group

Lorentz: not to be confused with 'Lorenz'

Lorentzian function → Cauchy distribution

Lorenz asymmetry coefficient

Lorenz asymmetry coefficient → Gini coefficient

Lorenz attractor

Lorenz attractor → de Bruijn graph

Lorenz curve

Lorenz curve → Gini coefficient
Lorenz: not to be confused with 'Lorentz'
loss → guaranteed loss → Dutch book
loss → without loss of generality
lot → number of defectives in a lot
lottery
lot-testing
lot-testing → number of defectives in a lot
lotto game
loudness → Fletcher-Munson curves
low dimensional → relevant low dimensional features
low dimensional → relevant low dimensional features → Topological Data Analysis
low point theorem → high point theorem
low-degree polynomial
low-degree polynomials → oblivious polynomial evaluation
low-degree polynomials → spline function
low-dimensional topology
lower bound
lower bound → lower bound on edge flows
lower bound → lower bound on edge flows → circulation problem
lower bound on edge flows → circulation problem
lower class boundary
lower class limit
lower cost
lower cost → sequential sampling
lower integral of a function
lower integral of a function → upper integral of a function
lower semi-continuous
lower sum of a function for a given partition
lower sum of a function for a given partition → upper sum of a function for a given partition
lower upper → LU
lower-triangular matrix
lowest degree → gonality
L^p space
L-series
L-shaped → first vibrational mode of a thin L-shaped membrane, clamped at the edges
LU → lower upper
LU decomposition
LU decomposition → matrix decomposition
Lucas sequence
lumpability
lumpability → Probability Theory
lumping together of all points → indiscrete topology
m (beginning of entries for M)
M (formerly meant thousand, now means million)

M (million)

$m > n > 0 \rightarrow$ primitive Pythagorean triple

m and n are coprime and not both odd $\rightarrow$ primitive Pythagorean triple

$m^2 - n^2 \rightarrow$ primitive Pythagorean triple

$m^2 + n^2 \rightarrow$ primitive Pythagorean triple

Macdonald's function

Machin series

Machin's formula

Machine Learning

Machine Learning $\rightarrow$ algorithm

Machine Learning $\rightarrow$ Data Mining

machine-breakdowns $\rightarrow$ modeling machine-breakdowns $\rightarrow$ Renewal Theory

Maclane $\rightarrow$ Eilenberg-Maclane space

Maclaurin series

Maclaurin trisectrix

Maclaurin's theorem

macroscopic homogeneity and microscopic inhomogeneity $\rightarrow$ effective medium approximation

magic graph

magic square

magic square $\rightarrow$ Chinese Magic Square

magic square $\rightarrow$ Recreational Mathematics

magma

magma $\rightarrow$ alternative magma

magma $\rightarrow$ left-alternative magma

magma $\rightarrow$ partial magma

magma $\rightarrow$ right-alternative magma

magnitude

magnitude $\rightarrow$ order of magnitude

major axis

major axis $\rightarrow$ ellipse

majority

malicious party $\rightarrow$ oblivious polynomial evaluation

Mamikon's proof of the Pythagorean theorem

Mamikon's Theorem

Mamikon's Theorem $\rightarrow$ Visual Calculus

management $\rightarrow$ knowledge management $\rightarrow$ mathematical knowledge management

Mandelbrot set

Manhattan distance $\rightarrow$ Taxicab Geometry

manhole covers $\rightarrow$ why manhole convers are round

manifold

manifold $\rightarrow$ abstract manifold

manifold $\rightarrow$ almost a manifold $\rightarrow$ Singularity Theory

manifold $\rightarrow$ compact complex manifold

manifold $\rightarrow$ complex manifold

manifold $\rightarrow$ complex manifold $\rightarrow$ Picard-Lefschetz Theory

manifold → contractibility
manifold → contractible manifold
manifold → CR-manifold
manifold → differentiable manifold
manifold → embeddings of one manifold into another → Geometric Topology
manifold → Finsler manifold
manifold → Haken manifold
manifold → homeomorphic to R^3
manifold → homotopy manifold
manifold → immersion
manifold → index of elliptic operators on compact manifolds → Atiyah-Singer Index Theorem
manifold → Kähler manifold
manifold → non-orientable manifold
manifold → orbifold
manifold → orientable manifold
manifold → oriented manifold
manifold → real manifold → Morse Theory
manifold → Riemannian manifold
manifold → simply connected 1-dimensional complex manifold
manifold → smooth manifold
manifold → Surgery Theory
manifold → topological manifold
manifold → two-dimensional compact manifold without boundary
manifold → vector field on a manifold
manifold → Whitehead manifold
manipulation → algebraic manipulation
Mann-Whitney U test
mantissa
map
map → diffusion map
map → Horseshoe Map
map → inclusion map
map → mapping
map → projection map
map → self-organizing map
map → structure-preserving map
map-coloring
mapping → contraction mapping
mapping → map
mapping → Sammon mapping
mapping → self-intersecting mapping
mapping class group (in Geometry Topology)
mapping from the set of positive integers → countability
mapping into three-dimensional space

mapping into three-dimensional space → Roman mapping
marginal → posterior marginals
marginal value
Marginal Value Theorem
markdown
Markov → Gauss-Markov Theorem
Markov → hidden Markov model
Markov → Markov model
Markov → statistical Markov model
Markov brothers' inequality
Markov chain
Markov matrix
Markov model
Markov process
markup
martingale
martingale → martingale convergence theorem
martingale → partial sum forms a martingale → Walsh series
martingale → semimartingale
martingale → submartingale
martingale → supermartingale
martingale → Theory of Martingales
martingale convergence theorem
martingale convergence theorem → Theory of Stochastic Processes
mass → point mass → Dirac delta function
material → deformation of material → hodograph
material implication
mathematical convenience → special form chosen for mathematical convenience
mathematical expectation
Mathematical Finance
Mathematical Finance → Itô integral
mathematical formulation of Quantum Mechanics
mathematical induction
mathematical induction → regular mathematical induction
mathematical induction → simple mathematical induction
mathematical induction → strong mathematical induction
mathematical induction → Well-Ordering Principle
mathematical jelly
mathematical knowledge management
mathematical limerick → Leigh Mercer's mathematical limerick
Mathematical Logic
Mathematical Logic
Mathematical Logic → Boolean Algebra
Mathematical Logic → Formal Logic
Mathematical Logic → Logic

Mathematical Logic → Logic
mathematical methods of game theory and economic theory
mathematical modeling
mathematical modeling → witch of Agnesi
Mathematical Morphology
Mathematical Olympiad → International Mathematical Olympiad
mathematical optimization
mathematical passion plays of Michael Fellows
mathematical passion plays of Michael Fellows → performance of proofs on the theatrical stage
mathematical structure
mathematical treatment of the axioms of Physics → Hilbert's 6th problem
Mathematics
Mathematics → Applied Mathematics
Mathematics → Pure Mathematics
Mathieu group
Matiyasevich's Theorem → Hilbert's 10th problem
matrix
matrix → adjacency matrix
matrix → adjoint matrix
matrix → adjugate matrix
matrix → augmented matrix
matrix → block diagonal matrix
matrix → Bose-Mesner algebra
matrix → cofactor matrix
matrix → column
matrix → conjugate matrix
matrix → conjugate transpose matrix
matrix → de Bruijn torus
matrix → defective matrix
matrix → diagonal matrix
matrix → diagonalizable matrix
matrix → eigendecomposition of a matrix
matrix → Hermitian matrix
matrix → idempotent matrix
matrix → invertible square matrix
matrix → Jordan matrix
matrix → Jordan normal form
matrix → Kac-Moody algebra
matrix → Linear Algebra
matrix → lower-triangular matrix
matrix → Markov matrix
matrix → normal matrix
matrix → orthogonal matrix
matrix → probability matrix

matrix → rank of a matrix

matrix → reduced row echelon form

matrix → rotation matrix

matrix → row

matrix → square matrix

matrix → stochastic matrix

matrix → symmetric matrix

matrix → trace of a matrix

matrix → transition matrix

matrix → translation matrix

matrix → transpose of a matrix

matrix → transpose of a matrix

matrix → unitary matrix

matrix → upper-triangular matrix

matrix addition

Matrix Algebra → Sylvester's Law of Inertia

matrix decomposition

matrix decomposition → Cholesky decomposition

matrix decomposition → LU decomposition

matrix decomposition → QR decomposition

matrix decomposition → rank factorization

matrix factorization → matrix decomposition

matrix multiplication

matrix of coefficients

matrix of coefficients → Gaussian elimination

Matrix Theory

Matrix Theory → Linear Algebra

Matrix Theory → rank-nullity theorem

maverick → Non-Well-Founded Set Theory

maxima

maximal ideal

maximal principle → Hausdorff Maximal Principle

maximal subgroup → O'Nan-Scott Theorem

maximizing the angle subtended by a picture hanging on a wall → picture-angle maximization

maximum

maximum → extrema → finding extrema of a function

maximum → greatest

maximum → high-point theorem

maximum area for a given perimeter

maximum area for a given perimeter → minimum perimeter for a given area

maximum fenced area, one side a wall

maximum flow problem

maximum flow problem → circulation problem

maximum flow problem → Optimization Theory

maximum likelihood estimation
maximum of the derivatives of a polynomial
maximum of the derivatives of a polynomial → Markov brothers' inequality
max-min inequality
May I have a large container of coffee? → mnemonic for π
maze
maze → labyrinth
mean
mean → arithmetic mean
mean → arithmetic mean → weighted arithmetic mean
mean → arithmetic-geometric mean
mean → generalized mean
mean → geometric mean
mean → geometric mean → weighted geometric mean
mean → harmonic mean
mean → harmonic mean → weighted harmonic mean
mean → Pythagorean mean
mean → quadratic mean
mean → regression toward the mean
mean → relationship between the mean, median, and mode
mean → root mean square
mean → sample mean
mean → weighted mean → weighted arithmetic mean
mean → weighted mean → weighted geometric mean
mean → weighted mean → weighted harmonic mean
mean →zero-mean → zero-mean random variable
mean long-term volatility → Heston model
mean proportionals to a given ratio → cissoid of Diocles
mean value → long-term mean value
mean-value theorem for derivatives
mean-value theorem for integrals
mean-zero random variable → zero-mean random variable
measurability
measurability rules out chaos → random variable
measurable cardinal
measurable function
measurable set
measure
measure → angle measure
measure → Biblical unit of measure → cubit
measure → blocking data in an experiment involving multiple measures
measure → complexity measure
measure → content
measure → convergence in measure

measure → degree angle-measure
measure → Haar measure
measure → invariant measure
measure → Measure Theory
measure → radian angle-measure
measure → Radon measure
measure → summary measures
measure → units of measure
measure → units of measure → imperial units of measure
measure → units of measure → metric units of measure
measure of a subtended angle
measure of complexity → complexity measure
Measure Theory
measure zero → of measure zero
measurement → proxy measurement
measures of central tendency and dispersion
measures of dispersion
measures of variability
Mechanics
Mechanics → Classical Mechanics
Mechanics → Classical Mechanics versus Quantum Mechanics → Bell's Theorem
Mechanics → Quantum Mechanics
mechanized mathematics
mechanized mathematics → fully mechanized mathematics
median
median → relationship between the mean, median, and mode
median of a triangle
medicine model → J curve
meet (of a lattice)
membership
membership → indicator function
membership → infinite membership chain
membership → set membership
membrane → first vibrational mode of a thin L-shaped membrane, clamped at the edges
membrane → vibrating membrane
memorizing large numbers → Allan Krill's technique for memorizing large numbers
memorylessness → Markov process
Menelaus's Theorem
Menelaus's Theorem → Ceva's Theorem
mental activity → constructive mental activity → Intuitionism
Mereology
Mergelyan's Theorem
meridian
meromorphic continuation
meromorphic continuation of a convergent integral

meromorphic continuation of a convergent integral $\rightarrow$ Hadamard regularization
meromorphic function
meromorphic function $\rightarrow$ Nevanlinna Theory
Mersenne prime
Mersenne prime $\rightarrow$ even perfect number
mesh
mesh $\rightarrow$ polygon mesh
mesokurtic distribution
Meta Mathematics
metacompact space
metaphor $\rightarrow$ models as metaphors $\rightarrow$ volatility
method $\rightarrow$ elementary method $\rightarrow$ Liouville's Theory of Elementary Methods
method $\rightarrow$ homotopy continuation method
method $\rightarrow$ method of undetermined coefficients
method $\rightarrow$ Variation of Parameters
method of cylindrical shells
method of Lagrange multipliers
method of least squares
method of least squares $\rightarrow$ finding the trend line or trend curve of a time series
method of semi-averages
method of semi-averages $\rightarrow$ separation of the data into two parts
method of undetermined coefficients
method of washers
methods $\rightarrow$ large-sampling methods
methods $\rightarrow$ simplified methods for computing
metric
metric $\rightarrow$ Cayley-Klein metric
metric $\rightarrow$ distance
metric $\rightarrow$ length
metric $\rightarrow$ pseudo-metric
metric $\rightarrow$ triangle inequality
metric generalization of Riemannian Geometry $\rightarrow$ Finsler Geometry
metric paper $\rightarrow$ A4 paper size
metric space
metric space $\rightarrow$ complete metric space
metric space $\rightarrow$ metrizability
metric system
metric system $\rightarrow$ metric units of measure
metric uniformity
metric units of measure
metric units of measure $\rightarrow$ metric system
metrics where lines are geodesics $\rightarrow$ Hilbert's 4th problem
metrizability
metrizability $\rightarrow$ metric space
metrizability $\rightarrow$ topological space

Meyer's relation

Michael line

microscopic inhomogeneity and macroscopic homogeneity → effective medium approximation

microscopy → phase-contrast microscopy → Zernike polynomials

middle → excluded middle → Law of the Excluded Middle

middle term → quadratic function

middle term → square of a binomial

middle term → square of half the coefficient of the middle term

middle-thirds set

midpoint

midpoint formula

Miller's rules → equivalence relation

Miller's rules (for which stellation forms should be considered 'properly significant and distinct')

Miller-Rabin primality test

million

mine → mining → Data Mining

miniature → homomorphism

minima (plural of minimum)

minimal growth of their Lebesgue constant → Padua points

minimal polynomial → Hall-Higman Theorem

minimal surface

minimal surface of revolution

minimally sufficient conditions

minimally sufficient conditions for Riemann integrability

minimax eversion → half-way model

minimax theorem

minimax theorem → Game Theory

minimize a sum → problem #6-IMO-1988

minimum

minimum → extrema → finding extrema of a function

minimum → least

minimum → smallest

minimum counterexample

minimum of two values → Leontief production function

minimum perimeter for a given area

minimum perimeter for a given area → maximum area for a given perimeter

minimum polynomial

minimum vertex cover

minimum-variance unbiased estimator

mining → Data Mining

mining → data mining model

Minkowski space

minor (in Linear Algebra)

minor axis

minor axis → ellipse

minuend

minus

minus → plus

minus-or-plus

minus-or-plus → plus-or-minus

miracle → Morley's Miracle

mirror-image → chirality

missing square puzzle

missing unit → dissection puzzle

mixed number

mixed number → fraction

mixing → topological mixing

mix-up → transposition of digits

MM → Mathematical Morphology

mnemonic for the order of operations → BODMAS

mnemonic for the order of operations → PEDMAS

mnemonic for the order of operations → Please excuse my dear aunt Sally.

mnemonic for π

Möbius function

Möbius group

Möbius strip

Möbius strip → cross-cap

Möbius transformation

mockery → ghosts of departed quantities

modal → free modal algebra

mode

mode → first vibrational mode of a thin L-shaped membrane, clamped at the edges

mode → relationship between the mean, median, and mode

model

model → 3/2 model

model → ARCH model

model → autoregressive moving average model

model → CEV model

model → data mining model

model → dispersion model

model → Eden growth model

model → explanatory model versus predictive model

model → framework for combining models and training data from multiple sources

model → framework for combining models and training data from multiple sources → B2B-DC

model → from inside the model → exogenous variable

model → from outside the model → exogenous variable

model → GARCH model

model → growth model

model → half-way model

model → Heston model
model → hidden Markov model
model → input-output model
model → Kuramoto model
model → latent Gaussian model
model → local volatility model
model → model of long-run economic growth
model → modeling → mathematical modeling
model → models → empirical models unsupported by theory → volatility
model → nested model
model → overfitting
model → predictive model versus explanatory model
model → SABR model
model → shortcomings of the Black-Scholes model
model → Solow-Swan model
model → statistical Markov model
model → stochastic volatility model
model of long-run economic growth
model validation technique
modeled by a special case
modeling → mathematical modeling
modeling machine-breakdowns → Renewal Theory
models → General Linear Models
models as metaphors → volatility
modular arithmetic
modular exponentiation
modular exponentiation → exponentiation
modular exponentiation → modular root-extraction
modular exponentiation → Public-Key Cryptography
modular form
modular function
modular function → connection between the monster group and modular functions
modular function → j-invariant
modular root-extraction
modular root-extraction → integer factorization
modular root-extraction → modular exponentiation
modular root-extraction → Public-Key Cryptography
modular symbol
module
module → crossed module
module → finitely generated modules → structure theorem for finitely generated modules ...
module → flat module
module → free module
moduli space

modulo a prime

modulo a prime → residue classes modulo a prime → field

modulus of a complex number

modulus of a congruence

modulus of a congruence → restriction on the number of solutions

modulus of continuity

modulus of continuity → Jackson's Inequality

modulus of continuity → Lipschitz condition

modulus of continuity → modulus of smoothness of order n

modulus of smoothness of order n

modulus of smoothness of order n → modulus of continuity

moment

moment → first moment

moment → sth moment about a given number

moment → undefined moment

moment coefficient of kurtosis

moment coefficient of skewness

moment-generating function

moment-generating function → alternative specification of a probability distribution

moment-generating function → generating function

moment-generating function → Not all random variables have moment-generating functions.

moment-generating function → not working directly with cumulative distribution functions

moment-generating function → not working directly with probability density functions

moment-generating function, lack of, → Cauchy distribution

moments → relation between moments

momentum operator

momentum operator → 4-momentum operator

money

money → graphical representation of income or wealth → Lorenz curve

money multiplier

money multiplier: not to be confused with 'fiscal multiplier'

monic polynomial

monochromatic clique (in a graph) → Ramsey's Theorem

monodromy

monodromy → Hilbert's 21st problem

monohedral tiling

monoid

monomial

monomial representation of a finite group

monotone → monotonic

Monotone Convergence Theorem

monotone convergent series

monotone divergent series

monotone series

monotonic collection of sets

monotonic function
monotonic sequence
monotonicity
monster group
monster group → connection between the monster group and modular functions
monstrous moonshine
monstrous moonshine → vertex operator algebra
Monte Carlo method
Monty Hall Problem
moonshine → monstrous moonshine
Moore plane
Moore space
more likely value → mode
more refined → a more refined notion of limit
Morita conjectures
Morley's Miracle
morphism
morphism → functor
morphology → Mathematical Morphology
Morse Theory
most famous irrational number
most famous irrational number → square root of 2
motion
motion → Brownian motion
motion → constrained motion under gravity
motion → constrained motion under gravity → brachistochrone
motion → constrained motion under gravity → pendulum
motion → constrained motion under gravity → tautochrone
motion → geometry of motion
motion → geometry of motion
motion → harmonic motion
motion → harmonic motion → complex harmonic motion
motion → linear motion → Tusi couple
motion → Newton's laws of motion and gravitation
motion → rigid motion
motion → scalar motion
motion of a planet → hodograph
motion of continua, from the atomistic view to the laws of → Hilbert's 6th problem
motion of the moon → Perturbation Theory
motive
motive → Algebraic Geometry
motive → Theory of Motives
movable singularity
movable singularity → when all movable singularities are poles → Painlevé property
movement → cyclical movement

movement → long-term movement
movement → motion
movement → random movement
movement → seasonal movement
moving average
moving average → autoregressive moving average model
moving average → average of a truncated running sum
moving average → reduction in the amount of variation in a set of data
moving average of order n
moving averages applied to a time series
moving averages applied to a time series → smoothing of a time series
moving-average method
moving-average method → finding the trend line or trend curve of a time series
MRDP Theorem
much earlier stage → conclusion reached at a much earlier stage
multigraph
multilinear function
multimodal distribution
multinomial distribution
multiple → least common multiple
Multiple and Partial Correlation
multiple commodities flowing through a network
multiple commodities flowing through a network → circulation problem
multiple measures → blocking data in an experiment involving multiple measures
multiple roots
multiple roots over infinite fields of nonzero characteristic
multiplication
multiplication → Associative Property for Multiplication
multiplication → Commutative Property for Multiplication
multiplication → fast multiplication → Karatsuba algorithm
multiplication chart
multiplication chart → multiplication table
multiplication operator
Multiplication Principle
multiplication table
multiplication table → multiplication chart
multiplicative function
multiplicative function → Euler's totient function
multiplicative function → Möbius function
multiplicative inverse
multiplicative inverse → identity element for multiplication
multiplicity of a zero
multiplicity of a zero → multiplicity of roots
multiplicity of roots
multiplicity of roots → multiplicity of a zero

multiplied by
multiplier
multiplier → factor of proportionality
multiplier → fiscal multiplier
multiplier → how much an endogenous variable changes in response to an exogenous variable
multiplier → Lagrange multiplier
multiplier → money multiplier
multiply transitive permutation group
multiplying fractions
multiset
multiset → counted with multiplicity
multivalued function
Multivariate Calculus
Mumford surface → fake projective plane
mutual acquaintances or strangers at a party problem
mutually disjoint sets
mutually-exclusive events
MVT → Marginal Value Theorem
MVUE → minimum-variance unbiased estimator
n (beginning of entries for N)
n → order n → moving average of order n
n things taken k at a time → combination
n things taken k at a time → permutation
n! → factorial
$n!/((k!(n-k)!) →$ binomial coefficient
$n!/(n-k)! →$ number of permutations of n things taken k at a time
$n(n-1)/2 →$ indefinite orthogonal group
$n/2 →$ Collatz conjecture
nabla
nabla → del
Naive Set Theory
Napierian logarithm
nappe
n-ary operation
Nash Theorems (in Differential Geometry)
natural choice to describe certain flows → hyperbolic coordinates
natural injection
natural logarithm
natural number
natural number → partition of a natural number
natural number → partition of a natural number → Young diagram
natural set of distributions to consider
natural set of distributions to consider → exponential family
Navier-Stokes equations
navigation → navigation problem → Zermelo's navigation problem

n-cube → singular n-cube

n-cube → standard n-cube

near 50% → Birthday Problem

near 50% → de Mere's Paradox

nearest neighbor

Nearest-Neighbor Algorithm

nearness → proximity space

necessarily the case

necessarily the case → necessity

necessarily the case → not necessarily the case

necessity

necessity → necessarily the case

needle triangle

needle triangle → degenerate triangle

negation → DeMorgan's Laws

negative

negative → minus

negative → positive

negative element → number of negative elements in the diagonal → Sylvester's Law of Inertia

negative exponent

negative one

negative powers of a group element

negative reciprocal → perpendicular line

negative reciprocal of the slope of the given line

negative-exponential curve → forgetting curve

neighborhood → tubular neighborhood

neighborhood of a point

neighborhood system

nephroid

nested intervals

nested model

nested model → Wilks' Theorem

nested sequence of increasing subsets

nested sequence of increasing subsets → Persistent Homology

net

network

network → flow network

network having the best performance on new data

Nevanlinna Theory

Nevanlinna-Pick interpolation theorem

new proof of an old result

new proof of an old result → Garfield's proof of the Pythagorean Theorem

new proof of an old result → Mamikon's proof of the Pythagorean Theorem

new technique in solving mathematical olympiad problems

new technique in solving mathematical olympiad problems → Vieta jumping

Newton number → kissing number
Newton polygon
Newton's Law of Cooling
Newton's laws of motion and gravitation
Newton's notation for the derivative → fluxion
Newton-Raphson iteration → Newton-Raphson method
Newton-Raphson method
Neyman-Pearson Lemma
Neyman-Pearson Lemma
n-fold root
nice function
Nielsen-Thurston classification
nil ideal
nilpotent and semisimple parts → Jordan-Chevalley decomposition
nilpotent element in a ring
nilpotent group
nilpotent ideal
nine → Casting Out Nines
nine-point circle
nine-point problem
no (proper) normal subgroups → simple group
no cardinal between those of Z and R → Continuum Hypothesis
no curvature → straight line
no infinite descending sequence → well-ordered set
no infinite membership chain
no moment-generating function → Cauchy distribution
no special nodes → circulation problem
no substitutability between factors
no substitutability between factors → Leontief production function
no such algorithm → Hilbert's 10th problem
no urelements → axiom of regularity
no-broadcast theorem
no-cloning theorem
node
node → arc
node → sink
node → source
node → special node
node → supersink
node → supersource
Noetherian ring
Noetherian ring → ascending chain condition on ideals
no-go theorem
noise → remove noise from data → smoothing operator
nominal and effective interest rates

nominal data

nominal data → level of measurement

non similarity of brick and box → de Bruijn's Theorem

non-abelian Lie group, ten-generator, → Poincaré group

non-algebraic property

non-Archimedean local field

non-associative algebra

noncentral chi-squared distribution

noncentral chi-squared distribution → chi-squared distribution

non-conservative oscillator → Van der Pol oscillator

non-convergence of a sequence of continuous functions to a continuous function

non-convex quadrilateral → arrow

nonconvex regular polyhedron

non-convex set

non-decreasing function

non-decreasing sequence

non-discrete topology

non-Euclidean geometry

non-existence of the derivative → critical point

nongravitational physical phenomena, classical and quantum setting for all → Lorentz group

nonhomogeneous (alternative form of inhomogeneous)

nonhomogeneous equation

nonhomogeneous equation → differential equation

non-increasing function

non-increasing sequence

nonlinear dimensionality reduction

Nonlinear Dynamics

non-linear generalization of Euclid's algorithm

non-linear generalization of Euclid's algorithm → Gröbner basis computation

nonlinear partial differential equation

nonlinear stability of numerical methods

nonlinear system

nonlinear system → output not proportional to input

non-Markovian functional of Brownian motion → Wiener sausage

non-monotonic function

non-monotonic function → Uncanny Valley

nonnegative

nonnegative integer

nonnegative powers of a group element

nonnegativity of the square of a real number

non-normal correlated data

non-occurrence of an event

non-occurrence of an event → zero-one law

non-orientable manifold

nonparametric test

nonstandard → Non-Well-Founded Set Theory
Nonstandard Analysis
non-uniform scaling
Non-Well-Founded Set Theory
Non-Well-Founded Set Theory
nonzero bias → biased
nonzero characteristic
norm
norm → inner product
norm → L^1 norm
norm → L^1 norm → Lebesgue's Dominated Convergence Theorem
norm → quasinorm
norm → semi-norm
norm → uniform norm
normal
normal → non-normal correlated data
normal → unit normal
normal → unit normal → outward unit normal
normal component of the curl → Stokes' Theorem
normal curve → confused with the normal curve → Hubbert curve
normal distribution
normal distribution → Central Limit Theorem
normal distribution → Empirical Rule
normal matrix
normal matrix → commutes with its adjoint
normal operator
normal operator → Functional Analysis
normal problem
normal problem → inverse problem
normal space
normal subgroup
normal to a curve at a point
normal topological space
normality
Normality assumes smoothness.
Normality assumes smoothness. → parallel curve
normally-distributed data sets
normally-embedded subspace
normed vector space
nose of a projectile → ogive
Not all random variables have moment-generating functions.
not connected → indefinite special orthogonal group
not how, only what → flow network
not necessarily the case
not necessarily the case → necessarily the case

not pejorative → bias
not working directly with cumulative distribution functions
not working directly with cumulative distribution functions → moment-generating function
not working directly with probability density functions
not working directly with probability density functions → moment-generating function
notation → del
notation → exponential notation for the power set → function space
notation → nabla
notation → Newton's notation for the derivative → fluxion
notation → Umbral Calculus
notion → a more refined notion of limit
No-Wandering Domain Theorem
nowhere-dense set
nowhere-dense set → Cantor set
nowhere-differentiable continuous function
NP-complete problem
NP-completeness
n-space
n-sphere
n^{th} partial sum
n^{th} partial sum → Gibbs phenomenon
n^{th} root of a number
n^{th}-Term Test of Convergence for an Alternating Series → Alternating Series Test
n^{th}-Term Test of Divergence
n-tuple
null distribution
null hypothesis
null hypothesis → alternative hypothesis
null hypothesis → free from vagueness and ambiguity
null hypothesis → hypothesis
null hypothesis → Inferential Statistics
null hypothesis → rejection of the null hypothesis
null hypothesis → speculated agent has no effect
null set
null set → empty set
nullary operation
nullity → rank-nullity theorem
number
number → about a given number
number → algebraic number
number → Artin root numbers
number → Bernoulli numbers
number → Betti number
number → bicomplex numbers
number → cardinal number

number → cipher
number → complex number
number → complex numbers → field of complex numbers → Frobenius Theorem
number → composite number
number → concrete number
number → Conway number
number → denominate number
number → Fermat number
number → Gaussian integer
number → given number → about a given number
number → Gödel number
number → Graham's number
number → highly composite number
number → hypercomplex numbers
number → hyperreal number
number → ideal number
number → imaginary number
number → integer
number → irrational number
number → irreducible semiperfect number
number → kissing number
number → kissing number → kissing number problem
number → Lefschetz number
number → mixed number
number → natural number
number → natural number → partition of a natural number
number → natural number → partition of a natural number → Young diagram
number → ordinal number
number → Pell number
number → perfect number
number → Perrin number
number → polygonal number
number → prime number
number → rational number
number → real number
number → real numbers → field of real numbers → Frobenius Theorem
number → Real numbers whose base 10 digits are even
number → semiperfect number
number → single number
number → split-complex numbers
number → square pyramidal number
number → superior highly composite number
number → surreal number

number → transcendent number
number → transcendental number
number → triangular number
number → winding number
number (up to isomorphism) of abelian groups of order n
number base → binary
number base → decimal
number base → duodecimal
number base → hexadecimal
number base → octal
number field → algebraic number field
number of combinations of n things taken k at a time
number of compounding periods per year
number of defectives in a lot
number of defectives in a lot → lot-testing
number of different maximal independent sets in an n-vertex cycle graph → Perrin number
number of divisors of a given positive integer
number of divisors of a given positive integer
number of dots in a region
number of double points concentrated at a point
number of double points concentrated at a point → delta invariant
number of fixed points of a continuous mapping
number of negative elements in the diagonal → Sylvester's Law of Inertia
number of observations in a sample
number of permutations of n things taken k at a time
number of points determining the curve
number of positive elements in the diagonal → Sylvester's Law of Inertia
number of possible outcomes
number of possible outcomes → Multiplication Rule
number of primes not exceeding x
number of primes not exceeding x → Prime Number Theorem
number of terms in an expression
number of time-steps → expected number of time-steps → Kemeny's constant
number of zeroes equals number of poles
number of zeroes equals number of poles → modular function
number on bottom → denominator
number on top → numerator
number system
Number Theory
Number Theory → abc conjecture
Number Theory → Analytic Number Theory
Number Theory → Bertrand's postulate
Number Theory → Collatz conjecture
Number Theory → coprime
Number Theory → Diophantine equation

Number Theory → effective results in Number Theory
Number Theory → Gaussian integer
Number Theory → Goldbach's Conjecture
Number Theory → Jacobi symbol
Number Theory → Kronecker symbol
Number Theory → Legendre symbol
Number Theory → Pell's equation
Number Theory → Probabilistic Number Theory
Number Theory → problem #6-IMO-1988
Number Theory → Pythagorean triples
Number Theory → Twin Prime conjecture
numbers → Allan Krill's technique for memorizing large numbers
number-theoretic function
number-theoretic function → arithmetic function
numeracy
numeral
numeral → Arabic numerals
numeral → Roman numerals
numerator
numerator → denominator
numerator → fraction
Numerical Analysis
Numerical Analysis → De Casteljau's Algorithm
Numerical Analysis → Perturbation Theory
numerical integration
numerical integration → Simpson's Rule
numerical integration → Trapezoidal Rule
Numerical Methods
numerical methods → nonlinear stability of numerical methods
numerically stable way to evaluate polynomials in Bernstein form → De Casteljau's Algorithm
o (beginning of entries for O)
O(p, q) → Lie group
O'Nan-Scott Theorem
O'Nan-Scott Theorem → Permutation Group Theory
obelus
obelus → divided by sign
object → exceptional object
object that retains enough information about the object of interest, a simpler → homotopy group
objective property of an estimator
oblate spheroid
oblivious polynomial evaluation
oblivious transfer
obscurity
obscurity → true features of the underlying space

observables → physical observables → C* algebra

observation → number of observations in a sample

observed → as soon as significant results are observed

obstacle

obstacle → barrier

obstacle → generic topographic obstacle in a flow in mathematical modeling → witch of Agnesi

obtuse angle

obtuse triangle

occurs simply by chance, or not → Inferential Statistics

octahedron

octal

odd → If the number is odd, multiply it by 3 and add 1. → Collatz conjecture

odd function

odd integer

odd perfect number

odd perfect number → any odd perfect number has at least 7 distinct prime factors

odd permutation

odds

odds → gambling

of finite character

of finite character → Tukey's Lemma

of interest, a simpler object that retains enough information about the object → homotopy group

of measure zero

ogive

ogive → cumulative frequency polygon

Oja's rule

olympiad → IMO

Olympiad → Mathematical Olympiad → International Mathematical Olympiad

once and only once → exactly once

one

one member → exactly one member → singleton

one of the first examples of determining the tangent to a curve → kappa curve

one-dimensional space

one-dimensional space → line

one-factor experiment

one-point compactification

one-sided surface

one-sided surface → Möbius strip

one-sided surface → real projective plane

one-sided test

one-to-one function → injective function

one-variable calculus

one-way classification

onion-peeling → true features of the underlying space

only a single triple point → Boy's surface

only what, not how → flow network
onto function
onto function → surjective function
open and closed set → clopen set
open class interval
open connected set
open connected set → domain
open cover
open cover → compactness
open disk
open interval
Open Mapping Theorem
open rectangle
open set
open set → clopen set
operation
operation → binary operation
operation → binary operation → partial binary operation
operation → function
operation → magma operation
operation → n-ary operation
operation → nullary operation
operation → row operation
operation → row operation → elementary row operation
operation → row operation → elementary row operation → Gaussian elimination
operation → ternary operation
operation → unary operation
Operations Research
Operations Research → flow network
operator
operator → adjoint operator
operator → closed operator
operator → closure operator
operator → compact self-adjoint operator
operator → differential operator
operator → differential operator
operator → elliptic operator
operator → Fredholm operator
operator → frontier operator
operator → Heaviside operator
operator → interior operator
operator → linear operator
operator → Mathematical Morphology
operator → momentum operator

operator → momentum operator → 4-momentum operator

operator → multiplication operator

operator → normal operator

operator → self-adjoint operator

operator → smooth operator

operator → smoothing operator

operator → Spectral Theory of Operators on a Hilbert Space

operator → unbounded operator

operator → vertex operator algebra

Operator Theory

operators on compact manifolds, index of elliptic → Atiyah-Singer Index Theorem

Oppermann's conjecture

opposing pairs of vectors → eutactic star

opposite of the Archimedean spiral → hyperbolic spiral

optical illusion

optical illusion → dissection puzzle

optical illusion → missing square puzzle

optimal apple-picking strategy → Marginal Value Theorem

Optimal Estimation

Optimal Estimation → Applied Statistics

optimization

optimization

optimization → Optimization Theory

optimization → reformulated as an optimization problem

optimization problem

optimization problem → conditional factor demand

Optimization Theory

Optimization Theory → maximum flow problem

or

or → exclusive or

OR → Operations Research

orbifold

orbit

orbit → elliptical orbit

orbit → elliptical orbit → derivation of elliptical orbits from Newton's laws of motion and ...

orbit → periodic orbit → infinite number of periodic orbits → Horseshoe Map

orbit → shape and orientation of the orbit of one astronomical body around another

orchard problem → orchard-planting problem

orchard-planting problem

orchard-planting problem → Discrete Geometry

orchard-planting problem → For all sufficiently large n, there are at most f(n) special objects.

order

order → infinite order

order → infinite order

order → infinite order → distribution of infinite order
order → partial order
order → Ramsey Theory
order → reduction of order
order → structure
order → structure
order of a group
order of a subgroup
order of a subgroup → Lagrange's theorem
order of a subgroup → theorem of Lagrange
order of an element
order of magnitude
order of operations
Order Theory
ordered basis
ordered pair
ordered triple
ordering
ordering → lexicographical ordering
order-preserving linear transformations → L-algebra
ordinal
ordinal → large countable ordinal
ordinal → Ordinal Analysis
Ordinal Analysis
ordinal association
ordinal association → rank correlation
ordinal data
ordinal data → level of measurement
ordinal number
ordinary annuity
ordinary differential equation
ordinary differential equation → linear system of ordinary differential equations
organizing → self-organizing map
orientable manifold
orientable surface
orientation
orientation → acyclic orientation
orientation → induced orientation
orientations → Padua points
oriented manifold
origami
origin
origin → issuing from a central origin → eutactic star
origin → value at the origin → Dirac delta function
orthocenter

orthogonal
orthogonal basis
orthogonal functions
orthogonal group
orthogonal group → indefinite orthogonal group
orthogonal group → indefinite special orthogonal group
orthogonal matrix
orthogonal polynomials
orthogonal polynomials → polynomials that are orthogonal on the unit disk → Zernike polynomials
orthogonal projection
orthogonal transformation
orthogonal transformation → Clifford algebra
orthonormal basis
orthonormal basis → Spectral Theorem
orthonormal vectors
oscillation at the edges of an interval → Runge's phenomenon
oscillator
oscillator → coupled oscillators
oscillator → coupled oscillators → Kuramoto model
oscillator → non-conservative oscillator → Van der Pol oscillator
oscillator → Van der Pol oscillator
osculating → kissing
osculating circle
osculating plane
osculation
osculation → osculating circle
osculation → osculating plane
outcome
outcome → possible outcomes → number of possible outcomes → Multiplication Rule
outlier
out-of-kilter algorithm
output
output → input
output → level of input required to produce a given level of output
output not proportional to input
output not proportional to input → nonlinear system
output proportional to input
output proportional to input → linear system
outside → zero outside of a compact set → compact support
outward unit normal
oval
oval → Cassini ovals
oval of Booth → hippopede
over a commutative ring
overdetermined differentiable system

overfitting

overfitting

overfitting → model

overfitting → prevention of overfitting

overshoot

overshoot → Gibbs phenomenon

overshoot → undershoot

overshoot does not die out as more terms are added → Gibbs phenomenon

oxygen-hemoglobin dissociation curve

p (beginning of entries for P)

p and 2p + 1 are both prime → Sophie Germain prime

packing → sphere packing

packing congruent rectangular bricks into larger rectangular boxes

packing congruent rectangular bricks into larger rectangular boxes → de Bruijn's Theorem

p-adic Analysis

p-adic Analysis → p-adic Number System

p-adic analysis → use of p-adic analysis to tell whether a quadratic form has a rational root

p-adic number

p-adic Number System

Padua points

Painlevé property

Painlevé transcendents

paint → swinging a punctured bucket of paint over a canvas → Lissajous figures

pair → ordered pair

pair of periods → fundamental parallelogram

pair of periods → fundamental parallelogram → function of a complex variable

pair set → unordered pair

pairing → axiom of pairing

pairing → Schröder-Bernstein Theorem

pairing → Wilson's Theorem

pairwise balanced design

pairwise balanced design → Combinatorial Design Theory

paper-folding → A4 paper size

paper-folding → flexagon

paper-folding → origami

parabola

parabola → cubic parabola

parabola → rectifying the parabola

parabola → semicubical parabola

parabolic cylinder functions

Parabolic Geometry

Parabolic Geometry → Euclidean Geometry

paracompact space

paradox

paradox → Banach-Tarski Paradox

paradox → Bertrand's box paradox
paradox → Helicopter Paradox
paradox → independence of starting state → Kemeny's constant
paradox → paradox regarding contingency tables → Simpson's paradox
paradox → problem
paradox → Russell's Paradox
paradox → Siegel's paradox
paradox → Simpson's paradox
paradox → Zeno's Paradoxes
paradox regarding contingency tables → Simpson's paradox
parallax
parallel curve
parallel lines
parallel lines → ambient space
parallel lines → skew lines
parallel lines cut by a transversal
Parallel Postulate
Parallel Postulate → Euclid's fifth postulate
parallel to the directrix → latus rectum
parallelepiped
parallelogram
parallelogram → elliptic function
parallelogram → fundamental parallelogram
parallelogram → fundamental parallelogram → function of a complex variable
parallelogram law of vector addition
parallelogram of periodicity
parameter
parameter → moduli space
parameter → parameters → Variation of Parameters
parameter → population parameter
parameter ecology
parameter space
parameter space → feasible region in the parameter space
parameterization
parameterization → independence of parameterization
parameterization → Teichmüller space
parameterized complexity
parametric curve → sampling of a parametric curve → Padua points
parametric equations
Pareto Principle
parity
parity check
part → aliquot parts
part → two parts → separation of the data into two parts
part versus whole

part versus whole → Mereology

partial

partial binary operation

partial converse

partial converse → converse

partial converse of the Borel-Cantelli Lemma → Second Borel-Cantelli Lemma

partial derivative

partial differential equation

partial differential equation of elliptic type

partial differential equation of elliptic type → Poisson's equation

partial differential equations → Hodge Theory

partial differential equations → Leray-Schauder degree

partial differential equations → Sobolev space

partial function

Partial Geometry

Partial Geometry → incidence structure

partial magma

partial order

partial order → po-group

partial recursive function

partial sum forms a martingale → Walsh series

partially ordered algebraic systems

partially ordered by inclusion

partially ordered by inclusion → Tukey's Lemma

partially ordered set

partially ordered sets → special kinds of partially ordered sets → Domain Theory

Particle Physics and Representation Theory

Particle Physics and Representation Theory → Wigner's classification

particular solution

particular solution of a differential equation

partition → coloring

partition → Dedekind cut

partition → equivalence relation

partition → graph partition

partition → graphical representation of a partition of a natural number → Young diagram

partition → lower sum of a function for a given partition

partition → partition of an interval

partition → Schläfli double six

partition → transversals of graph partitions

partition → upper sum of a function for a given partition

partition of a natural number

partition of a set

partition of an interval

partition of unity

partition of unity → shrinking space

Partition Theory

partitioned boundary

partitioning a sample of data into complementary subsets

partitioning a sample of data into complementary subsets → cross-validation

parts and the wholes they form → Mereology

Pascal → de Mere's Paradox

Pascal's triangle

Paschen's curve

path

path → expansion path

path → labyrinth

path → length of path of a bouncing ball

path → maze

path → polygonal path

path → same time for two paths → lemniscate of Bernoulli

path → shortest path problem

path → shortest path problem → Graph Theory

pathological distribution → Cauchy distribution

pattern → emergence of patterns as the scale of the objects grows → Ramsey Theory

Pattern Analysis and Recognition

patterns in juggling

patterns in juggling → Recreational Mathematics

patterns of five points → quincunx

PBD → pairwise balanced design

PCA → Principal Component Analysis

pdf → probability density function

peakedness of a curve → degree of peakedness of a curve

Peano's postulates

Pearson's correlation coefficient

PEDMAS

peeling an onion → true features of the underlying space

Peirce decomposition

pejorative → not pejorative → bias

Pell number

Pell's equation

Pell's equation → Diophantine equation

pencil → without lifting the pencil from the paper → nine-point problem

pencil (in Projective Geometry)

pendulum

pendulum → constrained motion under gravity

pendulum → spherical pendulum

Penrose tiles

pentagon

percent

percent change over time

percent decrease not offset by same percentage increase

percentage

percentage distribution

percentage histogram

percentage polygon

percentages → relatives

percentile

percentile rank

percolation

percolation threshold

perfect field

perfect number

perfect number → even perfect number

perfect number → odd perfect number

perfect number → odd perfect number → any odd perfect number has at least 7 prime factors

perfect set

perfect set property

perfect square

perfect square → Vieta jumping

performance of proofs on the theatrical stage

performance of proofs on the theatrical stage → mathematical passion plays of Michael Fellows

performance of theorems → performance of proofs on the theatrical stage

perimeter

perimeter → circumference

perimeter → finite perimeter

perimeter → finite perimeter → Caccioppoli set

perimeter → infinite perimeter → finite area with infinite perimeter → Koch Snowflake

perimeter → isoperimetric problem

perimeter → rectangle having greatest area for a given perimeter

perimeter → rectangle having smallest perimeter for a given area

period

period → base period

period → periodicity

period function → generalization of periodic functions to topological groups → automorphic form

periodic continued fraction

periodic function

periodic in two directions → elliptic function

periodic infinite decimal

periodic orbit

periodic wave-trains in nonlinear systems

periodic wave-trains in nonlinear systems → Benjamin-Feir instability

periodicity

periodicity → double periodicity

periodicity → double periodicity → fundamental parallelogram

periodicity → double periodicity → fundamental parallelogram → function of a complex variable periodicity → parallelogram of periodicity

permanent income hypothesis

permutation → equivalent up to permutation and isomorphism → Jordan-Hölder Theorem

permutation → number of permutations of n things taken k at a time

permutation group

permutation group → rank 3 permutation group

permutation group → transitive permutation group

permutation group → transitive permutation group → multiply transitive permutation group

Permutation Group Theory

Permutation Group Theory → O'Nan-Scott Theorem

perpendicular foot

perpendicular line → negative reciprocal of the slope of the given line

perpendicular lines

Perrin number

Persistent Homology

perspective

perturbation

Perturbation Theory

Perturbation Theory → Numerical Analysis

Pfaffian function

phase difference

phase-contrast microscopy → Zernike polynomials

phase-locked loop

phase-locked loop

phenomena, physical, classical and quantum setting for all (nongravitational) → Lorentz group

phenomenon → Runge's phenomenon

Phillips curve

phrase → a feasible region in the parameter space

phrase → as soon as significant results are observed

phrase → modeled by a special case

phrase → not working directly with cumulative distribution functions

phrase → not working directly with probability density functions

phrase → relationship between

phrase → weighted sum of random variables

phrase → without loss of generality

phrase → wolog

physical observables → C* algebra

physical phenomena, classical and quantum setting for all (nongravitational) → Lorentz group

Physics → mathematical treatment of the axioms of Physics → Hilbert's 6th problem

Physics → physical observables → C* algebra

Physics → Theoretical Physics → no-go theorem

pi → π

Picard group

Picard's theorem

Picard-Lefschetz Theory

pictorial representation → graphical representation

pictorial representation of data

pictorial representation of data → box and whiskers diagram

pictorial representation of data → dot plot

pictorial representation of data → scatterplot

pictorial representation of data → stem and leaf plot

picture hanging on a wall → Regiomontanus' Angle-Maximization Problem

picture-angle maximization (classical problem)

pie chart

piecewise continuously differentiable periodic function

piecewise continuously differentiable periodic function → Gibbs phenomenon

piecewise-continuous function

piecewise-defined

piecewise-defined → spline function

piecewise-smooth function

Pigeonhole Principle

pinch point

pinch point → cuspidal point

pinch point → singular point on an algebraic surface

Pinch Theorem

Pinch Theorem → Squeeze Theorem

placeholder

planar graph

planar graph → Fáry's Theorem

planar projection

planar projection → lemniscate of Gerono

planarity

planarity → Kuratowski's Theorem

plane

plane → a set is called plane

plane → a set is called plane → Cayley-Menger determinants

plane → affine plane

plane → complex plane

plane → complex projective plane

plane → Fano plane

plane → Geometry of Triangles in the Euclidean Plane

plane → half-plane

plane → Plane Geometry

plane → projective plane

Plane Geometry

planet → motion of a planet → hodograph

Platonic solid

platykurtic distribution

plausibility argument

Playfair's axiom

Please excuse my dear aunt Sally → order of operations
plot → dot plot
plot → pictorial representation of data
plot → scatterplot
plot winds from soundings of the Earth's atmosphere → hodograph
plurality
plus
plus → minus
plus-or-minus
plus-or-minus → minus-or-plus
$p_n > n(\log(n))$ → Rosser's theorem
po-group
Poincaré conjecture
Poincaré group
Poincaré group → group of Minkowski spacetime isometries
Poincaré Lemma
Poincaré Return Theorem
Poincaré's group → Wigner's classification
Poinsot's spirals
point
point → adherent point
point → all points on a line between two given points
point → antipodal points
point → collinear points
point → collinear points → Menelaus's Theorem
point → configuration of 30 points and 12 lines → Schläfli double six
point → critical point
point → cuspidal point
point → distance between two points
point → distance between two points → hypotenuse
point → distinct points
point → distinction between points
point → equispaced interpolation points
point → finite set of points → given a finite set of points in the plane → Sylvester-Gallai Theorem
point → fixed point
point → interpolation points
point → lattice point
point → number of double points concentrated at a point
point → number of double points concentrated at a point → delta invariant
point → Padua points
point → pinch point
point → point at infinity
point → point cloud
point → point discontinuity

point → point estimate

point → point of inflection

point → point process

point → point set

point → point set → point cloud → Pointless Topology

point → point set → unisolvent point set

point → Point Set Theory

point → point slope form of a linear equation

point → point where the solution of the equation behaves badly

point → pointed space

point → Pointless Topology

point → points → number of points determining a curve

point → points → patterns of five points → quincunx

point → points are on which lines

point → points are on which lines → incidence structure

point → point-slope form of a linear equation

point → pointwise convergence

point → pointwise limit

point → primitive dispersion point

point → saddle point

point → separating points from closed sets

point → singular point

point → singular point on an algebraic surface

point → stationary point

point → triple point → only a single triple point → Boy's surface

point → turning point

point → two distinct points

point at infinity

point cloud

point discontinuity

point estimate

Point Estimation

point mass → Dirac delta function

point of inflection

point process

point process → Poisson point process

point set

point set → unisolvent point set

Point Set Theory

Point Set Theory → Linear Point Set Theory

point where the solution of the equation behaves badly

point where the solution of the equation behaves badly → movable singularity

pointed graph → rooted graph

pointed space

Pointless Topology
points are on which lines
points are on which lines → incidence structure
point-slope form of a linear equation
pointwise convergence
pointwise limit
Poisson distribution
Poisson point process
Poisson process → Renewal Theory
Poisson's equation
Poisson's equation → Lane-Emden equation
Poisson's equation → Laplace's equation
polar axis → ray
polar coordinates
polar coordinates → converting between polar and rectangular coordinates
polar coordinates → pole
polar coordinates → ray
pole
pole → have at least 2 poles → elliptic function
poles → allowed poles → prescribed zeroes and allowed poles
poles → allowed poles → prescribed zeroes and allowed poles → Riemann-Roch Theorem
poles → number of zeroes equals number of poles → modular function
Polish space
political science model → J curve
polyform
polygamma function
polygamma function → digamma function
polygon
polygon → Euclidean tiling by convex regular polygons
polygon → frequency polygon
polygon → Jordan curve
polygon → Newton polygon
polygon → polygon mesh
polygon → polygons → dissections of polygons → Wallace-Bolyai-Gerwien Theorem
polygon → region bounded by a polygon
polygon mesh
polygonal number
polygonal path
polyhedra of equal volume → Hilbert's 3rd problem
polyhedron
polyhedron → toroidal polyhedron
polynomial
polynomial → Approximation by Polynomials
polynomial → Bernstein polynomial
polynomial → Bernstein polynomial

polynomial → Bernstein-Sato polynomial
polynomial → characteristic polynomial
polynomial → Chebyshev polynomial
polynomial → Chebyshev polynomial
polynomial → exponential polynomial
polynomial → homogeneous polynomial
polynomial → long division of polynomials → Remainder Theorem
polynomial → low-degree polynomials → spline function
polynomial → monic polynomial
polynomial → polynomials → Gauss's lemma on the factorization of polynomials
polynomial → polynomials → long division of polynomials
polynomial → polynomials → product of two primitive polynomials
polynomial → polynomials → Zernike polynomials
polynomial → primitive polynomial
polynomial → Racah polynomial
polynomial → separable and inseparable polynomials
polynomial → symmetric polynomial
polynomial → Weierstrass Approximation Theorem
polynomial → Wilson and Racah polynomials → Askey tableau
polynomial algorithm
polynomial algorithm → strongly polynomial algorithm
polynomial approximation → Mergelyan's Theorem
polynomial approximation → Runge's Approximation Theorem
polynomial approximation → Weierstrass Approximation Theorem
polynomial divisible by $x^2 + y^2$
polynomial divisible by $x^2 + y^2$ → circular algebraic curve
polynomial evaluation
polynomial evaluation → De Casteljau's Algorithm
polynomial evaluation → Horner's Method
polynomial evaluation → oblivious polynomial evaluation
polynomial interpolation
polynomial interpolation → Runge's phenomenon
polynomial interpolation of two variables
polynomial interpolation of two variables → Padua points
polynomial time
polynomial vector field
polynomial with integer coefficients
polynomials over a ring
polynomials that are orthogonal on the unit disk
polynomials that are orthogonal on the unit disk → Zernike polynomials
polyomino
polytope
polytropic process equation
Pontryagin duality

population
population mean
population parameter
population standard deviation
population variance
portmanteau → clopen set
POS → partially ordered set
posed → ill-posed problem
posed → well-posed problem
poset → partially ordered set
position
position, but no magnitude → point
positional notation
positive
positive → negative
positive → plus
positive definite binary quadratic form
positive element → number of positive elements in the diagonal → Sylvester's Law of Inertia
positive integer
positive integer → canonical representation of a positive integer
positive integer → Tarski's high-school algebra problem
positive semi-definite
possible outcomes → number of possible outcomes → Multiplication Rule
posterior marginals
postulate
postulate → axiom
postulate → Euclid's fifth postulate
power
power → statistical power
power → volume raised to a power → polytropic process equation
power law
power mean
power of a prime
power series
power set
power-associativity
powers of 2
practical number
precisely → is known, precisely
precision
precision → accuracy
precision → holding small numbers with great precision
pre-college mathematics contest → IMO
pre-defined condition
pre-defined stopping rule → pre-defined stopping time

pre-defined stopping time

pre-defined stopping time → sequential sampling

prediction → statistical inference

predictive model versus explanatory model

pre-norm → semi-norm

preparation for proving a theorem → lemma

prescribed zeroes and allowed poles

prescribed zeroes and allowed poles → Riemann-Roch Theorem

present value of a deferred annuity

present value of an annuity

presentational form

presentational form → rounding

present-value formula

preserving → structure-preserving map

President Garfield → Garfield's proof of the Pythagorean Theorem

pretending indices are exponents → Umbral Calculus

prevention of overfitting

price → future prices → Siegel's paradox

primality

primality → prime

primality test

primality test → Adleman-Pomerance-Rumley Primality Test

primality test → Baillie-PSW primality test

primality test → criterion for primality

primality test → deterministic primality test

primality test → Fermat primality test

primality test → Miller-Rabin primality test

primality test → Solovay-Strassen primality test

prime

prime → absolute pseudoprime

prime → Babbage's criterion for primality

prime → Euclid's Theorem

prime → existence of a prime in a certain place

prime → Fermat prime

prime → gaps between the primes

prime → how prime factors can be found by continued fractions

prime → infinitude of primes

prime → infinitude of the primes

prime → Kummer-Vandiver conjecture

prime → Mersenne prime

prime → Mersenne prime → even perfect number

prime → product of two distinct primes → Public-Key Cryptography

prime → pseudoprime

prime → search for prime divisors of a given number

prime → Sophie Germain prime
prime → sum of two odd primes
prime → sum of two odd primes → Goldbach's Conjecture
prime → Twin Prime conjecture
prime → Wilson's Theorem
prime congruent to 2 mod 3 → Eisenstein integer
prime factorization
prime ideal
prime meridian
prime number
Prime Number Theorem
Prime Number Theorem → J. E. Littlewood's Theorem of 1914
primes in arithmetic progression → Green-Tao theorem
primitive dispersion point
primitive of a function
primitive of a function → Darboux's theorem
primitive polynomial
primitive Pythagorean triple
primitive Pythagorean triple → fraction of primitive Pythagorean triples with perimeter < p
primitive recursive arithmetic
primitive recursive function
primitive roots of unity
principal axis theorem
Principal Component Analysis
principal ideal domain
principal value
principal value → Cauchy principal value
principal value → Hilbert transform
principle → Cavalieri's Principle
principle → Hardy-Weinberg Principle
principle → maximal principle → Hausdorff Maximal Principle
principle → Multiplication Principle
principle → Pareto Principle
principle → Pigeonhole Principle
principle → principle of factor sparsity
principle → Squeezing Principle
principle → unifying principle in Geometry → Group Theory
principle → Well-Ordering Principle
principle → Yao's Principle
principle ideal domain → structure theorem for finitely generated modules over a ...
principle of factor sparsity
principle of factor sparsity → Pareto Principle
prism
prismatoid
prismoid

privacy → oblivious polynomial evaluation
private equity model → J curve
Probabilistic Number Theory
probabilistic transition system
probability
Probability
probability → Bayesian Probability
probability → chance
probability → convergence in probability
probability → Monty Hall Problem
probability → posterior marginals
Probability axioms
Probability axioms → Probability Theory
probability density function
probability density function → not working directly with probability density functions
probability density function of the Cauchy distribution
probability density function of the Cauchy distribution → witch of Agnesi
probability distribution function
probability distribution function → distribution function
probability integral
probability matrix
Probability Theory
Probability Theory → convergence of random variables
Probability Theory → Cox's theorem
Probability Theory → Kolmogorov's axiomatics
Probability Theory → lumpability
Probability Theory → Probability axioms
Probability Theory → Renewal Theory
probable error
probe → sampling
probe → structuring element
probe → structuring element → Mathematical Morphology
problem #6-IMO-1988
problem #6-IMO-1988 → Vieta jumping
problem → 3 primes problem → Goldbach's Weak Conjecture
problem → Basel Problem
problem → Bernstein Problem (in Differential Geometry)
problem → Cannonball Problem
problem → circulation problem
problem → constrained motion under gravity
problem → constraint-satisfaction problem
problem → cost-minimization problem of producers
problem → Eight-Queens Problem
problem → extension problem

problem → forward problem
problem → Hilbert's problems
problem → ill-posed problem
problem → inverse Galois problem
problem → inverse problem
problem → inverse problem
problem → kissing number problem
problem → maximum flow problem
problem → Monty Hall Problem
problem → normal problem
problem → NP-complete problem
problem → optimization problem
problem → paradox
problem → problem #6-IMO-1988
problem → Problem of Apollonius
problem → problems about normal spaces → Morita conjectures
problem → puzzle → dissection puzzle
problem → reformulated as an optimization problem
problem → Regiomontanus' Angle-Maximization Problem
problem → shortest path problem
problem → Tarski's high-school algebra problem
problem → tractable problem
problem → traveling-salesman problem
problem → two envelopes problem
problem → uncertainty quantification problem
problem → utility-maximizing problem of consumers
problem → variational problem
problem → Waring's Problem
problem → well-posed problem
problem → Zermelo's navigation problem
Problem of Apollonius
problems about normal spaces
process
process → adapted process
process → Bernoulli process
process → Kaprekar process
process → point process
process → point process → Poisson point process
process → polytropic process equation
process → rinse and repeat
process → sequence
process → stochastic process
process → stochastic process → continuous time stochastic process
process → Wiener process

processing

processing → analysis and processing

processing → analysis and processing of geometrical structures → Mathematical Morphology

processing → signal processing → Hilbert transform

product → bilinear product

product → cup product

product → inner product

product → intersection product

product → multiplication table

product → scalar product of two vectors

product → scalar triple product

product → vector triple product

product → wedge product

product notation

product of an orthogonal matrix and an upper-triangular matrix

product of an orthogonal matrix and an upper-triangular matrix → QR decomposition

product of compact topological spaces → Tychonoff's Theorem

product of difference of squares → Markov brothers' inequality

product of roots → Vieta's formulas

product of the extremes

product of the extremes → fraction

product of the first n odd numbers → Markov brothers' inequality

product of the means

product of the means → fraction

product of two distinct primes → Public-Key Cryptography

product of two primitive polynomials

product rule → differential algebra

product rule → differential field

product rule → differential ring

product rule for derivatives

product topology

production → scale of production

production → scale of production → as the scale of production increases

production function

production function → Cobb-Douglas production function

production function → Leontief production function

production function → returns to scale

production rate of a resource over time

production rate of a resource over time → Hubbert curve

productive set

product-moment formula for the linear correlation coefficient

program → Erlangen program

program → Langlands program

progression

progression → sequence
project
project → data project
projection
projection → orthogonal projection
projection → planar projection
projection map
Projective Geometry
projective harmonic conjugate
projective line
projective plane
projective plane → fake projective plane
projective representation
projective variety
projective variety → algebraic geometry of complex projective varieties
projective variety → algebraic geometry of complex projective varieties → Hodge Theory
prolate spheroid
prolate trochoid
proof
proof → Automath
proof → contradiction
proof → converse
proof → Curry-Howard correspondence
proof → derivation
proof → how much axiomatic power you need to prove a particular theorem
proof → implication
proof → indirect proof
proof → new proof of an old result
proof → proof checking
proof → proof technique
proof → proof technique → Vieta jumping
proof → Proof Theory
proof → proof without words
proof → simple proof that π is irrational
proof → zero-knowledge proof
proof → ε-δ proof
proof checking
proof checking → automated proof checking
proof technique
proof technique → Vieta jumping
Proof Theory
proof without words
propagation
propagation → wave propagation
proper arithmetic progression

proper fraction

proper subset

properties of the standard deviation

property

property → additive property

property → an emergent property

property → an emergent property → synchronization

property → associative property

property → Associative Property for Addition

property → Associative Property for Multiplication

property → based on some useful algebraic properties

property → Commutative Property for Addition

property → Commutative Property for Multiplication

property → desired property of an estimator

property → Distributive Property

property → finite forking property

property → finite-intersection property

property → independence and identical distribution property

property → non-algebraic property

property → objective property of an estimator

property → Painlevé property

property → property of Baire

property → socks-shoes property

property of a topological space invariant under homeomorphisms → topological invariant

property of Baire

proportion

proportion → cumulative proportion → Lorenz curve

proportion → fixed proportions

proportional → output not proportional to input

proportional → output not proportional to input → nonlinear system

proportional → output proportional to input

proportional → output proportional to input → linear system

proportionality

proportionality → factor of proportionality

proportionality → inverse proportionality

proportions → sampling distribution of proportions

proposition

proximity space

proxy measurement

Prüfer group

p-series

pseudo vector

pseudo-Euclidean space

pseudo-metric

pseudoprime

pseudoprime → absolute pseudoprime

pseudorandom number generator → cryptographically secure pseudorandom number generator

pseudo-random-number generation

pseudo-random-number generation → random-number generation

pseudo-random-number generator → random-number generation

Public-Key Cryptography

Public-Key Cryptography → Cryptography

Public-Key Cryptography → Elliptic-Curve Cryptography

Public-Key Cryptography → modular exponentiation

Public-Key Cryptography → modular root-extraction

Public-Key Cryptography → RSA Public-Key Cryptosystem

Puiseux series

pump → water pump → Archimedes' screw

punctuated equilibrium

punctured disk

Pure Mathematics

purely-topological proof that the reals are uncountable

pursuit → curve of pursuit

pursuit curve → curve of pursuit

putting together → concatenation

puzzle → dissection puzzle

p-value

pyramid

Pythagorean means

Pythagorean means → relationships among the Pythagorean means

Pythagorean theorem

Pythagorean Theorem → Garfield's proof of the Pythagorean Theorem

Pythagorean Theorem → Mamikon's proof of the Pythagorean Theorem

Pythagorean triple

Pythagorean triple → primitive Pythagorean triple

q (beginning of entries for Q)

Q (set of rational numbers)

QR decomposition

QR decomposition → matrix decomposition

qu (misspelling of queue)

quadratic equation

quadratic equation → standard form of a quadratic equation

quadratic form

quadratic form → binary quadratic form

quadratic form → Clifford algebra

quadratic form → Hilbert's 11th problem

quadratic form → integral quadratic form

quadratic form → rational quadratic form

quadratic formula

quadratic function

quadratic mean

quadratic mean → root mean square

quadratic nonresidue

quadratic reciprocity

quadratic reciprocity → Law of Quadratic Reciprocity

quadratic residue

quadratic sieve

quadrature

quadrifolium

quadrilateral

quadrilateral → certain quadrilateral is a square → Finsler-Hadwiger Theorem

quadrilateral → non-convex quadrilateral → arrow

quadrilateral → quadrilaterals → taxonomy of quadrilaterals

qualitative result

quantification

quantification → existential quantification

quantification → uncertainty quantification problem

quantification → universal quantification

quantify → detect and quantify (a phenomenon)

quantify → detect and quantify (a phenomenon) → Topological Data Analysis

quantile

quantitative result

quantitative result → analytical result

quantum group

Quantum Mechanics

Quantum Mechanics → C* algebra

Quantum Mechanics → no-broadcast theorem

Quantum Mechanics → no-cloning theorem

Quantum Mechanics versus Classical Mechanics → Bell's Theorem

quantum, and classical, setting for all (nongravitational) physical phenomena → Lorentz group

quartic → bicircular quartic

quartic → Klein quartic

quartic equation

quartic plane curve

quartile

quasinorm

quaternions

queen → Eight-Queens Problem

questionable convergence

questionable convergence → Benjamin-Feir instability

queue

queue → Queueing Theory

queueing

queueing → queueing formula

queueing → queueing formula → fundamental queueing formula → Little's Law
queueing → Queueing Theory
queueing formula
queueing formula → Little's Law
Queueing Theory
Queueing Theory → Little's Law
Queueing Theory → queueing
quincunx
quincunx → bean machine
quincunx → Central Limit Theorem
quincunx → Galton board
quintic equation
quintic equation → Abel Ruffini Theorem
quotient
quotient → difference-quotient
quotient → Kolmogorov quotient
quotient → rationality
quotient → Stanley-Reisner ring
quotient group → automorphic function
quotient of functions → L'Hôpital's rule
quotient of sums of squares
quotient of sums of squares → Hilbert's 17th problem
quotient ring
quotient rule for derivatives
quotient space
quotient space → equivalence relation
quotient topology
r (beginning of entries for R)
R (set of real numbers)
R^3 → homeomorphic to R^3
Raabe integral of the gamma function
Raabe's Test
Racah polynomial
radian
radian angle-measure
radical
radical → surd
radical extensions
radical sign
radicand
radiodrome
radius
radius of convergence
radius of curvature
radix

radix → base
Radon measure
Radon measure → Haar measure
Radon transform
raffle
raising a fraction to higher terms
Ramanujan tau function
Ramanujan's sum
Ramanujan's sum → Ramanujan's sum
Ramification Theory
Ramsey Theory
Ramsey Theory → an emergent property
Ramsey Theory → General Systems Theory
Ramsey's Theorem
random
random → reverse engineering the seed of a linear congruential random number generator
random data → focal tendencies in random data
random destination state → transition from an initial state to a → Kemeny's constant
random experiment
random line → Crofton formula
random movement
random movement → component of a time series
random number
random number generator → Lehmer random number generator
random sampling
random sampling → Monte Carlo method
random selection
random selection → selection
random selection → urn
random time elapsed between two consecutive events
random time elapsed between two consecutive events → Renewal Theory
random variable
random variable → characteristic function
random variable → continuous random variable
random variable → convergence of random variables
random variable → dimensionality reduction
random variable → discrete random variable
random variable → infinite sequence of random variables
random variable → infinite sequence of random variables → Kolmogorov's Zero-One Law
random variable → k independent standard normal random variables
random variable → sequence of binary random variables
random variable → sequence of binary random variables → Bernoulli process
random variable → sums of dependent random variables
random variable → weighted sum of random variables
random variable → zero-mean random variable

random variables → convergence of expected values

random variation

random variation → component of a time series

random walk

randomization

randomized bocks

randomized versus deterministic algorithm, expected costs of → Yao's Principle

random-number generation

random-number generation → linear congruential random-number generator

random-number generation → pseudo-random-number generation

random-number generator → random-number generation

range → interquartile range

range of a function

range of a function → image

range of a set of numbers

rank

rank 3 permutation group

rank 3 permutation group → Finite Group Theory

rank correlation

rank correlation → Spearman's Formula for Rank Correlation

rank factorization

rank factorization → matrix decomposition

rank of a matrix

rank-nullity theorem

rank-nullity theorem → Matrix Theory

rapid calculation → Trachtenberg system of rapid calculation

rapid growth of the factorials

rapid growth of the factorials → 7!

rate → level

rate → production rate of a resource over time

rate → production rate of a resource over time → Hubbert curve

rate → related rates

ratio

ratio → aspect ratio → A4 paper size

ratio → can be expressed as the ratio of two holomorphic functions

ratio → can be expressed as the ratio of two holomorphic functions → meromorphic function

ratio → common ratio

ratio → common ratio → geometric progression

ratio → cross ratio

ratio → given ratio → mean proportionals to a given ratio → cissoid of Diocles

ratio → golden ratio

ratio → ratio data

ratio → ratio of the circumference of a circle to its diameter

ratio → Ratio Test

ratio → rational number

ratio → rise / run → slope

ratio → silver ratio

ratio data

ratio data → level of measurement

ratio of the circumference of a circle to its diameter

ratio of the circumference of a circle to its diameter → π

Ratio Test

rational curve

rational function

Rational Homotopy Theory

rational normal curve

rational number

rational number → fraction

rational number → ratio

rational number → Rational Root theorem

rational quadratic form

Rational Root theorem

rationality

rationality → quotient

ray

reactor → tank reactor → CSTR

Real Analysis

real benefit → just adding inconvenience, with no real benefit

real coordinate space

real eigenvalues → Hermitian matrix

real elements → If a matrix has only real elements, then its adjoint is equal to its transpose.

real manifold → Morse Theory

real number

real numbers → field of real numbers → Frobenius Theorem

Real numbers whose base 10 digits are even

real projective plane

real-valued function of a real variable

reciprocal → sum of the reciprocals of the win primes → Brun's Theorem

reciprocity

reciprocity → Hilbert's 9th problem

Recreational Mathematics

Recreational Mathematics → algorithmic and geometrical characteristics of origami

Recreational Mathematics → flexagon

Recreational Mathematics → fractal-generating software

Recreational Mathematics → Kaprekar's Constant

Recreational Mathematics → magic square

Recreational Mathematics → patterns in juggling

Recreational Mathematics → polyform

rectangle

rectangle → closed rectangle

rectangle → Latin rectangle

rectangle → open rectangle

rectangle → smallest area rectangle that encloses a given polygon → convex hull

rectangle chart

rectangle having greatest area for a given perimeter

rectangle having smallest perimeter for a given area

rectangular bricks → packing congruent rectangular bricks into larger rectangular boxes

rectangular coordinates

rectangular coordinates → axis

rectangular coordinates → converting between polar and rectangular coordinates

rectifiable curve

rectifiable path

rectifiable plane curve

rectification

rectification of a curve

rectifying the parabola

recurrence relation

recurrence relation → method of undetermined coefficients

recursion

Recursion Theory

recursive function

recursive function → partial recursive function

recursive function → primitive recursive function

recursively enumerable set

reduce problems in Abstract Algebra to problems in Linear Algebra → Representation Theory

reduced row echelon form

reducing a fraction

reducing a fraction to lowest terms

reducing the size

reducing the size of the state space

reduction

reduction → dimensionality reduction

reduction → dimensionality reduction

reduction → dimensionality reduction → nonlinear dimensionality reduction

reduction → row reduction → Gaussian elimination

reduction → Turing reduction

reduction in the amount of variation in a set of data

reduction in the amount of variation in a set of data → moving average

reduction of order

reductive space

reference triangle

refined → more refined → a more refined notion of limit

refinement

refinement of a partition

refinement of a partition of an interval
reflect changes over a period of time
reflect changes over a period of time → index
reflect changes over a period of time → time series
reflection
reflection → isometry
reflection about the horizontal axis
reflection about the origin
reflection about the vertical axis
reflection formula
reflection formula → functional equation
reflexive relation
reformulated as an optimization problem
Regiomontanus' Angle-Maximization Problem
region
region → feasible region
region bounded by a Jordan curve
region bounded by a polygon
region defined by two intersecting spheres
regression
regression → linear regression
regression → linear regression → heteroscedasticity-consistent standard errors
regression → ridge regression
Regression Analysis
regression toward the mean
regular → Fatou set
regular → functions regular in a disk → Landau theorems
regular 17-gon
regular convex polyhedron
regular convex polyhedron → Platonic solid
regular mathematical induction
regular problem
regular problem → Hilbert's 19th problem
regular space
regular topological space
regularity
regularity → Arens regularity
regularity axiom → axiom of regularity
regularization
regularization → Hadamard regularization
regularization → introducing additional information in order to solve an ill-posed problem
regularization → prevention of overfitting
Reidemeister torsion
Reidemeister torsion → analytic torsion
rejection

rejection → rejection criterion
rejection criterion
rejection criterion → rejection
rejection of the null hypothesis
related rates
relation
relation → anti-symmetric relation
relation → binary relation
relation → equivalence relation
relation → Meyer's relation
relation → recurrence relation
relation → reflexive relation
relation → symmetric relation
relation → transitive relation
relation → well-founded relation
relation between moments
relationship between
relationship between
relationship between consumption and disposable income → consumption function
relationship between definitions
relationship between definitions → uniform integrability
relationship between the mean, median, and mode
relationships among the Pythagorean means
relative change
relative dispersion
relative error
relative extremum
relative extremum → critical point
relative extremum → local extremum
relative frequency
relative positions of ovals, describe → Hilbert's 16th problem
relative standard deviation
relative standard deviation → coefficient of variation
relative topology
relative topology → subspace topology
relative-frequency distribution
relative-frequency histogram
relative-frequency polygon
relative-frequency table
relatively prime
relatively prime → coprime
relatives
relatives → linked relatives
relatives → percentages
relaxation

relevant low dimensional features

relevant low dimensional features → Topological Data Analysis

remainder

Remainder Theorem

removable discontinuity

remove noise from data

remove noise from data → smoothing operator

Renewal Theory

Renewal Theory → Probability Theory

renewal-reward process → Renewal Theory

renormalization group

repeating decimal

repelling set

repelling set → attractor

replacing subterms of a formula with other terms

replacing subterms of a formula with other terms → rewriting

replacing them with their complements

replication

representation → graphical representation of income or wealth → Lorenz curve

representation → induced representation

representation → integral representation of the logarithm

representation → monomial representation of a finite group

representation → pictorial representation of data → box and whiskers diagram

representation → pictorial representation of data → dot plot

representation → pictorial representation of data → scatterplot

representation → pictorial representation of data → stem and leaf plot

representation → projective representation

representation → representation of a positive integer as the sum of four squares

representation of a positive integer as the sum of four squares

representation theorem → Riesz Representation Theorem

representation theorem → Stone's representation theorem for Boolean Algebras

Representation Theory

Representation Theory → coherent set of characters

Representation Theory → faithful representation

representations → concrete representations versus abstract structure

requirement

requirement → level of input required to produce a given level of output

research

research → Operations Research

residue

residue → least residue

residue class

residue classes modulo a prime

residue classes modulo a prime → field

Residue Theorem

Residue Theory

resolution of singularities

resource → production rate of a resource over time

resource → production rate of a resource over time → Hubbert curve

resource-sharing → Cirquent Calculus

response → how much an endogenous variable changes in response to an exogenous variable

response variable

response variable → dependent variable

response variable → explanatory variable

restriction of a function to a proper subset of its domain

restriction on the number of solutions

restriction on the number of solutions → modulus of a congruence

result

result → alternative route to analytical results

result → analytical result

result → as soon as significant results are observed

result → corollary

result → new proof of an old result

result → qualitative result

result → quantitative result

result → same result → idempotence

result → theorem

result of performing some constructive generating process

result of performing some constructive generating process → enumerable set

result of performing some constructive generating process → Intuitionism

result of performing the same experiment a large number of times

result of performing the same experiment a large number of times → Law of Large Numbers

results not being obtainable in closed form

results not being obtainable in closed form → unbiased estimation of standard deviation

retains enough information about the object of interest, a simpler object that → homotopy group

retarded semilinear nonlocal differential equation

retract

Return Theorem → Poincaré Return Theorem

returns to scale

returns to scale → production function

Reuleaux triangle

reverse engineering the seed of a linear congruential random number generator

reverse kernelization

reversion to a long-term mean value

rewriting

rewriting → replacing subterms of a formula with other terms

rewriting → rewriting system

rewriting system

rewriting system → abstract rewriting system

rewriting system → rewriting

rhombus
RHS → LHS
RHS (right-hand side)
Ricci flow
riddle → paradox
ridge regression
Riemann Hypothesis
Riemann Hypothesis → Hilbert's 8th problem
Riemann integrability
Riemann integrability → minimally sufficient conditions for Riemann integrability
Riemann integrability → Riemann integral
Riemann integral
Riemann integral → Riemann integrability
Riemann Mapping Theorem
Riemann Mapping Theorem → Dirichlet's Principle
Riemann sphere
Riemann surface
Riemann zeta function
Riemannian Geometry
Riemannian Geometry → metric generalization of Riemannian Geometry → Finsler Geometry
Riemannian manifold
Riemannian manifold → Hodge Theory
Riemannian sphere → Riemann sphere
Riemann-integrability
Riemann-Roch Theorem
Riemann-Stieltjes integral
Riesz Representation Theorem
right angle
right circular cone
right curly brace
right- or left-handed → chirality
right strophoid
right strophoid → folium of Descartes
right triangle
right-hand side
right-sided limit
rigid body dynamics
rigid motion
rigid transformation → isometry
rigor
rigor → casualness
rigorous foundation → Hilbert's 15th problem
ring
ring → commutative ring
ring → commutator

ring → differential ring
ring → finite ring
ring → Jordan block over a ring
ring → nilpotent element in a ring
ring → Noetherian ring
ring → polynomials over a ring
ring → quotient ring
ring → ring homomorphism
ring → ring identity
ring → ring of integers
ring → ring of polynomials
ring → ring of quaternions
ring → Stanley-Reisner ring
ring → topological ring
ring homomorphism
ring identity
ring of integers
ring of quaternions
ring of symmetric functions
Ring Theory
Ring Theory → ideal
Ring Theory → nil ideal
Ring Theory → nilpotent ideal
rings → classification theorem for semisimple rings → Artin-Wedderburn Theorem
rings of polynomials
rinse and repeat
rinse and repeat → iteration
rinse and repeat → process
rise → rise / run → slope
rise / run → slope
rising factorial
Ritt's Theorem
Ritt's Theorem → unique factorization and...hold for the ring of exponential polynomials
R^n → n-space
R^n → usual basis of R^n
R^n → usual inner product on R^n
R^n → usual orientation for R^n
road-coloring theorem
rocket
rocket → rocket equation → Tsiolkovsky rocket equation
rocket equation
rocket equation → Tsiolkovsky rocket equation
Rolle's theorem
Roman numerals

Roman numerals → Arabic numerals
Roman surface
root
root → Artin root numbers
root → digital root
root → n-fold root
root → Rational Root theorem
root → root field
root → root flipping
root → root flipping → Vieta jumping
root → root mean square
root → root mean square → quadratic mean
root → root mean square deviation
root → root of a number
root → root of an equation
root → Root Test
root → rooted graph
root → roots of a polynomial → Vieta's formulas
root → roots of unity
root → square root
root → square root → hypotenuse
root field
root field → uniqueness of the root field
root flipping → Vieta jumping
root mean square
root mean square → quadratic mean
root mean square deviation
root of a number
root of an equation
Root Test
rooted graph
roots → multiplicity of roots
roots → product of roots → Vieta's formulas
roots → sum of roots → Vieta's formulas
roots of a polynomial → Vieta's formulas
roots of unity
root-swapping → Vieta jumping
root-swapping → Vieta jumping → problem #6-IMO-1988
rose (curve)
Rosenbrock's banana function
Rosser's theorem (in Number Theory)
rotation
rotation → isometry
rotation matrix

rotation of axes
rotation-estimation → cross-validation
Roth's theorem on 3-term arithmetic progressions
roulette
rounding
rounding → presentational form
rounding → rounding down
rounding → rounding to the nearest even digit
rounding → rounding up
rounding → truncation
rounding down
rounding to the nearest even digit
rounding up
route → alternative route to analytical results
row
row → column
row → matrix
row → row operation
row → row operation → elementary row operation
row → row operation → elementary row operation → Gaussian elimination
row operation
row operation → elementary row operation
row operation → elementary row operation → Gaussian elimination
row reduction → Gaussian elimination
RSA Public-Key Cryptosystem
RSA Public-Key Cryptosystem → Public-Key Cryptography
ruin → gambler's ruin
rule → Empirical Rule
rule → law
rule → Miller's rules
rule → Oja's rule
rule → Simpson's Rule
rule → stopping rule → stopping time
rule → Trapezoidal Rule
Rule of 70
ruled surface
ruler and compass construction
run
run → length of run
run → length of run → algorithm terminates within how many iterations
run → rise / run → slope
run for a long time → allowed to run for a long time → Ergodic Theory
Runge's Approximation Theorem
Runge's phenomenon

Runge's phenomenon → Gibbs phenomenon
running sum
running total → running sum
Russell's paradox
s (beginning of entries for S)
s → sample standard deviation
S over V ratio
s^2 → sample variance
SABR → stochastic alpha, beta, rho
SABR model
saddle point
salient point
salt-and-pepper function
same boundary → three disjoint open sets having the same boundary → lakes of Wada
same composition length and same composition factors → Jordan-Hölder Theorem
same cross-sectional area → Cavalieri's Principle
same experiment a large number of times → Law of Large Numbers
same result → idempotence
same time for two paths → lemniscate of Bernoulli
same times for descent → tautochrone
same volume → Cavalieri's Principle
Sammon mapping
sample
sample → number of observations in a sample
sample mean
sample size not fixed in advance
sample size not fixed in advance → sequential sampling
sample space
sample standard deviation
sample standard deviation → (n − 1) in denominator instead of n
sample standard deviation → s
sample variance
sampling
sampling → Exact-Sampling Theory
sampling → large-sampling methods
sampling → probe
sampling → random sampling
sampling → sequential sampling
sampling → structuring element
sampling → structuring element → Mathematical Morphology
sampling distribution
sampling distribution → standard deviation of a sampling distribution
sampling distribution of differences
sampling distribution of means
sampling distribution of proportions

sampling distribution of sums
sampling of a parametric curve → Padua points
Sampling Theory
sampling with and without replacement
Samuel compactification
Sandwich Theorem
Sandwich Theorem → Squeeze Theorem
Sanskrit prosody → de Bruijn sequence
Sarason interpolation theorem
Sard's Theorem
satisfies its own characteristic equation → Cayley-Hamilton Theorem
Sato → Bernstein-Sato polynomial
sausage → Wiener sausage
sawtooth function
scalar
scalar field
scalar motion
scalar product of two vectors
scalar product of two vectors → inner product
scalar triple product
scale
scale → economies of scale
scale → emergence of patterns as the scale of the objects grows → Ramsey Theory
scale → returns to scale
scale → sliding scale
scale line → expansion path
scale of production
scale of production → as the scale of production increases
scale-invariant group
scale-invariant sequence
scalene triangle
scaling
scaling → homogeneous dilation
scaling → inhomogeneous dilation
scaling → non-uniform scaling
scaling → uniform scaling
scattered line
scattered set
scatterplot
Schauder Fixed-Point Theorem
scheme
scheme → association scheme
Schläfli double six
Schreier conjecture (theorem)
Schreier conjecture (theorem) → Finite Group Theory

Schröder-Bernstein Theorem
Schubert Calculus
Schubert Calculus → Hilbert's 15th problem
Schur multiplier
Schur multiplier → Group Theory
Schur-Zassenhaus Theorem
Schur-Zassenhaus Theorem → Finite Group Theory
Schwarz triangle
Schwarz triangle → tessellations of the sphere
Schwarz's inequality
scissors congruence
scissors congruence → dissections of polygons
scissors congruence → dissections of polygons → Wallace-Bolyai-Gerwien Theorem
scissors congruence → Wallace-Bolyai-Gerwien Theorem
scope of a variable
score
screw → Archimedes' screw
search for prime divisors of a given number
seasonal index adjustments
seasonal movement
seasonal movement → component of a time series
seasonal variation
seasonal variation → component of a time series
sec → secant
secant
secant → hyperbolic secant → Poinsot's spirals
secant cubed → integral of secant cubed
secant line
secant squared → derivative of the tangent
second axiom of countability
Second Borel-Cantelli Lemma
second moment of area
second-countable space
second-derivative test
second-order differential equation
secret writing → cryptography
secret writing → Cryptography
section
section → conic section
section → cross section
section → toric section
secure two-party computation
seed → reverse engineering the seed of a linear congruential random number generator
seed of a random number generator
segment

segment → line segment
segment → line segment → directed line segment → equipollence
selection
selection → choice → Axiom of Choice
selection → random selection
selection → urn
selection with replacement
selection without replacement
self-adjoint linear transformation
self-adjoint operator
self-adjoint operator → Spectral Theorem
self-intersecting mapping
self-intersecting mapping → Roman surface
self-intersection
self-intersection → cross-cap
self-organizing map
self-similarity
semi-analytic set
semi-averages → method of semi-averages
semi-continuity
semicubical parabola
semigroup
semi-honest party → oblivious polynomial evaluation
semimartingale
semimartingale → martingale
semiperfect number
semiperimeter
semiperimeter → Heron's formula
semisimple algebras, classification theorem for → Artin-Wedderburn Theorem
semisimple and nilpotent parts → Jordan-Chevalley decomposition
semisimple rings, classification theorem for → Artin-Wedderburn Theorem
sensitivity to initial conditions → chaos
separability → linear separability
separable and inseparable polynomials
separable Banach space with no basis → Walsh series
separable differential equation
separable extension
separable space
separated sets
separated space
separating points from closed sets
separation axiom
separation of the data into two parts
separation of the data into two parts → method of semi-averages
separation of variables

sequence
sequence → bounded sequence
sequence → bounded sequence → Kaprekar process
sequence → Cauchy sequence
sequence → de Bruijn sequence
sequence → decreasing sequence
sequence → Farey sequence
sequence → Fibonacci sequence
sequence → Følner sequence
sequence → increasing sequence
sequence → infinite sequences of abstract symbols → Symbolic Dynamics
sequence → Lucas sequence
sequence → monotonic sequence
sequence → nested sequence of increasing subsets
sequence → non-decreasing sequence
sequence → non-increasing function
sequence → process
sequence → progression
sequence → scale-invariant sequence
sequence → sequence of binary random variables
sequence → sequence of binary random variables → Bernoulli process
sequence → sequence of decreasing fractions
sequence → sequence of decreasing fractions → depreciation
sequence → sequence of functions
sequence → sequence of functions → Lebesgue's Dominated Convergence Theorem
sequence → sequence of partial sums
sequence → sequence of random variables
sequence → sequence of reciprocals of positive integers
sequence → subsequence
sequence → subsequence → convergent subsequence
sequence → subsequence → convergent subsequence → uniformly convergent subsequence
sequence of binary random variables
sequence of binary random variables → Bernoulli process
sequence of decreasing fractions
sequence of decreasing fractions → depreciation
sequence of elementary row operations
sequence of elementary row operations → Gaussian elimination
sequence of functions
sequence of functions → Lebesgue's Dominated Convergence Theorem
sequence of partial sums
sequence of reciprocals of positive integers
Sequent Calculus
sequential sampling
sequential sampling → pre-defined stopping time

sequential sampling → Statistics
sequentially compact
serial correlation → autocorrelation
series
series → alternating series
series → benchmark series → test of convergence
series → convergent series → monotone convergent series
series → divergent series
series → divergent series → Cesàro summation
series → divergent series → monotone divergent series
series → divergent series → Summability Theory
series → Eisenstein series
series → formal power series
series → Fourier series
series → Laurent series
series → Machin series
series → Maclaurin series
series → monotone series
series → power series
series → radius of convergence
series → Taylor series
series → telescoping series
series → test of convergence
series → time series
series → Walsh series
serpentine curve
Serre duality
set
set → Asymmetric Cantor set
set → bounded set
set → Caccioppoli set
set → Cantor set
set → carrier set
set → closure of a set
set → computationally unrealistic set
set → convex set
set → countable set
set → creative set
set → dense set
set → empty set
set → enumerable set
set → equality of sets
set → exterior of a set
set → Fatou set

set → finite set
set → finite set of points → given a finite set of points in the plane → Sylvester-Gallai Theorem
set → Generalized Cantor set
set → generating set of a group
set → Hyperset Theory
set → i-connected set
set → infinite set
set → interior of a set
set → intersection of sets
set → Julia set
set → Kuratowski's 14-Set Theorem
set → large set
set → level set
set → linearly-ordered set
set → multiset
set → non-convex set
set → Non-Well-Founded Set Theory
set → null set
set → partially ordered set
set → partition of a set
set → perfect set
set → point set
set → power set
set → productive set
set → range of a set of numbers
set → recursively enumerable set
set → repelling set
set → scattered set
set → semi-analytic set
set → set of algebraic numbers
set → set of integers
set → set of natural numbers
set → set of nonnegative integers
set → set of positive integers
set → set of rational numbers
set → set of real numbers
set → set of real numbers that is not Lebesgue measurable
set → set of transcendental numbers
set → set of true formulas about indiscernibles
set → set of true formulas about indiscernibles → zero sharp
set → Set Theory → Hyperset Theory
set → Set Theory → Non-Well-Founded Set Theory
set → sets → mutually disjoint sets

set → sets → separated sets
set → simple set
set → singleton
set → Smith-Volterra-Cantor set
set → solution set
set → sparse set
set → star-shaped set
set → sub-analytic set
set → subset → nested sequence of increasing subsets
set → sum-free set
set → unbounded set
set → uncountable set
set → underlying set
set → union of sets
set → universal set
set → Vitali set
set → well-ordered set
set function
set function → content
set function → measure
set having a lower bound
set having an upper bound
set inclusion
set membership
set membership → indicator function
set of algebraic numbers
set of all continuous functions on [0,1]
set of continuous maps between two topological spaces → compact-open topology
set of distributions
set of distributions → natural set of distributions to consider
set of integers
set of measure zero
set of natural numbers
set of nonnegative integers
set of rational numbers
set of real numbers
set of real numbers that is not Lebesgue measurable
set of real numbers that is not Lebesgue measurable → Vitali set
set of transcendental numbers
set of true formulas about indiscernibles → zero sharp
Set Theory
Set Theory → Linear Point Set Theory
Set Theory → Naive Set Theory
Set Theory → Non-Well-Founded Set Theory
Set Theory → Point Set Theory

Set Theory → Topology → Pointless Topology
Set Theory → urelement
setting the derivative to zero
setting the derivative to zero → finding extrema of a function
setting, classical and quantum, for all (nongravitational) physical phenomena → Lorentz group
seven number summary
seven number summary → five number summary
several complex variables → Theory of Functions of Several Complex Variables
shape
shape → first vibrational mode of a thin L-shaped membrane, clamped at the edges
shape → form
shape → Geometry
shape → ogive
shape → shape of data
shape → shape of stories
shape → star-shaped set
shape analysis → convex hull
shape and orientation of the orbit of one astronomical body around another
shape and size → structuring element
shape of data
shape of data → Topological Data Analysis
shape of stories
sharing of subcomponents → Cirquent Calculus
sharp → zero sharp
sheaf
sheaves (plural of sheaf)
Sheppard's Correction
Sheppard's Correction → grouping error
shift operator
shifting base
shifting base → sliding scale
shoes and socks
shortcomings of the Black-Scholes model
shortcomings of the Black-Scholes model → stochastic volatility model
shorten a brute force attack on a code → de Bruijn sequence
shortest distance between two points
shortest distance between two points → straight line
shortest path problem
shortest path problem → Graph Theory
shortest path problem → sum of the weights of the edges is minimized
shrinking space
Siegel's paradox
Sierpiński curve
sieve → Brun sieve
sieve → Fundamental Lemma of Sieve Theory

sieve → general number field sieve
sieve → Legendre sieve
sieve → quadratic sieve
sieve → Sieve Theory
sieve of Eratosthenes
Sieve Theory
Sieve Theory → Fundamental Lemma of Sieve Theory
sigma additivity
sigma algebra
sigmoid
sigmoid → Gompertz curve
sign
sign → algebraic sign
sign → sign function
sign → sign test
sign function
sign test
signal processing → Hilbert transform
signalizer functor theorem
signature
signature → signature of a quadratic form
signature of a quadratic form
signed measure
significance
significance → exact test
significance → statistical significance
significant digit
significant digit → Benford's Law
significant results
significant results → as soon as significant results are observed
silver ratio
similar triangles
similarity transformation
similarity transformation → homothecy
simple aggregate index
simple closed plane curve → Jordan curve
simple complex Lie group
simple extension
simple group
simple group → finite simple group
simple interest
simple Lie group
simple mathematical induction
simple mathematical induction → mathematical induction
simple plane path

simple pole
simple proof that π is irrational
simple set
simpler object that retains enough information about the object of interest, a → homotopy group
simplest of all orthogonal series → Walsh series
simplicial complex
simplicial complex → abstract simplicial complex
simplification → Rational Homotopy Theory
simplified methods for computing
simplified methods for computing → computational formula
simply connected 1-dimensional complex manifold
simply-connected space
Simpson's paradox
Simpson's Rule
Sims conjecture (theorem)
simultaneous congruences
simultaneous congruences → Babbage's criterion for primality
simultaneous congruences → Chinese Remainder Theorem
simultaneous equations
sin → sine
sin A / A = sin B / B → Law of Sines
sine
sine → hyperbolic sine
sine wave
Singer → Atiyah-Singer Index Theorem
single number
single number → index
single singularity with delta invariant three
single singularity with delta invariant three → butterfly curve
single-sided surface → Möbius strip
singleton
singular exponents
Singular Homology
singular n-cube
singular point
singular point → analytic structure of an algebraic curve in the neighborhood of a singular point
singular point on an algebraic surface
singularity
singularity → classification of singularities
singularity → cusp
singularity → essential singularity
singularity → information about the topology of singularities → algebraic curve
singularity → monodromy
singularity → movable singularity
singularity → resolution of singularities

singularity → single singularity with delta invariant three

singularity → single singularity with delta invariant three → butterfly curve

singularity → singularities → classification of singularities

singularity → singularities → topology of singularities

singularity at the origin → bean curve

Singularity Theory

sink

sink → flow network

sink → node

sink → source

sink → supersink

sink → supersink → flow network

sinusoidal curve

situation → algorithm terminates within how many iterations

situation → conclusion reached at a much earlier stage

situation → just adding inconvenience, with no real benefit

situation → little now versus more later

situation → no moment-generating function

situation → Normality assumes smoothness.

situation → Not all random variables have moment-generating functions.

situation → not necessarily the case

situation → output not proportional to input

situation → output proportional to input

situation → points are on which lines

situation → special form chosen for mathematical convenience

situation → statistical convention that the alternative hypothesis is assumed to be wrong

situation in which the derivative of volume equals the surface area → sphere

six → double six → Schläfli double six

size → Is it bigger than a bread box?

size → order of magnitude

size → reducing the size

size and shape → structuring element

size function

size function → Topological Data Analysis

skew lines

skew lines → parallel lines

skew symmetry

skew symmetry → skew symmetry constraint

skew symmetry constraint

skew symmetry constraint → flow network

skewed distribution

slant asymptote

slant height

slide rule

slide rule → abacus
slide rule → calculation device
sliding scale
sliding scale → shifting base
slope
slope field
slope field → direction field
slope formula
slope-intercept form of a linear equation
slow rise of the logarithm
small group of Lie type
small stellated dodecahedron
small stellated dodecahedron → great icosahedron
small triangle inside a larger triangle
small triangle inside a larger triangle → Morley's Miracle
smallest → least
smallest → minimum
smallest area rectangle that encloses a given polygon
smallest area rectangle that encloses a given polygon → convex hull
smallest box
smallest box → smallest area rectangle that encloses a given polygon → convex hull
smallest element of a set
smallest infinite cardinal → aleph-null
smallest number that can be made from a given set of digits → Kaprekar's Constant
smallest perimeter → rectangle having smallest perimeter for a given area
smallest topology on a set
smallest topology on a set → indiscrete topology
Small-Sampling Theory
Small-Sampling Theory → Exact-Sampling Theory
Small-Sampling Theory → Student's t-distribution
smile → volatility smile
Smith-Volterra-Cantor set
smooth completion → hyperelliptic curve
smooth function
smooth manifold
smooth operator
smoothing
smoothing → averaging
smoothing → curve fitting
smoothing of a time series
smoothing of a time series → moving averages applied to a time series
smoothing operator
snake-shaped curve → serpentine curve
snow → Snow Plow Problem
snow → snowflake

snow → snowflake → Koch snowflake
Snow Plow Problem
snowflake
snowflake → Koch Snowflake
SO(p, q) → indefinite special orthogonal group
soap bubbles
Sobolev space
socks-and-shoes illustration of the Axiom of Choice
socks-shoes property
sofa around a corner (classical problem)
Solid Geometry
solid of revolution
Solovay-Strassen primality test
Solow-Swan model
solution
solution → approximate solution
solution → closed-form solution
solution → dimension of space of solutions → Atiyah-Singer Index Theorem
solution → particular solution
solution → solutions → constraint on rational solutions
solution → solutions → constraint on rational solutions → Rational Root Theorem
solution → space of solutions
solution → Superposition Principle
solution set
solution set → extraneous root
solutions to homogeneous linear differential equations
solvability
solvability → exact solvability
solvability by radicals
solvability by radicals → constructability
solvable group
some → for some → existential quantification
soon → as soon as significant results are observed
Sophie Germain prime
soul theorem
soul theorem → Riemannian Geometry
soundings → plot winds from soundings of the Earth's atmosphere → hodograph
source
source → flow network
source → node
source → sink
source → supersource
source → supersource → flow network
Souslin's theorem
space → 0-dimensional space

space → 1-dimensional space

space → 2-dimensional space

space → 3-dimensional space

space → 3-space → torsion of a curve in 3-space

space → adjunction space

space → affine space

space → algebraic space

space → ambient space

space → Banach space

space → bicompact space

space → bordering of a space

space → comb space

space → compact Hausdorff space

space → complete metric space

space → completely normal space

space → connected space

space → coordinate space

space → deleted comb space

space → discreate topological space

space → dogbone space

space → door space

space → Dowker space

space → Eilenberg-Maclane space

space → extremally-disconnected space

space → fiber space

space → first-countable space

space → Fréchet space

space → function space

space → half-space

space → Hausdorff space

space → Hausdorff space → compact Hausdorff space

space → Hilbert space

space → Lindelöf space

space → locally-compact Hausdorff space

space → locally-convex space

space → mapping into three-dimensional space

space → metacompact space

space → metric space

space → moduli space

space → Moore space

space → normal space

space → paracompact space

space → parameter space

space → parameter space → feasible region in the parameter space

space → proximity space

space → pseudo-Euclidean space

space → reductive space

space → regular space

space → second-countable space

space → separable space

space → separated space

space → shrinking space

space → simply-connected space

space → Sobolev space

space → space of continuous functions on a compact Hausdorff space

space → Spectral Theory of Operators on a Hilbert Space

space → state space

space → Stone space

space → Stone space of the free modal algebra

space → symmetric space

space → tangent space

space → Teichmüller space

space → topological features of a space

space → topological space

space → totally-bounded metric space

space → totally-bounded uniform space

space → true features of the underlying space

space → underlying space

space → uniform space

space → uniformizable space

space → vanish above the dimension of a space → Betti number

space → webbed space

space filling curve

space filling curve → Butz Algorithm

space group

space of continuous functions on a compact Hausdorff space

space of continuous functions on a compact Hausdorff space → Stone-Weierstrass Theorem

space of solutions

space of solutions → dimension of space of solutions

space travel

space travel → Tsiolkovsky rocket equation

spacial (not to be confused with special)

spacial (spelling of spatial often used in mathematics)

spacial resolutions → various spacial resolutions

Spanier-Whitehead duality

Spanier-Whitehead duality → Alexander duality

sparse data

sparse data → Topological Data Analysis
sparse graph
sparse linear system
sparse matrix
sparse set
sparsity → principle of factor sparsity → Pareto Principle
spatial → spacial
Spearman's Formula for Rank Correlation
Spearman's rank correlation
special case
special case → modeled by a special case
special case of a pair → singleton
special case of the circulation problem → maximum flow problem
special case of the gamma distribution → chi-squared distribution
special divisors → Clifford's theorem on special divisors
special form chosen for mathematical convenience
special form chosen for mathematical convenience → exponential family
special functions
special functions → Painlevé transcendents
special kinds of partially ordered sets → Domain Theory
special linear group
special node
special node → no special nodes → circulation problem
special node → node
special orthogonal group → indefinite special orthogonal group
species-area curve
species-area curve → species-discovery curve
species-discovery curve
species-discovery curve → species-area curve
specification
specification → alternative specification
spectral energy distribution → witch of Agnesi
spectral properties of random Schrödinger operators → Wiener sausage
Spectral Theorem
Spectral Theorem → orthonormal basis
Spectral Theory
Spectral Theory of Operators on a Hilbert Space
Spectrum of the Fibonacci Hamiltonian
speculated agent has no effect → null hypothesis
speculative hypothesis → alternative hypothesis
speech recognition → hidden Markov model
speed
speed → average speed
speed → average speed → weighted harmonic mean
speed math → Trachtenberg system of rapid calculation

sphere
sphere → exotic sphere
sphere → hemisphere
sphere → intersection of a sphere and a cylinder → Viviani's curve
sphere → Lie Sphere Geometry
sphere → n-sphere
sphere → n-sphere → volume of the n-sphere
sphere → Riemann sphere
sphere → sphere packing
sphere → sphere with handles
sphere → spheres → Dandelin spheres
sphere → tangent to a sphere → Viviani's curve
sphere eversion
sphere packing
sphere with handles
sphere-packing bound → Hamming bound
spherical basis
spherical harmonics
spherical pendulum
spherical symmetry
spherical triangle
Spherical Trigonometry
spheroid
spheroid → oblate spheroid
spheroid → prolate spheroid
spheroidal coordinates
spiral
spiral → Archimedean spiral
spiral → Cotes's spiral
spiral → epispiral
spiral → hyperbolic spiral
spiral → logarithmic spiral
spiral → Poinsot's spirals
Spirograph
spline function
split orthogonal group
split-complex numbers
splitting field
spoiler → counterexample
spoiler → disproof
spoiler → Euler spoiler
spoiler → Euler spoiler → Graeco-Latin square
sporadic group
sporadic group → monster group
square

square → certain quadrilateral is a square → Finsler-Hadwiger Theorem
square → difference of two squares
square → factorization of the difference of two squares
square → Graeco-Latin square
square → group of symmetries of the square
square → inscribed-square problem
square → iterating the square → Horseshoe Map
square → Lagrange's 4-square theorem
square → Latin square
square → magic square
square → Pell's equation
square → perfect square
square → perfect square → Vieta jumping
square → product of difference of squares → Markov brothers' inequality
square → root mean square
square → squares → representation of a positive integer as the sum of four squares
square → squares → two squares that share a vertex
square → squares → two squares that share a vertex → Finsler-Hadwiger Theorem
square → sum of first n odd numbers
square → sum of reciprocals of the squares → Basel Problem
square → sums of squares → quotient of sums of squares → Hilbert's 17 problem
square → Toeplitz' conjecture
square generated from two given squares
square generated from two given squares → Finsler-Hadwiger Theorem
square matrix
square matrix → invertible square matrix
square matrix over a commutative ring → Cayley-Hamilton Theorem
square of a binomial
square of half the coefficient of the middle term
square of half the coefficient of the middle term → quadratic equation
square of the hypotenuse
square pyramidal number
square pyramidal number → Cannonball Problem
square root
square root → hypotenuse
square root → search for prime divisors of a given number
square root of 2
square root of 2 → most famous irrational number
square root of 2 → Pell number
square root of 5
square root of 5 → Binet's formula
square root of the variance
square root of the variance → Heston model
square torus → de Bruijn torus

square wave
square wave function
square-free number
square-integrable function
squares → method of least squares
squaring the circle
squaring the circle → Archimedean spiral
squeeze mapping
squeeze mapping → hyperbolic coordinates
Squeeze Theorem
Squeeze Theorem → Squeezing Principle
squeezing → uniform squeezing and stretching → Horseshoe Map
Squeezing Principle
Squeezing Principle → Squeeze Theorem
squiggly curves → Lissajous figures
squircle
S-shaped curve → sigmoid
S-shaped function → sigmoid
stability
stability → algebraic stability
stability → A-stability
stability → B-stability
stability → instability
stability → nonlinear stability of numerical methods
stability → volatility
stable algorithm
stable distribution
stable homotopy theory
stacking dominoes over the edge of a table
stage → conclusion reached at a much earlier stage
standard Borel space
standard deviation
standard deviation → population standard deviation
standard deviation → relative standard deviation
standard deviation → sample standard deviation
standard deviation → unbiased estimation of standard deviation
standard deviation → within one standard deviation from the mean → Empirical Rule
standard deviation → within three standard deviations from the mean → Empirical Rule
standard deviation → within two standard deviations from the mean → Empirical Rule
standard deviation of a sampling distribution
standard deviation of a sampling distribution → standard error
standard error
standard error → standard deviation of a sampling distribution
standard errors
standard form of a linear equation

standard form of a quadratic equation
standard n-cube
standard scores
standardized variable
Stanley-Reisner ring
star → appearance of a star in a telescope → Airy functions
star → eutactic star
star refinement
star-shaped → stellated polyhedron
star-shaped set
starting from the exact solution of a related, simpler problem
starting from the exact solution of a related, simpler problem → Perturbation Theory
starting state → independence of starting state
start-value → seed of a random number generator
state → starting state → independence of starting state
state → transition from an initial state to a random destination state → Kemeny's constant
state function
state space
stationary distribution
stationary point
stationary point → critical point
statistic
statistic → Statistics
statistic → U-statistic
statistical analysis of experimental data
statistical convention
statistical convention that the alternative hypothesis is assumed to be wrong
Statistical Decision Theory
statistical decisions and hypotheses
Statistical Estimation Theory
statistical hypothesis testing
statistical inference
statistical inference → information on how good the inference is
statistical Markov model
statistical power
statistical significance
statistical significance → statistical significance test
statistical significance test
statistical significance test → statistical significance
Statistical Theory
Statistical Theory → Statistics
Statistical Theory → U-statistic
Statistics
Statistics → Applied Statistics
statistics → bar graph

statistics → box and whiskers diagram

statistics → Descriptive Statistics

Statistics → Descriptive Statistics

statistics → dot plot

Statistics → heteroscedasticity-consistent standard errors

statistics → Inferential Statistics

Statistics → Inferential Statistics

statistics → posterior marginals

statistics → scatterplot

Statistics → sequential sampling

Statistics → Statistical Theory

statistics → Statistics

statistics → stem and leaf plot

steering wheel, locked → osculating circle

Steinberg group

Steiner surface → Roman surface

Steiner's enlarging process

stellated dodecahedron → small stellated dodecahedron

stellated polyhedron

stellated polyhedron → small stellated dodecahedron

stellation → great icosahedron

stellation → Miller's rules

stellation → small stellated dodecahedron

stem and leaf plot

stem and leaf plot → dot plot

stem and leaf plot → scatterplot

step function

stereographic projection

s^{th} moment about a given number

Stieltjes integral

Stirling's formula

Stirling's formula → asymptotic representation of the gamma function

stochastic alpha, beta, rho

Stochastic Calculus

Stochastic Calculus → Itô Calculus

stochastic matrix

stochastic process

stochastic process → adapted process

stochastic process → continuous time stochastic process

stochastic process → Theory of Stochastic Processes

stochastic variable

stochastic variable → random variable

stochastic volatility

stochastic volatility → 3/2 model

stochastic volatility → stochastic volatility model

stochastic volatility model

stock market → Black-Scholes equation

Stokes' Theorem

Stone space

Stone space of the free modal algebra

Stone's representation theorem for Boolean Algebras

Stone-Čech compactification

Stone-Weierstrass Theorem

stop → as soon as significant results are observed

stopping rule → stopping time

stopping time

stopping time → pre-defined stopping time

Størmer's Theorem

story → shape of stories

straight → a set is called straight

straight → a set is called straight → Cayley-Menger determinants

straight line

straight line → Fáry's Theorem

straight line → shortest distance between two points

straight line depreciation

strain → stress-strain curve

stress-strain curve

stretching → uniform squeezing and stretching → Horseshoe Map

strictly decreasing function

strictly increasing function

string

string → harmonics of a plucked string

string → vibrating string

string-manipulation → consequences of certain string-manipulation rules → Formalism

strip → Möbius strip

strong mathematical induction

strong pseudoprime

strong test case → Rosenbrock's banana function

strong topology

strongly polynomial algorithm

strongly polynomial algorithm → polynomial algorithm

strophoid

strophoid → right strophoid

structural complexity

structural support

structural support → inverted catenary arch

structure

structure → abstract structure versus concrete representations

structure → algebraic structure

structure → analytic structure
structure → combinatorial structure
structure → geometrical structure
structure → gradient flow structure
structure → incidence structure
structure → mathematical structure
structure → order
structure → Ramsey Theory
structure → structure theorem for finitely generated modules over a principal ideal domain
structure → substructure
structure theorem for finitely generated modules over a principal ideal domain
structure-preserving map
structuring element
structuring element → Mathematical Morphology
structuring element → sampling
Student's t-distribution
Sturm-Liouville Theory
sub base of a topological space
subadditive function
subadditivity
sub-analytic set
subcomponent → sharing of subcomponents → Cirquent Calculus
subdivision of a graph
subformula-sharing → Cirquent Calculus
subgraph
subgraph → graph
subgraph → induced subgraph
subgroup
subgroup → coset
subgroup → maximal subgroup → O'Nan-Scott Theorem
subgroup → normal subgroup
subgroup → trivial subgroup
submartingale
subsequence
subsequence → Ascoli Theorem
subset
subset → cocountable subset
subset → cofinite subset
subset → inclusion
subset → inclusion → partially ordered by inclusion → Tukey's Lemma
subset → indicator function
subset → proper subset
subset → subsets → nested sequence of increasing subsets
subspace → normally-embedded subspace

subspace topology

subspace topology → relative topology

substitutability

substitutability → fungibility

substitutability → no substitutability between factors

substitution effect

Substitution Theorem for Integrals

Substitution Theorem for Integrals → Change of Variables Formula

substructure

substructure → extension

substructure → structure

substructure → superstructure

subtangent

subtangent → function having a constant subtangent

subtangent → function having a constant subtangent → exponential function

subtended angle

subtended angle → picture-angle maximization

subtracted from

subtraction

subtrahend

success → exactly two possible outcomes

success → exactly two possible outcomes → Bernoulli trial

successor ordinal

such that

sufficiency

sufficiently-large

sum → addition table

sum → check sum

sum → connected sum

sum → minimize a sum → problem #6-IMO-1988

sum → Ramanujan's sum

sum → running sum

sum → squares → representation of a positive integer as the sum of four squares

sum → sum of powers

sum → sum of powers → Waring's Problem

sum → telescoping sum

sum → weighted sum of random variables

sum from 1 to 100

sum of a geometric sequence

sum of a subset of the divisors of a number → practical number

sum of an initial segment of an arithmetic sequence

sum of digits

sum of first n odd numbers

sum of four squares → representation of a positive integer as the sum of four squares

sum of powers

sum of powers → Waring's Problem
sum of reciprocals of the squares → Basel Problem
sum of roots → Vieta's formulas
sum of the divisors of a given positive integer
sum of the interior angles of a polygon
sum of the reciprocals of the twin primes → Brun's Constant
sum of the reciprocals of the twin primes → Brun's Theorem
sum of the squares of the legs of a right triangle
sum of the weights of the edges
sum of the weights of the edges is minimized → shortest path problem
sum of two odd primes
sum of two odd primes → Goldbach's Conjecture
sum of two squares
sum-free set
summability → summation
Summability Theory
summary → five number summary
summary → seven number summary
summary measures
summary measures → mean
summary measures → median
summary measures → mode
summation → Cesàro summation
summation → summability
summation → Tauberian theorems
summation notation
summation symbol
sum-of-the years-digits method of depreciation
sums → sampling distribution of sums
sums of dependent random variables
sums of four squares
sums of squares → quotient of sums of squares → Hilbert's 17th problem
sums of two squares
superior highly composite number
supermagic graph
supermartingale
superposition of solutions
Superposition Principle
superset
supersink
supersink → flow network
supersink → node
supersink → sink
supersink → supersource
supersource

supersource → flow network
supersource → node
supersource → source
supersource → supersink
superstructure → extension
superstructure → substructure
supplementary angles
supply
supply → demand
supply curve
support
support → compact support
supremum
supremum → limsup
surd
surd → radical
surface
surface → algebraic surface
surface → algebraic surface → singular point on an algebraic surface
surface → Bolza surface
surface → Boy's surface
surface → closed surface
surface → closed surface → classification theorem for closed surfaces
surface → hypersurface
surface → isometric surfaces
surface → Klein quartic
surface → minimal surface
surface → Mumford surface → fake projective plane
surface → Roman surface
surface → Teichmüller space
surface → two-dimensional surface in 3-space
surface → two-dimensional surface in 3-space → cross-cap
surface area → situation in which the derivative of volume equals the surface area → sphere
surface area of a solid of revolution
surface area of a sphere
surface area of the helicoid
surface with constant curvature
surface-area over volume ratio → S over V ratio
Surgery Theory
surjective function
surjective function → onto function
surprising divergence → harmonic series
surreal number
Suzuki-Ree group

swapping → root-swapping → Vieta jumping → problem #6-IMO-1988
sweeping generalization
sweeping generalization → Atiyah-Singer Index Theorem
sweeping line
sweeping line → sweeping tangent
sweeping tangent
sweeping tangent → sweeping line
swinging a punctured bucket of paint over a canvas → Lissajous figures
Sylow theorems
Sylow theorems → Finite Group Theory
Sylvester's Law of Inertia
Sylvester-Gallai Theorem
symbol → Jacobi symbol
symbol → Kronecker symbol
symbol → Legendre symbol
symbol → Legendre's symbol
symbol → modular symbol
symbolic computation
symbolic computation → computer algebra
Symbolic Dynamics
Symbolic Dynamics → Horseshoe Map
symbolic integration
Symbolic Method → Blissard's Symbolic Method → Umbral Calculus
symmetric curve → idealized symmetric curve → Hubbert curve
symmetric difference of two sets
symmetric events
symmetric events → Hewitt-Savage Zero-One Law
symmetric function
symmetric function → ring of symmetric functions
symmetric matrix
symmetric matrix → equal to its transpose
symmetric polynomial
symmetric polynomial → Vieta's formulas
symmetric relation
symmetric space
symmetry
symmetry → anti-symmetry
symmetry → asymmetry
symmetry → axis of symmetry
symmetry → circular symmetry
symmetry → cylindrical symmetry
symmetry → high degree of symmetry → Roman surface
symmetry → skew symmetry
symmetry → skew symmetry → skew symmetry constraint
symmetry → skew symmetry → skew symmetry constraint → flow network

symmetry → spherical symmetry
symmetry group
symmetry group → Euclidean group
symplectic geometry
synchronization
synchronization → an emergent property
synchronization → Kuramoto model
synthetic division
synthetic division → long division of polynomials
Synthetic Geometry
system
system → abstract rewriting system
system → deep-inference system
system → differentiable system
system → differentiable system → overdetermined differentiable system
system → dynamical system
system → integrable system
system → lacunary system
system → metric system
system → nonlinear system
system → rewriting system
system → transition system
system → transition system → probabilistic transition system
system of equations
system of linear equations
system of linear equations → Gaussian elimination
system of polynomial equations
system of polynomial equations over the real or complex numbers
system of simultaneous equations
Systems Theory
Systems Theory → General Systems Theory
Szpiro's conjecture
t (beginning of entries for T)
T_0 space
T_0 space → topologically distinguishable points
T_1 space
T_2 space
T_3 space
T_4 space
table
table → addition table
table → dominoes stacked over the edge of a table
table → multiplication table
table → truth table
tableau → Askey tableau

tableau → Young tableau
tabular data
tac node
tagged partition
tail
tail event
tail event → Kolmogorov's Zero-One Law
tail of a distribution
tail of a distribution → tail event
tails
taken k at a time
taken k at a time → binomial coefficient
taken k at a time → permutation
taking limits
taking limits → L'Hôpital's rule
tally mark
tan → tangent
tangent
tangent → envelope
tangent → horizontal tangent → Rolle's theorem
tangent → hyperbolic tangent
tangent → sweeping tangent
tangent bundle
tangent circle
tangent circle → osculating circle
tangent cluster
tangent cluster → Mamikon's Theorem
tangent line
tangent space
tangent sweep
tangent sweep → Mamikon's Theorem
tangent to a sphere → Viviani's curve
tangent vector
tangential component
tangential component → Stokes' theorem
tank reactor → CSTR
Tannaka-Krein duality
Tarski's algebra problem → Tarski's high-school algebra problem
Tarski's high-school algebra problem
Tarski's Undefinability Theorem
tau → Ramanujan tau function
Tauberian theorems
taut string
taut string → imaginary taut string
taut string → imaginary taut string

taut string → imaginary taut string → involute

tautochrone

tautochrone → constrained motion under gravity

tautology

tautology → conditional tautology → Sequent Calculus

tax on those who don't know mathematics → lottery

taxation → Laffer curve

taxicab → Hardy's taxicab number

taxicab → Taxicab Geometry

Taxicab Geometry

taxonomy of quadrilaterals

Taylor series

Taylor's theorem

TDA → Topological Data Analysis

t-distribution → Student's t-distribution

tea → lady tasting tea → Fisher's Exact Test

technique

technique → mathematical induction

technique → Mathematical Morphology

technique → model validation technique

technique → new technique in solving mathematical olympiad problems

technique → new technique in solving mathematical olympiad problems → Vieta jumping

technique → proof technique → Vieta jumping

Teichmüller space

telephone traffic → Erlang distribution

telescoping series

telescoping sum

ten

ten degrees of freedom → Minkowski space

tendency → focal tendencies in random data

ten-generator non-abelian Lie group → Poincaré group

tensile loading

tensile loading → stress → stress-strain curve

tensor

Tensor Calculus

term

term → expression

term → factoring

term → middle term → quadratic function

term → middle term → square of a binomial

term → middle term → square of half the coefficient of the middle term

term → replacing subterms of a formula with other terms

term → rewriting

term → term algebra

term algebra
terminating decimal
termination
termination → algorithm terminates within how many iterations
termination → as soon as significant results are observed.
termination → stopping time
termination → terminating decimal
termination → truncation
ternary operation
ternary set → Cantor set
tessellation
tessellation → corona
tessellation → Penrose tiles
tessellation → tiling
tessellations of the sphere
tessellations of the sphere → Schwartz triangle
test → approximate test
test → chi-squared test
test → exact test
test → Fisher's Exact Test
test → Friedman test
test → Kolmogorov-Smirnov Goodness-of-Fit Test
test → Likelihood Ratio Test
test → nonparametric test
test → primality test → Adleman-Pomerance-Rumley Primality Test
test → second-derivative test
test → statistical significance test
test → test of convergence
test → testing → statistical hypothesis testing
test → White test
test case → strong test case → Rosenbrock's banana function
test data
test of convergence
test of convergence → Alternating Series Test
test of convergence → Comparison Test
test of convergence → Dirichlet's Test
test of convergence → Integral Test
test of convergence → Kummer's Test
test of convergence → Limit Comparison Test
test of convergence → n^{th}-Term Test of Divergence
test of convergence → Raabe's Test
test of convergence → Ratio Test
test of convergence → Root Test
test of convergence → Test of Convergence of a Geometric Series

test of convergence → Test of Convergence of a p-Series
Test of Convergence of a Geometric Series
Test of Convergence of a p-Series
test statistic
testing → statistical hypothesis testing
tests involving normal distributions
tests involving sample differences
tests of hypotheses and significance
tetraflexagon
tetrahedron
the classical and quantum setting for all (nongravitational) physical phenomena → Lorentz group
The function itself need not be injective, only its derivative.
the problem of points
The sample standard deviation is not unbiased for the population standard deviation.
the various exogenous variables one is faced with
theft → fraud-detection → Benford's Law
their true face → true features of the underlying space
theorem
theorem → Ahlfors Finiteness Theorem
theorem → Arrow's Impossibility Theorem
theorem → Artin-Wedderburn Theorem
theorem → Ascoli's Theorem
theorem → Atiyah-Singer Index Theorem
theorem → Bayes' Theorem
theorem → Bell's theorem
theorem → Bertrand's Theorem
theorem → Bohr-Mollerup theorem
theorem → B-theorem
theorem → Cayley-Hamilton Theorem
theorem → Central Limit Theorem
theorem → Ceva's Theorem
theorem → classification theorem
theorem → classification theorem for closed surfaces
theorem → convergence theorem
theorem → convergence theorem → Lebesgue's Dominated Convergence Theorem
theorem → corollary
theorem → Cramer's theorem on algebraic curves
theorem → Divergence Theorem
theorem → Enriques-Kodaira classification
theorem → Finsler-Hadwiger Theorem
theorem → Frobenius Theorem
theorem → fundamental theorem
theorem → Fundamental Theorem of Calculus
theorem → fundamental theorem of symmetric polynomials

theorem → Gauss-Markov Theorem

theorem → Gödels' Incompleteness Theorem

theorem → Hadwiger's Theorem

theorem → Hall-Higman Theorem

theorem → impossibility theorem

theorem → index theorem

theorem → index theorem → Atiyah-Singer Index Theorem

theorem → Inverse Function Theorem

theorem → Jordan-Hölder Theorem

theorem → Kronecker-Weber Theorem

theorem → Krylov-Bogolyubov Theorem

theorem → Kuratowski's 14-Set Theorem

theorem → Landau theorems

theorem → Lebesgue's Dominated Convergence Theorem

theorem → Lefschetz Fixed-Point Theorem

theorem → lemma

theorem → Little's Law

theorem → Matiyasevich's Theorem

theorem → minimax theorem

theorem → Monotone Convergence Theorem

theorem → MRDP Theorem

theorem → Nash Theorems (in Differential Geometry)

theorem → Nielsen-Thurston classification

theorem → no-broadcast theorem

theorem → no-cloning theorem

theorem → no-go theorem

theorem → No-Wandering-Domain Theorem

theorem → O'Nan-Scott Theorem

theorem → Pinch Theorem

theorem → Poincare Return Theorem

theorem → Pythagorean Theorem

theorem → Ramsey's Theorem

theorem → rank-nullity theorem

theorem → Remainder Theorem

theorem → result

theorem → Riemann-Roch Theorem

theorem → Riesz Representation Theorem

theorem → Ritt's Theorem

theorem → Rolle's Theorem

theorem → Runge's Approximation Theorem

theorem → Sandwich Theorem

theorem → Sard's Theorem

theorem → Schauder Fixed-Point Theorem

theorem → Schröder-Bernstein Theorem
theorem → Sims conjecture (theorem)
theorem → Spectral Theorem
theorem → Squeeze Theorem
theorem → Stone-Weierstrass Theorem
theorem → structure theorem for finitely generated modules over a principal ideal domain
theorem → Sylow theorems
theorem → Sylvester-Gallai Theorem
theorem → Tarski's Undefinability Theorem
theorem → Tauberian theorems
theorem → Tits alternative
theorem → Von Neumann-Morgenstern Utility Theorem
theorem → Wallace-Bolyai-Gerwien Theorem
theorem → Weierstrass Approximation Theorem
theorem → Well-Ordering Theorem
theorem → Wilks' Theorem
theorem → Wilson's Theorem
theorem of Lagrange
theorem of Lagrange → divisor of the order of a group
theorem of Lagrange → order of a subgroup
theorem proving → Automath
theorem proving → Curry-Howard correspondence
theorem-enactment → performance of proofs on the theatrical stage
Theoretical Physics → no-go theorem
theory
theory → Algebraic Number Theory
theory → Algorithm Theory
theory → Approximation Theory
theory → Catastrophe Theory
theory → Character Theory
theory → Class Field Theory
theory → Combinatorial Design Theory
theory → Combinatorics
theory → Computational Complexity Theory
theory → Design of Experiments
theory → Domain Theory
theory → duality theory
theory → Elimination Theory
theory → empirical models unsupported by theory → volatility
theory → Ergodic Theory
theory → Estimation Theory
theory → Exact-Sampling Theory
theory → Filtering Theory
theory → Finite Group Theory

theory → Galois Theory
theory → Game Theory
theory → General Systems Theory
theory → Graph Minor Theory
theory → Graph Theory
theory → Group Theory
theory → Handle Theory
theory → Hodge Theory
theory → Hyperset Theory
theory → Index Theory
theory → Information Theory
theory → Intersection Homology
theory → Intersection Theory
theory → Interval Estimation
theory → Iteration Theory
theory → K-Theory
theory → Lie Theory
theory → Liouville's Theory of Elementary Methods
theory → Mathematical Finance
theory → Mathematical Morphology
theory → Matrix Theory
theory → Measure Theory
theory → Morse Theory
theory → Naive Set Theory
theory → Nevanlinna Theory
theory → Non-Well-Founded Set Theory
theory → Number Theory
theory → Operations Research
theory → Operator Theory
theory → Optimization Theory
theory → Order Theory
theory → Partition Theory
theory → Percolation Theory
theory → Perturbation Theory
theory → Picard-Lefschetz Theory
theory → Point Estimation
theory → Probability Theory
theory → Proof Theory
theory → Queueing Theory
theory → Ramification Theory
theory → Ramsey Theory
theory → Rational Homotopy Theory
theory → Recursion Theory

theory → Renewal Theory
theory → Representation Theory
theory → Residue Theory
theory → Ring Theory
theory → Set Theory
theory → Sieve Theory
theory → Singular Homology
theory → Singularity Theory
theory → small-sampling theory
theory → Spectral Theory
theory → Spectral Theory of Operators on a Hilbert Space
theory → stable homotopy theory
theory → Sturm-Liouville Theory
theory → Summability Theory
theory → Surgery Theory
theory → Systems Theory
theory → Systems Theory → General Systems Theory
theory → Theory of Association Schemes
theory → theory of biquadratic forms
theory → Theory of Functions of Several Complex Variables
theory → Theory of Markov Processes
theory → Theory of Martingales
theory → Theory of Motives
theory → Theory of Stochastic Processes
theory → Valuation Theory
Theory of Association Schemes
Theory of Association Schemes → Analysis of Variance
Theory of Association Schemes → association scheme
Theory of Association Schemes → Design of Experiments
theory of biquadratic forms
Theory of Functions of a Complex Variable
Theory of Functions of Several Complex Variables
Theory of Linear Spaces
Theory of Markov Processes
Theory of Martingales
Theory of Motives
Theory of Stochastic Processes
Theory of Stochastic Processes → martingale convergence theorem
Theory of Vibrations
there exists → existential quantification
there exists a $\delta > 0$
thin → first vibrational mode of a thin L-shaped membrane, clamped at the edges
thinking outside the box → nine-point problem
thousand

three cusps → deltoid curve
three disjoint open sets having the same boundary → lakes of Wada
Three Sigma Rule → Empirical Rule
three-dimensional space
three-dimensional space → 3-space
three-dimensional space → mapping into three-dimensional space
threshold
threshold → percolation threshold
through a focus → latus rectum
thrust → Tsiolkovsky rocket equation
Thurston's geometrization conjecture
T_i space → topological space
tiling
tiling → anisohedral tiling
tiling → convex uniform tiling of the Euclidean plane
tiling → corona
tiling → Euclidean tiling by convex regular polygons
tiling → isohedral tiling
tiling → monohedral tiling
tiling → Penrose tiles
tiling → tessellation
tiling → wallpaper group
tilted algebra
time
time → allowed to run for a long time → Ergodic Theory
time → continuous time Gaussian process
time → continuous time stochastic process
time → holding time
time → holding time → Renewal Theory
time → reflect changes over a period of time
time → stopping time
time between events in a Poisson point process → exponential distribution
time derivative
time derivative → fluxion
time rate of change → fluxion
time series
time series → averaging
time series → reflect changes over a period of time
time series → smoothing of a time series
Time Series Analysis
Time Series Analysis → heteroscedasticity-consistent standard errors
Time Series Analysis → y = T × C × S × R
time-average
time-average → Little's Law

times → multiplication

time-steps → expected number of time-steps → Kemeny's constant

time-varying volatility

Tits alternative

Tits group

Toeplitz' conjecture

together → lumping together of all points → indiscrete topology

together → putting together → concatenation

toilet roll → length of a toilet roll

Tonelli's theorem

top

top → Euler top

top → Goryachev-Chaplygin top

top → gyroscope

top → Kovalevskaya top

top → Lagrange top

topographic obstacle in a flow in mathematical modeling → witch of Agnesi

topological convergence

topological data

topological data → topological index → Atiyah-Singer Index Theorem

Topological Data Analysis

topological entropy

topological features of a space

topological features of a space → Persistent Homology

topological field

topological group

topological group → generalization of periodic functions to ... → automorphic form

topological index

topological index → Atiyah-Singer Index Theorem

topological indistinguishability

topological invariant

topological invariant → homeomorphism

topological isomorphism → homeomorphism

topological manifold

topological manifold → Handle Theory

topological mixing

topological proof of a non-topological result

topological proof of a non-topological result → Furstenberg's proof of the infinitude of the primes

topological proof of the Abel Ruffini Theorem

topological property → topological invariant

topological ring

topological space

topological space → basic shape of a topological space → homotopy group

topological space → closure

topological space → holes in a topological space → homotopy group

topological space → i-connectedness
topological space → space
topological vector space
topologically distinguishable points
topologically distinguishable points → T_0 space
topologically indistinguishable points
topologically indistinguishable points → identification
topologist's sine curve
Topology
topology
topology → coarsest topology
topology → coherent topology
topology → compact-open topology
topology → complete metric space
topology → Differential Topology
topology → discrete topology
topology → families of topologies on a fixed set
topology → final topology
topology → flat topology
topology → Geometric Topology
topology → identification topology
topology → indiscrete topology
topology → induced topology
topology → initial topology
topology → non-discrete topology
topology → Pointless Topology
topology → problems about normal spaces → Morita conjectures
topology → product topology
topology → quotient topology
topology → relative topology
topology → strong topology
topology → subspace topology
topology → topological space
topology → Topology
topology → trivial topology
topology → weak topology
topology of singularities
tori (plural of torus)
toric section
toric section → conic section
toric variety
toroidal coordinates
toroidal polyhedron
Torricelli's trumpet → Gabriel's horn

torsion of a curve in 3-space

torus

torus → de Bruijn torus

torus → square torus → de Bruijn torus

total frequency

total function

total length of path → length of path of a bouncing ball

total variation of a function

totality

totality → binary relation

totality → partially ordered set

totally-bounded metric space

totally-bounded uniform space

totally-disconnected set

totient function

totient function → Euler's totient function

tower

toy → Spirograph

trace

trace of a fixed point of a small circle that rolls within a larger circle → hypocycloid

trace of a fixed point of a small circle that rolls within a larger circle

trace of a matrix

trace of a matrix

Trachtenberg system of rapid calculation

tractable problem

tractable problem → closed-form expression

tractrix

trade away your preferred consumption goods → Siegel's paradox

trailing digits

trailing digits → leading digits

training data

trajectory

trajectory → cannonball trajectory

transcendence

transcendence of e

transcendence of π

transcendent number

transcendent number → algebraic number

transcendental number

transcendental number → Baker's Theorem

transcendental number → four exponentials conjecture

transcendental number → Hilbert's 7th problem

transcendents → Painlevé transcendents

transfer → Becker-Gottlieb transfer

transfer → oblivious transfer

transfinite induction

transform

transform → Hilbert transform

transform → hit or miss transform

transform → hit or miss transform → Mathematical Morphology

transform → integral transform

transformation → homothetic transformation

transformation → linear transformation

transformation → linear transformation → order-preserving linear transformation → L-algebra

transformation → Möbius transformation

transformation → orthogonal transformation

transformation → rigid transformation → isometry

transformation of nonlinear partial differential equations to linear

transition from an initial state to a random destination state → Kemeny's constant

transition matrix

transition system

transition system → directed graph

transition system → probabilistic transition system

transitive relation

transitivity

transitivity → edge-transitivity

transitivity → face-transitivity

transitivity → vertex-transitivity

translation

translation → isometry

translation matrix

translation of axes

transportation network → flow network

transpose

transpose → conjugate transpose matrix

transpose → If a matrix has only real elements, then its adjoint is equal to its transpose.

transpose of a matrix

transpose of a matrix

transposition of digits

transposition of digits → Casting Out Nines

transversal

transversal of a graph partition

transverse wave

transverse wave → longitudinal wave

Trapezoidal Rule

travel

travel → distance of travel

travel → space travel → Tsiolkovsky rocket equation

travel through a network of nodes

travel through a network of nodes → flow network

traveling-salesman problem

traveling-salesman problem → Graph Theory

traveling-salesman problem → Nearest-Neighbor Algorithm

traveling-salesman problem → Sierpiński curve

treatment

treatment → coordinate-free treatment

tree

tree-planting problem → orchard-planting problem

trefoil knot

trend

trend → component of a time series

trend → long-term movement

trend curve

trend line

trial

trial → Bernoulli trial

trial divisor

triangle

triangle → acute triangle

triangle → equiangular triangle

triangle → equilateral triangle

triangle → Geometry of Triangles in the Euclidean Plane

triangle → Gergonne triangle

triangle → inequality regarding a triangle → Hadwiger-Finsler inequality

triangle → isosceles triangle

triangle → needle triangle

triangle → obtuse triangle

triangle → Pascal's Triangle

triangle → right triangle

triangle → scalene triangle

triangle → Schwarz triangle

triangle → small triangle inside a larger triangle → Morley's Miracle

triangle → spherical triangle

triangle → spherical triangle → Schwarz triangle

triangle → triangle inequality

triangle → triangle wave function

triangle → Trigonometry

triangle center

triangle center → Apollonius center

triangle center → de Longchamps point

triangle formed by intersecting trisectors → Morley's Miracle

triangle inequality

triangle inequality → metric

triangle wave function

triangular matrix
triangular number
triangulation
tricircular plane algebraic curve of degree six → Watt's curve
trident curve
trifolium
trigonometric function
trigonometric function → circular function
trigonometric identity
trigonometric substitution
Trigonometry
trigonometry → Spherical Trigonometry
trinomial
triple
triple → ordered triple
triple → Pythagorean triple
triple → Pythagorean triple → primitive Pythagorean triple
triple point → only a single triple point → Boy's surface
triple point at the origin → bow curve
triple product → scalar triple product
triple product → vector triple product
trisection → angle trisection → cubic parabola
trisection → angle trisection → limaçon trisectrix
trisection → angle trisection → Maclaurin trisectrix
trisection of angles
trisection of angles → Morley's Miracle
trivial subgroup
trivial topology
trivial topology → indiscrete topology
trochoid
true class limit
true face → their true face → true features of the underlying space
true features of the underlying space
true features of the underlying space → Persistent Homology
true formulas → set of true formulas about indiscernibles → zero sharp
true value
truncation
truncation → rounding
truncation → termination
truth
truth → arithmetical truth
truth table
truth value
Tschirnhausen cubic
Tsiolkovsky rocket equation

tubular neighborhood
Tukey's Lemma
Tukey's Lemma → Axiom of Choice
Tukey's Lemma → Hausdorff Maximal Principle
Turán's brick factory problem
Turing degree
Turing reduction
turning a sphere inside out → sphere eversion
turning point
Tusi couple
Twin Prime conjecture
twin primes
twin primes → Goldbach's Conjecture
twin primes → sum of the reciprocals of the twin primes → Brun's Theorem
two circles → generated by two circles → Watt's curve
two circles → Tusi couple
two distinct points
two distinct points → construction of a line
two distinct points → line
two envelopes problem
two nodes as singularities → bicuspid curve
two squares that share a vertex
two-dimensional analog of the vibrating string → vibrating membrane
two-dimensional compact manifold without boundary
two-dimensional space
two-dimensional space → plane
two-dimensional surface in 3-space
two-dimensional surface in 3-space → cross-cap
two-factor experiment
two-point compactification
two-sided incompressible surface → Haken manifold
two-sided test
two-tailed and one-tailed tests
two-way classification
Tychonoff cube
Tychonoff's Theorem
Tychonoff's Theorem → Axiom of Choice
type → Lie type → group of Lie type
type 1 error
type 2 error
u (beginning of entries for U)
U → unbiased
U.S. President Garfield → Garfield's proof of the Pythagorean Theorem
ultrafilter
ultrafilter → filter

ultranet
Umbral Calculus
unary operation
unbiased
unbiased → zero bias
unbiased estimate
unbiased estimate → biased estimate
unbiased estimation of standard deviation
unbiased estimator
unbiased estimator → biased estimator
unbiased estimator → minimum-variance unbiased estimator
unbiasedness
unbounded function
unbounded operator
unbounded set
Uncanny Valley
Uncanny Valley → J curve
uncertainty
uncertainty quantification problem
uncountability
uncountability → uncountable set
uncountability → uncountable set → Cantor set
uncountability of the real numbers
uncountable → purely-topological proof that the reals are uncountable
uncountable cardinal number
uncountable set
uncountable set → Cantor set
undefinability → Tarski's Undefinability Theorem
undefined → ill defined
undefined expected value and variance → Cauchy distribution
undefined moment
undefined variance and expected value → Cauchy distribution
underlying set
underlying space
underlying space → true features of the underlying space
undershoot
undershoot → overshoot
undetermined → method of undetermined coefficients
Undetermined Coefficients Method → method of undetermined coefficients
unemployment versus wage hikes → Phillips curve
unequal areas → missing square puzzle
unexpected divergence → harmonic series
unicursal curve → rational curve
uniform → homogeneous
uniform approximation

uniform approximation → Weierstrass Approximation Theorem
uniform continuity
uniform convergence
uniform distribution
uniform integrability
uniform limit
uniform norm
uniform scaling
uniform space
uniform space → gage of a uniform space
uniform space → totally-bounded uniform space
uniform squeezing and stretching → Horseshoe Map
uniformily (misspelling of uniformly)
uniformity
uniformity → averaging
uniformity → diagonal uniformity
uniformity → homogeneity
uniformity → homogenization
uniformity → metric uniformity
uniformity in all orientations
uniformity in all orientations → isotropy
uniformizable space
uniformization of analytic relations → Hilbert's 22nd problem
uniformly continuous function
uniformly convergent subsequence → Ascoli Theorem
unifying principle in Geometry → Group Theory
unimodal distribution
union
union → intersection
union of a collection of sets
union of sets
union of two sets
unioned with
unique factorization
unique factorization and...hold for the ring of exponential polynomials → Ritt's Theorem
uniqueness
uniqueness → exclusive or
uniqueness → singleton
uniqueness → uniqueness existential quantifier
uniqueness existential quantifier
uniqueness of identity and inverses
uniqueness of the root field
unirational but not rational → Enriques-Kodaira classification
unisolvent point set
unit

unit → experimental unit
unit → imaginary unit
unit → unit normal
unit → unit normal → outward unit normal
unit circle
unit hyperbola
unit normal
unit normal → outward unit normal
unit of measure → Biblical unit of measure → cubit
unital algebra
unitary divisor
unitary group
unitary matrix
units of measure
units of measure → imperial units of measure
units of measure → metric units of measure
units-of-production method of depreciation
unity
unity → eigenvalue of unity → stationary distribution
unity → partition of unity
unity → primitive roots of unity
unity → roots of unity
univariate calculus
Universal Algebra
universal enveloping algebra
universal enveloping algebra → Casimir operator
universal enveloping algebra → Lie algebra
universal enveloping algebra → Verma module
universal quantification
universal set
unknown
unknown → variable
unknown data
unordered pair
unpredictable → nonlinear system
unprovable identity → Tarski's high-school algebra problem
unraveling a knot
unrealistic → computationally unrealistic set
unsolvability
unsolvability → degree of unsolvability → Turing degree
unsolvability of the quintic → Abel Ruffini Theorem
unwanted fluctuations
unwanted fluctuations → distracting fluctuations
up to permutation and isomorphism, equivalent → Jordan-Hölder Theorem
upper bound

upper class boundary

upper class limit

upper integral of a function

upper integral of a function $\rightarrow$ lower integral of a function

upper semi-continuous

upper sum of a function for a given partition

upper sum of a function for a given partition $\rightarrow$ lower sum of a function for a given partition

upper-triangular matrix

upper-triangular matrix $\rightarrow$ Gaussian elimination

urelement

urn

urn $\rightarrow$ random selection

urn $\rightarrow$ selection

Urysohn's Lemma

use of base 3 $\rightarrow$ Cantor set

use of cross ratio $\rightarrow$ Cayley-Klein metric

use of determinants $\rightarrow$ Eight-Queens Problem

use of p-adic analysis to tell whether a quadratic form has a rational root

use of the logarithm $\rightarrow$ Cayley-Klein metric

used in fixed proportions

used in fixed proportions $\rightarrow$ fixed proportions

used in fixed proportions $\rightarrow$ Leontief production function

useful algebraic properties $\rightarrow$ based on some useful algebraic properties

user-friendly presentation of random data $\rightarrow$ Descriptive Statistics

U-shaped curve

U-statistic

U-statistic $\rightarrow$ Estimation Theory

U-statistic $\rightarrow$ Statistical Theory

usual basis of R^n

usual inner product on R^n

usual norm for the plan

usual orientation for R^n

usual uniformity on R

u-substitution

utility $\rightarrow$ Von Neumann-Morgenstern Utility Theorem

utility function

utility function $\rightarrow$ curvature of an individual's utility function

utility function $\rightarrow$ Friedman-Savage utility function

utility graph

utility-maximizing problem of consumers

utility-maximizing problem of consumers $\rightarrow$ indifference curve

v (beginning of entries for V)

$V - E + F = 2 \rightarrow$ Euler's equation

vagueness $\rightarrow$ free from vagueness and ambiguity

validation

validation → cross-validation

validation → model validation technique

validation data

valley → Uncanny Valley

valuation

Valuation Theory

valuations on convex bodies in R^n

valuations on convex bodies in R^n → Hadwiger's Theorem

value

value → expected value

value → mean value → long-term mean value

value → principal value

value → principal value → Cauchy principal value

value → true value

value at the origin

value at the origin → Dirac delta function

valued field

Van der Pol oscillator

Vandermonde's identity

Vandiver → Kummer-Vandiver conjecture

vanish above the dimension of a space → Betti number

variability → measures of variability

variable

variable → bound variable

variable → continuous variable

variable → dependent variable

variable → dependent variable

variable → dependent variable → response variable

variable → dimensionless variable

variable → discrete variable

variable → dummy variable

variable → endogenous variable

variable → exogenous variable

variable → explanatory variable

variable → explanatory variable → independent variable

variable → free variable

variable → independent variable

variable → independent variable

variable → independent variable → explanatory variable

variable → random variable

variable → random variable → k independent standard normal random variables

variable → random variable → weighted sum of random variables

variable → response variable

variable → response variable → dependent variable

variable → scope of a variable
variable → standardized variable
variable → unknown
variable constant → Kemeny's constant
variance
variance → Analysis of Variance
variance → minimum-variance unbiased estimator
variance → population variance
variance → sample variance
variance and expected value are undefined → Cauchy distribution
variation
variation → coefficient of variation
variation → cyclical variation
variation → difference of two functions of bounded variation
variation → random variation
variation → reduction in the amount of variation in a set of data
variation → seasonal variation
variation → variations → Calculus of Variations in the Large
variation between treatments
variation of a function
Variation of Parameters
Variation of Parameters → inhomogeneous linear ordinary differential equation
variation within treatments
variational problem
variety → abelian variety
variety → algebraic variety
variety → toric variety
various spacial resolutions
various spacial resolutions → Persistent Homology
vector
vector → equipollence
vector → Laplace-Runge-Lenz vector
vector → Laplace-Runge-Lenz vector → shape and orientation of the orbit of one ...
vector → orthonormal vectors
vector → pseudo vector
vector → quaternions
vector → tangent vector
vector → vectors → opposing pairs of vectors → eutactic star
Vector Calculus
vector field
vector field on a manifold
vector flow
vector flow → Hamiltonian vector flow
vector space

vector space → dimension of a vector space

vector space → finite-dimensional vector space

vector space → locally-convex topological vector space

vector space → modular symbol

vector space → solutions to homogeneous linear differential equations

vector space → topological vector space

vector spaces applied to the study of field extensions

vector triple product

vector-valued function

vector-valued function → Jacobian matrix

velocity

velocity diagram

velocity diagram → hodograph

velocity diagram → hodograph → transformation of nonlinear partial differential equations to linear

Venn diagram

Verma module

Verma module → universal enveloping algebra

versus → Bernstein-Sato polynomials versus Bernstein polynomials used in approximation

versus → Dynamics versus Kinematics

versus → expansion path versus income-consumption curve

versus → explanatory model versus predictive model

versus → factor demand function versus conditional factor demand function

versus → part versus whole

versus → part versus whole → Mereology

versus → predictive model versus explanatory model

versus → rectangle having greatest area... versus rectangle having smallest perimeter...

versus → whole versus part

versus → whole versus part → Mereology

vertex

vertex → two squares that share a vertex

vertex → vertex operator algebra

vertex cover

vertex cover problem

vertex cover problem → minimum vertex cover

vertex of a ray

vertex operator algebra

vertex operator algebra → monstrous moonshine

vertex-transitivity

vertical asymptote

vertical bar chart

vertical intercept

vibrating membrane

vibrating membrane → Can you hear the shape of a drum?

vibrating membrane → vibrating string

vibrating string

vibrating string → harmonics of a plucked string

vibrating string → vibrating membrane

vibration → first vibrational mode of a thin L-shaped membrane, clamped at the edges

vibration of a fixed-string

Vieta jumping

Vieta jumping → problem #6-IMO-1988

Vieta's formulas

Vinogradov's theorem

Vinogradov's theorem → Harald Helfgott's proof of Goldbach's Weak Conjecture

Visual Calculus

Visual Calculus → hodograph

Visual Calculus → Mamikon's Theorem

Vitali set

Viviani's curve

volatility

volatility → evolution of the volatility of an underlying asset

volatility → evolution of the volatility of an underlying asset → Heston model

volatility → implied volatility

volatility → local volatility

volatility → mean long-term volatility → Heston model

volatility → stability

volatility → stochastic volatility → 3/2 model

volatility → stochastic volatility model

volatility → time-varying volatility

volatility clustering

volatility smile

volatility smile → SABR model

voltage → breakdown voltage → Paschen's curve

Volterra → Smith-Volterra-Cantor set

volume

volume → Cavalieri's Principle

volume → cube

volume → situation in which the derivative of volume equals the surface area → sphere

volume bound → Hamming bound

volume element

volume of a cone

volume of a cylinder

volume of a solid of revolution

volume of a sphere

volume of the n-sphere

volume oi an ellipsoid

volume raised to a power → polytropic process equation

Von Neumann-Morgenstern Utility Theorem

Vonnegut → Kurt Vonnegut → shape of stories

Voronoi diagram

Voronoi diagram → distance to points in a specific subset of the plane

vortex

w (beginning of entries for W)

wage hikes versus unemployment → Phillips curve

walk → random walk

wall → ladder against a wall

wall → maximum fenced area, one side a wall

wall → picture hanging on a wall

Wallace-Bolyai-Gerwien Theorem

Wallis' infinite product

Wallman compactification

wallpaper group

Walsh series

wandering domain

wandering domain → No-Wandering-Domain Theorem

Waring's Problem

water → water pump → Archimedes' screw

water pump → Archimedes' screw

water wave → cross section of a single water wave → witch of Agnesi

Watt's curve

wave

wave → longitudinal wave

wave → sine wave

wave → square wave function

wave → transverse wave

wave → triangle wave function

wave → water wave → cross section of a single water wave → witch of Agnesi

wave → wave propagation

wave propagation

waveform

waves on deep water → periodic wave-trains in nonlinear systems

weak divisor

weak topology

weak topology generated by a set of maps

weak topology generated by the family of subspaces

wealth → graphical representation of income or wealth → Lorenz curve

webbed space

Weber's integral

Wedderburn's Theorem

wedge product

Weibull distribution

Weierstrass Approximation Theorem

weight

weight → sum of the weights of the edges

weighted aggregate index

weighted arithmetic mean
weighted geometric mean
weighted harmonic mean
weighted harmonic mean → average speed
weighted mean
weighted mean → weighted arithmetic mean
weighted mean → weighted geometric mean
weighted mean → weighted harmonic mean
weighted sum of random variables
well-founded relation
well-order
well-ordered set
Well-Ordering Principle
Well-Ordering Principle → mathematical induction
Well-Ordering Principle → problem #6-IMO-1988
Well-Ordering Theorem
Well-Ordering Theorem → Axiom of Choice
well-posed problem
well-posed problem → ill-posed problem
Weyl-Kac character formula
what → only what, not how → flow network
wheel, locked steering → osculating circle
when all movable singularities are poles → Painlevé property
where two edges meet → vertex
whether singularities of solutions occur only at singularities of the equation
Which one was first?
White test
Whitehead continuum → Whitehead manifold
Whitehead manifold
Whittaker functions
whole versus part
whole versus part → Mereology
why banks don't mind compounding daily → boundedness of compound interest
why manhole covers are round
width
width → curve of constant width
Wiener process
Wiener sausage
wiggliness → topologist's sine curve
Wigner's classification
Wigner's classification → Particle Physics and Representation Theory
Wigner's classification → Poincaré's group
Wigner's Theorem
Wigner's Theorem → Hilbert space of states
Wigner's Theorem → mathematical formulation of Quantum Mechanics

Wijsman convergence

Wilcoxon signed-rank test

Wilks' Theorem → approximate test

Wilks' Theorem → nested model

Wilks's Theorem

Willmore energy

Willmore functional

Wilson and Racah polynomials → Askey tableau

Wilson's Theorem

win → guaranteed win → Dutch book

wind → winds → plot winds from soundings of the Earth's atmosphere → hodograph

winding number

witch of Agnesi

witch of Agnesi → density function of the Cauchy distribution

within one standard deviation from the mean → Empirical Rule

within three standard deviations from the mean → Empirical Rule

within two standard deviations from the mean → Empirical Rule

without boundary → two-dimensional compact manifold without boundary

without divisors of zero → Frobenius Theorem

without lifting the pencil from the paper → nine-point problem

without loss of generality

without loss of generality → wolog

wolog → without loss of generality

wood being easier to split along its grain than across it

wood being easier to split along its grain than across it → anisotropy

word problem

wordless → proof without words

worn-out widget, best strategy for replacing a → Renewal Theory

writing → secret writing → cryptography

writing the equation of a line

wrong → statistical convention that the alternative hypothesis is assumed to be wrong

Wronskian

x (beginning of entries for X)

$-x$ → additive inverse

$x_1, x_2, x_3, \ldots x_n, \ldots$ → sequence

$x_1 x_2 x_3 \ldots x_n$ → Vieta's formulas

$x^2 - y^2$ → difference of two squares

x^2 → square

$x^2 + y^2 = r^2$ → circle

$x^2 = 4py$ → parabola

$x^2/a^2 - y^2/b^2 = 1$ → hyperbola

$x^2/a^2 + y^2/b^2 = 1$ → ellipse

$x^3 - y^3$ → difference of two cubes

x^3 → cube

x-axis → horizontal axis

xe^x

x^x

y (beginning of entries for Y)

$y = T \times C \times S \times R$

$y = T \times C \times S \times R$ → Time Series Analysis

$y(xx) = (yx)x$ → right-alternative magma

Yao's Principle

Yates' correction for continuity

y-axis → vertical axis

yield → effective yield

You can't comb a hairy ball smooth. → fixed point

Young diagram

Young diagram → Young tableau

Young tableau

Young tableau → Young diagram

Young's inequality

z (beginning of entries for Z)

Z (set of integers)

Zariski topology

zed

Zeno's Paradoxes

Zermelo's navigation problem

Zernike polynomials

zero

zero → divisor of zero

zero → multiplicity of a zero

zero → setting the derivative to zero

zero bias

zero bias → unbiased

zero derivative → Rolle's theorem

zero derivative → stationary point

zero divisor

zero of a function

zero of a function → Riemann Hypothesis

zero outside of a compact set → compact support

zero sharp

zero-dimensional space

zero-dimensional space → 0-dimensional space

zero-divisors

zeroes → number of zeroes equals number of poles → modular function

zeroes → prescribed zeroes and allowed poles

zeroes → prescribed zeroes and allowed poles → Riemann-Roch Theorem

zero-knowledge proof

zero-mean

(end of document)